the literary reputation of Hemingway in Europe

THE LITERARY REPUTATION OF HEMINGWAY IN EUROPE

edited by
Roger ASSELINEAU

with an introduction by
Heinrich STRAUMANN

New York University Press
1965

© 1965 by Lettres Modernes
Library of Congress Catalog Card Number: 65-22740
Manufactured in the United States of America

TABLE OF CONTENTS

3   Introduction
       by Heinrich STRAUMANN

9   Hemingway's English Reputation
       by D. S. R. WELLAND

39   French Reactions to Hemingway's Works between the two World Wars
       by Roger ASSELINEAU

73   The Critical Reception of Hemingway's Works in Germany since 1920
       by Helmut PAPAJEWSKI

93   Hemingway in Italy
       by Mario PRAZ

127   Hemingway in Norway
       by Sigmund SKARD

151   Hemingway in Sweden
       by Lars ÅHNEBRINK

177   Hemingway's Revival in the Soviet Union : 1955-1962
       by Stephen Jan PARKER

Appendix :

197   Not Spain but Hemingway
       by Arturo BAREA

211   NOTES on contributors

the literary reputation of Hemingway
in Europe

INTRODUCTION

by Heinrich STRAUMANN

THE reception of a writer's books in his own country, the ups and downs of his fame during his lifetime and after, the changing emphasis in the elucidation of particular aspects of his work, have long been, and will always be, of special interest to those who are worried over the vagaries of critical evaluation and interpretation. If one compares the present estimates of a Melville or a Longfellow with those at the beginning of this century, one cannot but wonder where and when a critic's responsibility begins and ends, and whether and how any more or less permanently valid judgements can ever be made. And yet the very discrepancies of critical opinion may at the same time be of considerable help in the understanding of the complexities of a literary situation. The appearance of new styles and new tastes invariably points towards essential changes in the sense of values, in attitudes towards life and in concepts of being. This becomes even more obvious when one examines the fame of a writer outside his own country. The often noted paradox that a writer may be even more highly thought of abroad and in translations than at home and in his own language is only an especially striking result of the apparently inextricable web of operations making for the cultural status of a given age.

The attempt to disentangle some of these operations lies at the basis of the following essays. Their subject is the position of Hemingway's work in some major and some minor European literatures. Although naturally associated with comparative literary history, the essays are not in any way bound to a definite method but are held together by a common purpose, which, however, as such, appears only indirectly in the essays themselves. This purpose is the interpretation of what has been referred to as the European image of the United States of America, especially between the two World Wars. It has by now become common knowledge that the way in which the bulk of Europeans perceived America in its political, economic, social and cultural aspects was determined by a number of elements as heterogeneous, one-sided or accidental as any. There was, after the catastrophe of the First World War and the high hopes set on American co-operation by victors and defeated alike, the shock of the American defection from the League of Nations. There was the abysmal disappointment over what was considered the failure of Woodrow Wilson. And there was, above all, the general collapse of the remnants of Victorian values together with a profound skepticism about anything that remotely resembled the ideals of the pre-war world. The theme of disillusionment appears in some form or other in every literature of Europe and the underlying attitude was bound to affect the critical reception of American writing.

There is little doubt that the two serious American novelists who at that time belonged among the most widely read authors were Sinclair Lewis and Upton Sinclair, i.e., two writers expressing direct and outspoken criticism especially of certain social aspects of their country. Mencken was admired for his brilliant and merciless attacks on similar points, while the subtler and more indirect criticism implied in the writings of Ezra Pound and T. S. Eliot was at that time appreciated only by a comparatively small circle of intellectuals. Other contemporary American poets were hardly known in Europe. Faulkner's world would remain, for some time to come, largely undiscovered, and the plays of O'Neill had only just begun to be performed in some European theatres.

In this set-up the appearance and appreciation of Hemingway's work was bound to be of special significance. Unlike others

Hemingway was actively connected with events of vital influence on the future history of Europe. He had participated in the fighting on the Italian front. As a newspaper man he covered the Rapallo Conference and the Ruhr Conflict. He witnessed the horrors of the Greco-Turkish war in its final stages with the Greek retreat on Smyrna and the appalling misery of the refugees. He met Mussolini and watched the growth of the Fascist movement in Italy. In other words he became so intensely aware of the role of violence in human existence and of what the ever present consciousness of death can do to Man that only the basic appetites, the craving for food and drink and sexual satisfaction seemed to count as against any traditionally conceived values except those of honesty towards oneself and of solidarity with others. Working backward from *The Old Man and the Sea* one might even be inclined to say that more and more Hemingway's attitude seemed to reflect " *Man's lonely exhausting struggle for a belief in some achievement as a value, which, after being obtained, will be torn to shreds by a hostile world but will keep its significance for him who fought for it.* "

At the same time, however, Hemingway was in touch with writers and artists and acutely perceptive of their enhanced sensibilities about the emotional implications of the age. Through Sherwood Anderson he had been introduced to Gertrude Stein and her circle in Paris. He knew Lincoln Steffens and especially Ezra Pound whose poetry he admired as much as T. S. Eliot's. In this way his style of writing, which naturally emerged from the tough genre of newspaper reporting, almost imperceptibly changed into that metallic quality for which it became famous. Apparently bare and callous, subtly terse and strangely balanced in its reiterative elements, it exactly corresponded to the concepts behind his stories. It seems probable that the extraordinary unity of content, attitude and expression was the main reason for the special appeal of Hemingway's work to his own " lost " generation in Europe. It precisely confirmed what that generation largely felt about the shattered hopes of a better world and strengthened them in their belief that only absolute honesty towards themselves and their appetites would permit of anything like a new beginning. On the other hand Hemingway's work also helped towards a new interpretation of the image of America. Not, of course, in the way of a direct presentation as in the case of a Sinclair Lewis, but through the much more concealed method of setting an American character, often in the role of the narrator, against a foreign background. Unrecognized by the author himself, this important aspect was, in the inter-war period, hardly noticed by European critics. One could even say that Hemingway, by designing provocative characters of Italian, French, Austrian and Spanish origin, distracted readers from a conscious view of his American characters. Nevertheless it would, retrospectively, be difficult to deny that, despite his being an expatriate, or perhaps rather on account of it, he considerably contributed towards the reshaping of the European image of American men and women. It was an image more fundamentally human in its elementary and often inarticulate aspects and therefore closer to his contemporaries of the Old World.

In the following essays, written by some of the best experts on the subject for each literature, it becomes evident that the reception of Hemingway's work varies very clearly from country to country. It would be rash to try and summarize, let alone explain, the possible reasons for it. There is, of course, the whole range from enthusiastic praise to total denunciation and from extraordinary insight to complete misjudgement. But quite as remarkable is that the work of a good translator and the recommendation of one single eminent critic, as in France and Italy, may be sufficient to start the ball rolling, just as the absence of these two elements may be of fatal consequence for an early recognition in a foreign country Equally important seems to be the general cultural situation of the country in question. It is remarkable that Scandinavia, Holland and Switzerland, i. e., countries which had not undergone the experience of war, were much slower in picking up the thread, whilst in Germany the process of early recognition was abruptly stopped with the beginnings of the Hitler Régime, and when it could start again after the end of World War II the situation had fundamentally changed. The most direct effect, in content and manner, on the writers of a foreign tongue can be perceived in Italy, whilst the subtler but equally vigorous heritage of a narrative technique which permits of dissolving the boundary line between the objective and subjective worlds has been noticed amongst modern French writers. In England, partly as a result of some uneasy associations with the art and reputation of Kipling, a prolonged tendency towards "*suspended judgement*" made itself felt, but there is surely some deeper sense in the fact that both an English and a French critic recall the name of Lord Byron to find an adequate metaphor for the stamp which Hemingway left on at least a decade of contemporaries.

Finally it will be well to recall that the essays here collected have grown out of a symposium of the European Association of American Studies held at the Villa Serbelloni in Bellagio on the Lago di Como in September 1960. There were two other sections, one on *American Educational Theories and the European Mind*, and the other on *Woodrow Wilson's Reputation in Europe from April 1917 to his Death*. Most of the papers delivered in those two sections were published separately in various journals. The literary section had originally planned a discussion of *The Lost Generation Writers in Europe*, but decided to concentrate its efforts on the critical reception of Hemingway's work. All the members of the Conference were present at and took part in the discussion of each individual paper. The result of these efforts is the present book.

To complete the panoramic view of Hemingway's European reception, the editor has added to the symposium Dr. Stephen Jan Parker's chronicle of this novelist's fluctuating fortunes in Russia and in appendix the late Arturo Barea's essay, representing a liberal Spanish view.

HEMINGWAY'S ENGLISH REPUTATION

by D. S. R. WELLAND

To Hemingway's reputation and literary influence in England might be applied the iceberg image that he applied to his own art: only one-eighth of it is above water. This essay can only try to gauge the whole by concentrating on the verifiable eighth and guessing at the unassessable bulk below. Hemingway is the one author of whose work all undergraduates embarking on American literature courses will have read something; but the statistical value of such a statement can (and would) be instantly nullified by many critics with a sneer at adolescent tastes. There have been two books on Hemingway by British writers: the first, John Atkins's *The Art of Ernest Hemingway* appeared in 1952 but does not compare well with Philip Young's study which came out in America in the same year. A work of avowed enthusiasm, its critical value is seriously undermined by the brashness of its tone, the haphazardness of its organization, and its persistent denigration of criticism as an art. Mr. Atkins invents his own rules as he goes along, arbitrarily brushing aside opposition by elevating prejudice into principle: "*No critic has the right to quarrel with a character's behaviour, because human behaviour is infinitely variable,*" and "*although I believe moral values can and should be kept out of criticism, it is not really possible to exclude emotion.*" A more useful book is Stewart Sanderson's *Hemingway*, published in the "Writers and Critics" series in 1961; far less pretentious than Atkins, it is a solid, straightforward introduction to Hemingway's work in which admiration is tempered by judgment; at the same time, it is not in any major sense a new contribution to Hemingway criticism.

Surveying literary periodicals we find, if we exclude reviews, only four significant essays on Hemingway in the thirty-five years since *In Our Time* was published in this country, and two of those are reprints of articles by Americans.[1] It would, however, be a curious distortion of the truth to base an estimate of Hemingway's impact on English fiction on Wyndham Lewis's "The Dumb Ox" and D. S. Savage's "Ernest Hemingway," even if they were reinforced by Atkins and Sanderson. Surveys of modern fiction have proliferated in the past thirty years, but a study of them would be no better guide to Hemingway's role. In many of them, if he is mentioned at all, it is in the most cursory way: in one, in 1934, he figures merely in a roll-call of writers influenced by Gertrude Stein; in another, in 1946, only three out of six contributors to a symposium on *The Future of Fiction* refer to him at all and then only to deplore the work of his imitators.[2] Yet, when his death was reported on 3 July 1961, the obituary in *The Times* pronounced pontifically: "*No history of the literature of our time will be able to ignore his achievement or his far-reaching influence.*" As if to underline his importance, *The Times* also devoted its third leader to him, but the more equivocal tone that that leader adopted is so representative of the British attitude to Hemingway as to justify reproducing it in its entirety:

For many people the main shock of Ernest Hemingway's death will come from learning that he was only sixty-one. There was not merely the grizzled beard, the likeness to that other wanderer, Odysseus, which has been mentioned more than once. There was also the fact that his last masterpiece, *The Old Man and the Sea*, seemed to have that wise simplicity supposed to come with great age. He had been before the public, and something of a legendary character, for a long time. Views about him had changed from the early days; his reputation had settled. The youthful pioneer of a new style of American writing had long since ceased to experiment. No one knew whether yet another fine work would not come. No one would have expected it to set a new course or break new ground.

For a writer supposed to be so influential, and regarded as having founded a school, his output was not large. The youth of his nation tried to copy him; he remained a solitary both in achievement and style. The growth of the legend depended more on deeds than on words. He has been compared rather extravagantly to Herman Melville; there was at least this to be said for the parallel : both men drew the seeds of their best work from direct experience. Hemingway's two enduring novels, *A Farewell to Arms* and *For Whom the Bell Tolls*, had their sources in war. He wrote about it with pity and tenderness; these are the qualities that will keep his work alive long after the toughness is forgotten. They were the truest part of the man himself.

It is almost too characteristic to be true : the three works that it names are the three most likely to command widespread approval in England, least likely to provoke embarrassment or disagreement. There is the complacent assurance that the volcano has been extinct for some time, and how right we were not to be overawed by it : the toughness will be forgotten (though how and why are not specified, nor is there any apparent recognition that the "*pity and tenderness*" are functions of the toughness). A bland scaling-down is in process : "*supposed to be so influential... his output was not large... more on deeds than on words... compared rather extravagantly...*" and so on. Above all, there is the sustained impression of him as a foreigner : "*pioneer of a new style of American writing... the youth of his nation tried to copy him.*" The whole tenor of Paleface disparagement of this Redskin's influence gives itself away by this transparent pretence that 'Cowboys and Indians' is played by the youth of one nation only. The grudging praise, the insularity, the distinction between legend and achievement, and, in the final sentence, the innuendo that some parts of the man were less true, even bogus — all these characteristics recur constantly in English comment on Hemingway from the 'twenties onward.

Sometimes his gift for understatement seems to have influenced his admirers too greatly : thus Graham Greene, paying tribute to him in the B.B.C.'s memorial programme, acknowledged "*He meant a great deal to us when we began to write*" but got little further in amplification of this. Sometimes one hand takes away what the other has given : thirty years ago, in the opening essay of *Music at Night*, Aldous Huxley with quiet firmness seemed to take Hemingway's greatness for granted : " *Proust, D. H. Lawrence, André Gide, Kafka, Hemingway — here are five obviously significant and important contemporary writers... They are at one only in this: that none of them has written a pure tragedy, that all are concerned with the Whole Truth.*" Yet later in the same volume when the praise is repeated it is qualified in a way that provoked Hemingway to an irritated rejoinder. [3] "*In A Farewell to Arms, Mr. Ernest Hemingway ventures, once, to name an Old Master. There is a phrase, quite admirably expressive (for Mr. Hemingway is a most subtle and sensitive writer), a single phrase, no more, about 'the bitter nail-holes' of Mantegna's Christs; then quickly, quickly, appalled by his own temerity, the author [...] passes on shamefacedly to speak once more of Lower Things.*" To plead irony is not satisfactorily to excuse the faintly patronising tone of this passage, but it well illustrates the dilemma of English criticism in 1931 where Hemingway is concerned : on the one hand, an unfeigned respect for his subtlety and sensibility ; on the other, an uneasiness at the preoccupation with alcohol, sex and violence that had led so many readers to recoil from *Fiesta* (under which title, for some reason, *The Sun Also Rises* has always been published in England).

This uneasiness found its spokesman in Wyndham Lewis, whose essay " The Dumb Ox ; a study of Ernest Hemingway " appeared in April 1934 in *Life and Letters*. Its incorporation into *Men Without Art* brought it again to public attention in the same year. The frequency and the glee with which subsequent critics borrow the title is evidence of its impact. Lewis's main attack is on what he calls " *the unfortunate impressionability of Hemingway.* " Not only has he been far too readily impressed by Gertrude Stein ; this is only a symptom of a more serious disease. Like the characters in his novels " *He is in the multitudinous ranks of* those to whom things happen — *terrible things of course, and of course stoically borne,* " but " *His world of men* *and women (*in violent action, *certainly) is completely empty of will.*" Pater's definition of Mérimée, Lewis argues, "*the enthusiastic amateur of rude, crude, naked force in men and women wherever it could be found,*" is applicable to Hemingway only so long as this reservation is emphasised. "*Hemingway comes from a pretty thoroughly 'levelled' nation, where personality is the thing least liked. The rigid organization of the communal life as revealed in* Middletown, *for instance* [...] *is akin to the military state. So will, as expressed in the expansion of the individual, is not a thing we should expect to find illustrated by a deliberately typical American writer.*" Insisting on Hemingway as "*an American nationalist by temperament,*" Lewis goes on to deprecate the effect on the English language of "*Americanization — which is also for England, at least, proletarianization*" and to censure Hemingway's part in a process which "*is too far advanced to require underlining.*" Lewis deplores the "*cheap and coarse*" matter which is, "*considered in isolation, valueless as writing,*" but "*the cumulative effect is impressive,*" and he pays tribute to its skill.

If you say *anyone could write it*, you are mistaken there, because, to obtain that smooth effect, of commonplace reality, there must be no sentimental or other heightening, the number of words expended must be proportionate to the importance and the length of the respective phases of the action, and any false move or overstatement would at once stand out and tell against it. If an inferior reporter to Hemingway took up the pen, that fact would at once be detected by a person sensitive to reality... This is the voice of the 'folk', of the masses, who are the cannon-fodder, the cattle outside the slaughter-house, serenely chewing the cud — *of those to whom things are done*, in contrast to those who have executive will and intelligence... That does not affect its quality as art. The expression of the soul of the dumb ox would have a penetrating beauty of its own, if it were uttered with genius (and in the case of Hemingway that is what has happened)... But... if we take this to be the typical art of a civilization — and there is no serious writer who stands higher in Anglo-Saxony today than does Ernest Hemingway — then we are by the same token saying something very definite about that civilization.

Certainly Lewis is right in seeing 1934 as marking the peak of Hemingway's reputation up to that time. *Winner Take Nothing* had just been published, and in the inside front cover of the issue of *Life and Letters* containing Lewis's article appears a publisher's advertisement for it, quoting reviews by David Garnett and Gerald Gould. The latter hails him as "*the most brilliant story-writer of his generation*" and likens him at his best to Maupassant, a comparison Edwin Muir had drawn when reviewing *Fiesta* seven years earlier. That Garnett's review had been the full-page leading review ("Books in General") of *The New Statesman* for 10 February is indicative of the importance attached to Hemingway. David Garnett had written the introduction to the English edition of *The Torrents of Spring* in 1933, praising it as a "*high-spirited, good-tempered and good-natured parody*" but finding it chiefly interesting as "*a parody of Hemingway himself, and in the light which it throws on his other work;*" it "*shows that he is a conscious artist who knows just what he is doing.*" Though disappointed in *Winner Take Nothing* as a reversion to "the early heavy manner," Garnett in this review continues to insist on Hemingway's artistry, and ranks some of the stories in *Men Without Women* "*with the very finest stories written in recent times.*" From the later collection he picks out "Fathers and Sons" for particular praise, commenting: "*Some readers may find a touch of sentimentality here; I find only extreme vividness and extreme beauty.*" In similar vein William Plomer had epitomised Hemingway in the Spring number of *Now and Then* as "*the most interesting contemporary American short-story writer. Vivid, adroit, and an expert in brevity, he can put more point into an anecdote than many writers can into a novel*"; Hemingway's nihilism he saw as "*the nihilism of our time*" and also "*the nihilism that so often goes with vitality.*" Yet a few months earlier, writing in the January 1934 number of *The English Review* Miss Storm Jameson had, while discussing "The Craft of the Novelist," advanced an explanation of Hemingway's popularity altogether less flattering:

It is this simplicity, this appeal to our crudest interests, which explains Hemingway's success. He appeals especially to the oversophisticated, by offering them the illusion of living by violent and sensual impulses. In England at least his success has been largely with the intellectuals. They have praised his simplicity, his directness, without perceiving that he is simple because he has so little to say.

Contrasting him unfavourably with T. F. Powys and D. H. Lawrence, she finds " *Hemingway's capacity for feeling is clumsy and insensitive ;* " but she does not deny the attention he commands.

Whether one liked it or not, then, Hemingway was established by 1934, and this makes a useful watershed from which to survey the vicissitudes of his reputation. *In Our Time* had been published in England in September 1926 without attracting a great deal of attention. The *Times Literary Supplement* was noncommittal, finding it " *difficult to analyze Mr. Hemingway's method* " in stories that " *achieve their effect by novel and rather puzzling means* " but, despite that, " *are very interesting examples of a fresh and sincere psychology.* " In *The Observer* Gerald Gould recognized " *a new writer, with a vision and a technique of his own* " and even " *a touch of genius,* " but was put off by " Indian Camp " which he felt indulged a cruelty greater than art can legitimately allow itself. The most perceptive review of *In Our Time* came in April 1927 from the pen of D. H. Lawrence. [4] While deprecating the " *mottoes* " as " *a little affected,* " Lawrence saw the book's thematic unity : " *these few sketches are enough to create the man and all his history : we need know no more.* " He welcomed its honesty and its rejection of sentimentalism, thus going at once to the two aspects of Hemingway's writing that have occasioned most debate, and ended with this prophecy : " *In the end he'll be a sort of tramp, endlessly moving on for the sake of moving away from where he is. This is a negative goal, and Mr. Hemingway is really good, because he's perfectly straight about it.* " This is saying as much as many critics have said after Hemingway had been writing for a further quarter of a century.

Hemingway's "*negative goal*" was a major stumbling block to reviewers of *Fiesta* which came out in June 1927. Worried by its amorality, the *Times Literary Supplement* dismissed it as "*frankly tedious* [...] *an unsuccessful experiment* [...] *in which he abandons his vivid impressionism for something much less interesting*"; its conversation was "*crude, meaningless*" and there seemed "*hardly any point in putting it in a novel.*" This was to remain substantially the English view of this novel, but in *The Nation and Athenaeum* Edwin Muir was more sympathetic: "*His observation is so exact that it has the effect of imagination* [...] *his dialogue is by turns extraordinarily natural and brilliant, and impossibly melodramatic* [...] *he neither turns away from unpleasant details nor does he stress them.*" About Brett he was less certain: she "*might have stepped out of* The Green Hat" [Michael Arlen's best-selling romance]; "*she is the sentimentally regarded dare-devil, and she never becomes real.*" Although this novel shows "*a lack of artistic significance,*" Muir ends optimistically by seeing in it "*hopes of remarkable achievement.*"

For English critical opinion these hopes were not to be fulfilled by *Men Without Women*. Although the English edition (with slight textual differences from the original) did not come out until April 1928, two reviews appeared in 1927. To one of them, Cyril Connolly's, I shall return later. The other, though not published in this country, is of particular interest, being written for the *New York Herald Tribune* by Virginia Woolf. [5] A superficial judgment might have suggested that Hemingway would be unacceptable to the sensibilities of Bloomsbury, and that the Bloomsbury cult would have been in collision with the Hemingway cult. That some readers had no difficulty in reconciling the two is demonstrated by Stephen Spender, who began reading Hemingway as an undergraduate at Oxford at about this time:

> Joyce, Virginia Woolf and Hemingway revealed to me areas of sensibility of which I had hardly been conscious before reading them. For example, the sensibility which can enable one to think about what one is thinking while one is thinking it. Hemingway made me

aware of a quality and texture in the words upon a page which are like the rough surface of a plaster wall.⁶

To have Mrs. Woolf's own testimony, written at the time, is doubly valuable. She admits only a slight acquaintance with his earlier work, and comments on *Fiesta* that "*if Mr. Hemingway is 'advanced,' it is not in the way that is to us most interesting.*" Like Edwin Muir, she compares his characterisation to Maupassant, but finds no "*fundamental novelty in his conception of the art of fiction.*" His "*candour is modern and it is admirable;*" his style is bare but effective : "*Each word pulls its weight in the sentence.*" Yet "*there is something faked, too, which turns bad and gives an unpleasant feeling;*" the characters are "*indeed, terribly afraid of being themselves, or they would say things simply in their natural voices. So it would seem that the thing that is faked is character.*" Arguably, Virginia Woolf makes insufficient allowance here for the brittle, self-conscious, sophisticated affectation that is not faked but built deliberately into the characters; if so, she is not alone in her error. Of *Men Without Women* she deplores the "*self-conscious virility*" ("*ferocious virility*", Connolly called it) but finds it less violent than in Lawrence, Joyce and Norman Douglas. The stories she considers competent but marred by "*an excessive use of dialogue*" which upsets the proportions of the story and blurs its effect. In her opinion "*his talent has contracted rather than expanded; compared with his novel his stories are a little dry and sterile;*" she foresees that "*his is a talent which may contract and harden still further! it may come to depend more and more upon the emphatic moment; make more and more use of dialogue, and cast narrative and description overboard as an encumbrance.*" For all its reservations, however, this is a review that, for its date, shows considerable confidence in Hemingway's courage and skill, even though the remark "*he is modern in manner but not in vision*" is unexpected. Clearly there was a receptive audience awaiting proof of Hemingway's genius, and this it found in November 1929 in *A Farewell to Arms*.

This novel had one immediate advantage in its ready appeal to an existing taste and an expanding demand for war memoirs, factual or fictitious. Siegfried Sassoon's *Memoirs of a Fox-Hunting Man* had appeared in September 1928 and had gone into five impressions in three months. Edmund Blunden's *Undertones of War* had followed in November, with a second impression a month later. In September 1929 Richard Aldington's *Death of a Hero* came out, to be reprinted twice before the year ended, and Robert Graves's *Goodbye to All That* was being advertised by Cape simultaneously with *A Farewell to Arms* which they announced as " The first novel about the Italian front. " This was to guarantee it an immediate public but was also to do it a disservice. *The Spectator*, for example, was inclined to impose on its readers as something of a penance the reading of " *this tale of weariness, so laconically written ;* " to commend the novel in the following terms is hardly to focus on its main virtues as literature : " *There may be cruder war books, but there are none gloomier than this very great one, which deserves a shelf of its own... so that it can be used as an antidote to the sickly poison of glory and glamour.* " *The Times* praised the author's " *very powerful talent* " and thought that the novel " *even in these days of many War novels, stands out as something entirely original with the grim dryness of its humour, the sensual realism of its episodes, and the unrelieved pessimism of its view of life.* "

The Times Literary Supplement made the same point, finding " *the actual scenes of war* [...] *biting and brilliant ; they are so vivid and yet effortless that it is hard to believe one is reading fiction.* " More far-seeing, perhaps, were Gerald Gould in *The Observer* who saw it as a " *novel of adventure and passion which happens to touch a corner of the war,* " and the reviewer in *The New Statesman* who, recognising that, for all the accuracy of its reporting, it was more than merely another war book, praised the way in which Frederick and Catherine " *simply emerge from the war.* " Within two weeks of its publication *The Observer* bracketed it with *Goodbye to All That* as the best-sellers of the week. Arnold Bennett hailed it as " *tremendously effective [...] a superb performance."* J. B. Priestley (whose *Good Companions* had appeared in the same year) explained in *The Book Society's Review* that the Book Society Committee had recommended Mazo de la Roche's *Whiteoaks* instead of it only because " A Farewell to Arms, *far rougher and more outspoken, a brutally masculine performance, is not everybody's book.* " Priestley, however, is quick to condemn " *the fashionable mistake of supposing that this limitation necessarily makes Mr. Hemingway more important than he already is.* "

In the general consensus of praise three things are picked out for comment by most of the reviewers : the handling of the love affair, the effective combination of brutality and tenderness, and the idiom, especially in dialogue. To more than one critic Catherine seemed a silly, rather unintelligent girl, but all of them were affected by the harsh realism of her death even more than by the war-scenes. There is an encouragingly liberal note about these reviews : instead of the outraged morality that one might have expected, there is a recognition that the ending, though painful, is dramatically right, and a sympathetic response to the emotional situation that is best expressed in *The New Statesman* :

I have seen the epithet 'coarse' applied to Mr. Hemingway's treatment of his theme, but it seems to me extraordinarily out of place. He indicates with unusual delicacy, in phrases not reticent indeed but by no means elaborated, how a real and worthy companionship grew up between these two out of the practice of the mutual pleasures of the body.

The *Times Literary Supplement* considered " *the frankly sensual love-relation* [...] *remarkable, not for any loftiness, but for its beautiful precision* ", and to Gerald Gould it was " *an eager and beautiful love-affair.* " There was ready admiration too for the range of effect he could achieve with his dialogue, building up an entire character like Rinaldi wholly by means of it.

Yet the admiration is accompanied by perhaps too prompt and emphatic an insistence on Hemingway as, in the words of *The Times Literary Supplement* " *distinctively and absolutely American*

[...] *Nobody but an American could have his staccato style, his particular turn of dialogue, his power of rejecting everything that is extraneous to his keen but selective vision, his dismal animation, his unrationalized pessimism.*" Priestley, while applauding the heightening of the "*beautiful tenderness and pathos* [...] *by the cunning suggestion throughout of inarticulacy,*" is so convinced of its Americanness as to urge upon Hemingway the necessity of returning at once and writing about life in the States. In short, *A Farewell to Arms* seems to establish Hemingway rather as a novelist for English readers to enjoy than as one for English novelists to model themselves on. In this connection the reception in 1932 of *Death in the Afternoon* need not detain us: it was reviewed by *aficionados* of the bull-fight who were either indifferent to Hemingway as a writer or actively hostile. The *Times Literary Supplement* reviewer considered "*his supercharged 'he-manishness'* [sic] *is brutal and infuriating*" and demanded in an angry parenthesis what the literary conversations with the Old Lady were "*doing in this galley,*" as though they were some sort of printer's error.

So far, then, there had been an acceptance, more general than might be expected, of Hemingway as a sensitive and skilful literary artist. The calibre and reputations of the writers who reviewed him are also indicative. Chronologically this is the period of Huxley's praise of him, and in 1933 he was to receive T. S. Eliot's characteristically qualified approval in the pages of *The Criterion* :[7]

Even Mr. Ernest Hemingway — that writer of tender sentiment, and true sentiment, as in 'The Killers' and *A Farewell to Arms*... has been taken as the representative of hard-boiling... Mr. Hemingway is a writer for whom I have considerable respect; he seems to me to tell the truth about his own feelings at the moment when they exist. He does not belong in the class in which I have placed [Anatole] France, and Gide, and (tentatively) Mr. Aldous Huxley. He has, at the moment, a popularity which I think (it is a high compliment) is largely undeserved.

If the last, somewhat cryptic, observation implies a faith in Hemingway's potentialities, this quotation may be taken as marking the apogee of Hemingway's undisputed reputation in England and as tacit recognition that he and Eliot had some literary aims in common. In *Death in the Afternoon*, after parodying Marvell, he had joked about having " *learned how to do that by reading T. S. Eliot,* " but his account, in the opening pages, of his literary apprenticeship is not facetious. The celebrated passage about the quest for " *the real thing, the sequence of motion and fact which made the emotion* " is demonstrably parallel to Eliot's theory of the « objective correlative » adumbrated in his essay on *Hamlet* in 1919. Hemingway's observation on this is reported to have been " *Mr. Eliot works his side of the street and I work mine,* " but at least in 1933 it looked like the same street.

If the later 'thirties saw something of a reaction against Hemingway (and it was by no means unanimous) it is not exclusively attributable to Wyndham Lewis. Three other factors need discussion : the imitations of Hemingway, a change in the temper of the times, and Hemingway's own contribution. About this time begin the complaints about the cheap and superficial imitators of Hemingway's toughness of attitude and laconic directness of style ; thus in 1934 F. Tennyson Jesse begins a favourable review of James M. Cain's *The Postman Always Rings Twice* : " *Mr. Ernest Hemingway is responsible for much* " and goes on to criticise " *two-dimensional books* " written in unintelligent imitation of him. This sort of complaint — by no means unjustified — swells as the years pass to a chorus that need not be documented here (one critic even indicts " *a more subtle writer, yet much under Hemingway's influence [...] the prolific William Faulkner* "). The danger is that although so much of this imitation is in the realm of pulp-fiction, and candidly recognised as such by many critics, Hemingway is sometimes caught in the back-wash of guilt by association : a barbed " Profile " in *The Observer* in 1950 credited him with " *an enormous influence [...] — quantitatively perhaps a wider influence than that of any other contemporary novelist. But the imitators of Hemingway have been pygmy figures.* " The damage is done by the word "*quantitatively*" and by the innuendo that pygmy imitators must betoken a pygmy criginal.

The changing temper of the age may be conveniently illustrated from Cecil Day Lewis's "Letter to a Young Revolutionary" of 1933.[8] He deprecates

the contagion of those years immediately after the war — the era' in England, of physical exhaustion and psycho-analysis. We only allowed two virtues then, courage and 'intellectual honesty' — which meant that it doesn't matter what you do as long as you know you're doing it, and preferably, why you're doing it. We had not begun to take Lawrence seriously, you see. Hemingway is the *locus classicus* for the spirit of those times.

This definition of "*intellectual honesty*" differs from Eliot's praise of Hemingway's truthfulness much less in content than it does in tone, and the contrasting of Lawrence with Hemingway is also symptomatic. To a generation for whom, in Thomas Mann's phrase, "*the destiny of man presents its meaning in political terms*" Hemingway could have little to say. One of Wyndham Lewis's complaints against Hemingway had been of political indifference and it is a complaint that, re-stated in differing terms, recurs constantly over the next ten years at least.

Nor did Hemingway do much to help himself. *The Green Hills of Africa*, in 1936, was sympathetically received as a travel book by *The Observer* and *The Times Literary Supplement* but David Garnett in *The New Statesman*, who had had mixed feelings about *Winner Take Nothing*, confessed himself disappointed : "*I wish he would lift his head from the trail.*" In 1937 came *To Have and Have Not* : for most English critics Hemingway emerged as, in talent, a " *have not.* " Ralph Straus in *The Sunday Times* found it "*extraordinarily exciting*" and *The Times Literary Supplement* commended its dialogue and "*effective understatement*" but neither would go much further. Both commented in suspiciously non-committal tones on its "*frankness,*" and the *Supplement* gave the game away by its opening remark : "*For Mr. Hemingway toughness is all.*"

About the political awareness implied in the title there was an obviousness and an immaturity that the somewhat disconcerting form of the tales did little to redeem. Edwin Muir made as gallant a case as he could for it in *The Listener*, stressing Hemingway's "*complete honesty and very considerable skill,*" but even he admits that Harry is "*a flagrantly romantic figure;*" he notes that Hemingway "*still distrusts thought, but he is also concerned about the state of the world, and his technique, fashioned exclusively to deal with the world of sensation, does not quite know how to deal with the change.*" Hemingway's apparent distrust of thought now began to cause more misgivings than it had done before: it began to look as though Wyndham Lewis had been right, and "*the dumb ox*" came to be used with increasing frequency even by critics hitherto sympathetic. This, of course, is directly parallel to and in some ways a reflection of the changing American view: John K. M. McCaffery defines this as the "*period marked by critical attacks of the most notable savagery.*" [9] Writing in 1936 on *The Novel Today* Philip Henderson summed up "*these charming, brilliant and empty novels*" as "*a deliberate over-simplification of the complex cross-currents of his environment;*" their brilliance is seductively exhilarating until one realises that "*there can be no such simplification of life through 'direct action' as Hemingway offers us.*" Much the same criticism was to be made more fully and more damningly by *Scrutiny* in 1939 when the appearance of *The Fifth Column* was made the occasion for a review of Hemingway's work as a whole under the title "Hollywooden Hero." Its tone was valedictory: Hemingway has been over-rated but now he "*has grown a little dusty.*" The reissue of *A Farewell to Arms* in the Penguin Library had done no more than "*feebly re-animate the relics with a tawdry glow*" so that we could now see "*how simple and how extravagantly emotional the values of toughness really are.*" The best that could be said for Hemingway was that he was "*a true if limited artist*" writing prose of a "*banal simplicity*" as "*a means of avoiding the complexity of human relations, of avoiding the necessity of living.*" For full measure Faulkner's

work is bracketed with Hemingway's for condemnation as
" *a dishonest perversion* [...] *an attempt to pump tragic significance
into a conception of life that is quite as banal as Hemingway's,
and much more confused.*" A very similar moral indignation
later led *Scrutiny's* editor, F. R. Leavis, to a rejection of Hemingway in his introduction to Marius Bewley's *The Complex
Fate* :

> In Hemingway we have, it may be granted, something positively
> American. But it is hard to see why, in this, he should be thought
> to promise well for an American literary future — in saying which
> one is registering the portentous distance between Hemingway and
> Mark Twain. The author of *Huckleberry Finn* writes out of a full
> cultural heritage. The life he depicts is not crude — with the case
> presented by Hemingway in sight, the critic would be very improvident to use that adjective in connection with *Huckleberry Finn*.
> Compared with the idiom cultivated by Hemingway, Huck's language, as he speaks it, it is hardly excessive to say, is Shakespearian
> in its range and subtlety.

By 1939, then, there was a fairly prevalent disillusion in
Hemingway which *The First Forty-nine Stories* did little to
relieve. "*The picture itself is always fine, but — you begin
to wish for something a little less raw and bleeding*", complained
Straus in *The Sunday Times*, while *The Times Literary Supplement* modified its approval of one or two of the stories by echoing
Wyndham Lewis : "*what the dumb ox says is so peculiarly
uninteresting; and all that goring does get monotonous* [...] *And,
of course, there is sentimentality...*" One of the very few critics
of significance to remain faithful to Hemingway was Cyril Connolly. In *The New Statesman* in 1927 he had seen *Men Without
Women* as "*irritating, but very readable and full of a power and
freshness*" that showed the author to be "*obviously capable
of a great deal of development before his work reaches maturity.*"
The Green Hills of Africa, which he reviewed for *The Sunday
Times*, disturbed him by its attitude to the reader which "*is
getting more self-conscious and aggressive, and results in the facetiousness which is perhaps his worst fault,*" and he joined in the
general chorus of deprecation of the imitators "*who have*

everywhere cashed in on the Hemingway technique. [...] *ignoring his craftsmanship and quality of thought."* His considered opinion was still that *" Hemingway is probably a great writer. Certainly he is a great verbal artist, and there can be very few other writers living who unite such purity of emotional content with such mastery of form."* More sympathetic than most to *To Have and Have Not*, he wrote candidly of it in *The New Statesman* : *" Morally I find the book odious "* but *" he is still a delight to read* [...] *These three stories are not very new, but they show an admirable handling of his material, within its limitations."* Connolly's most important comment at this stage was the prediction that Hemingway is *" obviously the person who can write the great book about the Spanish war. And in Spain he will not be able to write about people who feel without writing about people who think* [...] *and consequently he can get rid of his antihighbrow complexes. He will have to write about people like himself. ' Cojones ' are not enough."*

With *For Whom the Bell Tolls* in 1941 Hemingway's flagging reputation received a new lease of life, Connolly's prophecy seemed fulfilled, and there was a general and generous expression of satisfaction at the improvement. Straus in *The Sunday Times* found it *" harrowing "* and with *" tricks of style which may irritate, but you will not deny its stark grandeur* [...] *it seems as if all Spain and all its troubles were here, and it is impossible not to admire the manner in which this immense feat has been accomplished."* *The Observer* considered it *" a great novel* [...] *ruggedly honest* [...] *filled with a truth and loving kindness which is deeply moving "* and *" a greater sustained effort "* than *A Farewell to Arms*. E. M. Forster summarised it in *The Listener* as *" full of courage and brutality and foul language. It is also full of tenderness and decent values* [...] *It is a book for grown-up people."* The general mood was well caught by V. S. Pritchett in *The New Statesman*: Hemingway, who seemed to have become simply *" sex, guns, booze and sons of bitches, "* had now produced *" the most adult and humane piece of writing he has done ; " " if you cut out Jordan's romance, the Spanish war has restored* to Hemingway his seriousness as a writer," as he has at last "*found a background of ideas he can respect.*" Even *Scrutiny* was partially won over. W. H. Mellers, who had written so scathingly a couple of years earlier, reviewed it as a book which, though not great, turned "*reporting, as he has so often done, into a small kind of art.*" His main objection, that it was "*extraordinarily boring to read at long stretches,*" he countered by the recognition that "*the boringness is maybe the condition of a certain kind of success, the slow unfolding of action paralleling the slow exfoliation of the prose.*" The most dissident voice was that of *The Times Literary Supplement*, highlighting the most controversial aspect of this novel. Pritchett had praised, as had others, the "*astonishingly real Spanish conversation,*" but to this reviewer the "*steady flow of dialogue in the manner of a literal translation*" and "*the unwearied suggestion of oathbesprinkled Spanish speech*" were worrying and distasteful.

This criticism was developed and deepened in an important review-article in *Horizon* by Arturo Barea under the title "Not Spain But Hemingway." Recognising its honesty "*in so far as it renders Hemingway's real vision,*" Barea finds himself "*awkwardly alone in the conviction that, as a novel about Spaniards and their war, it is unreal and, in the last analysis, deeply untruthful.*" He then demonstrates in convincing detail the unsureness of Hemingway's grasp of Spanish idiom which leads him to turns of phrase unintentionally offensive or which substitute for genuine dignity a "*hollow and artificial solemnity.*" Although there are some "*Spanish scenes and characters which are excellently observed,*" he cannot allow that Pilar and Pablo would ever have been admitted as leaders or that the group-violence of lynchings and mass rape referred to are in keeping with the Spanish character. Above all, he lends support to critical misgivings about the love-story by demonstrating that Hemingway's unfamiliarity with the psychology of the Spanish woman makes Maria "*the most unreal character of the book*". Cyril Connolly, of course, was editing *Horizon* and he

published the article with the editorial promise that he would
" *also gladly publish the best letter we receive on Barea's review* [...]
*for we feel that this most original article neglects the literary and
dramatic qualities of the book, and Arthur Koestler, who was to
have replied to it, is now in the Pioneer Corps.* " That this offer
was not taken up may be a tribute to the success of Barea's
demolition-work or a sign of public indifference ; it may more
probably reflect the shortage of space in war-time periodicals
and the military preoccupations of other writers as well as
Koestler. Certainly some part of the popularity of *For Whom
the Bell Tolls*, as of *A Farewell to Arms*, must be attributed to
its appeal to a mood of the moment. Not only was there a
considerable sympathy for the Spanish struggle against Fascism
but no doubt many of those who read it in the armed forces
would respond to the love-story more sympathetically than they
might otherwise have done.

The next ten years see the most sustained critical attention
to Hemingway in this country, particularly in the literary
periodicals that flourished during and after the war. Stephen
Spender contributed to *Penguin New Writing* a regular article
on " Books and the War " : in April 1941 he detected an advance
in Hemingway, whose short stories he had hitherto found
disappointing because " *Unrelated lumps of experience are ultimately as tedious as unrelated moralizing sermons.* " " But
the Spanish War seems to have provided Hemingway with a
genuine experience " and led him to the realization that " *man's
struggle against his own nature has more significance than his
nature itself.* " In the autumn of 1942, under the title of " Literature and Public Events," he took up the cudgels against
Edwin Muir who had published " The Natural Man and the
Political Man " in the summer number of *New Writing and
Daylight*. Muir's thesis, interestingly developed, had been
that in contemporary literature older concepts of the natural
man were giving way to newer and more socially-oriented views
of political man exercising a responsibility for his own social
destiny. Despite his earlier admiration for Hemingway, Muir

was unconvinced by his attempt to effect this transition in *For Whom the Bell Tolls*.

> The man Mr. Hemingway describes in this book is still the natural man, fighting and lusting. He has merely added a few words to his vocabulary; the words liberty, fraternity and equality. They are sufficient in themselves to give him an aim beyond his appetites; but his way to them is still the way of the natural man... This sentimentality of violence is implicit in the work of all writers who conceive Utopia as a kingdom to be taken by storm. Mr. Hemingway's first frustrated men were far more real.

Wisely, Spender does not seek, in reply, to credit Hemingway with any particular political sagacity : instead he argues that Hemingway "*is corrupt in his values to the extent that his age is corrupt* [...] *the main problem of literature — that of recreating lived experience in living forms of art, is not simply to be solved by the novelist or poet adopting a morally correct and superior attitude.*" This is the familiar battle perennially fought over Hemingway : how is the artist to be evaluated who restricts his art to the faithful delineation of the life he sees ? Attack is often easier and more entertaining than defence of such a writer, and in the Winter 1942-3 number of *New Writing and Daylight* John Hampson had a great deal of fun hurling all the old accusations of fake toughness, sentimentalism, limited articulation and anti-intellectualism not only at Hemingway but at most contemporary American writers : it is done too indiscriminately and with too much venom to convert anyone, but those who are of that persuasion seem never to weary of reiteration.

Of the criticism so far discussed, much is a campaigning over old battlegrounds ; the appearance of each new novel has extended the front without radically changing the nature of the campaign or of the weapons employed. A landmark in Hemingway criticism is reached with D. S. Savage's essay in *Focus Two* (1946). It represents a responsible and systematic examination of the Hemingway canon and an attempt to adjudicate between, so to speak, the Muir and the Spender positions.

This is done by accepting one of Wyndham Lewis's points; Hemingway represents " *a special form of that which might be termed the* proletarianization *of literature : the adaptation of the technical artistic conscience to the sub-average human consciousness.* " Savage sees " *some points of similarity between the Heroic Ages of the past and our own blood-stained epoch as it moves into an increasingly bleak future,* " and Hemingway is the bard of this age, though a disparity between him and Homer is fully recognized. He compares the two " *novels of love and war,* " declaring in favour of the " *nihilistic despair* " of *A Farewell to Arms* and against the " *subdued, lyrical ecstasy of acceptance* " which mars *For Whom the Bell Tolls*. There has been no positive development in Hemingway between the two books : indeed, the second is " *a* retrogressive recapitulation *of an essentially identical theme,* " marked by " *a certain loss of sincerity and asceticism of style, the proneness to a peculiar sentimentalism, and the readiness to entertain the cheap substitutes for thought manufactured by political factions.* " It is a severe view but not an unfair one, and Savage documents it well with extracts from the novels. His conclusion is one that many English readers would in large part accept : " *If the earlier and typical Hemingway* [...] *represents an aspect of the widespread sickness of our civilization, the Hemingway of* For Whom the Bell Tolls *reveals that sickness in an advanced stage, sickness masquerading as health, and, accepted as such, precluded from the possibility of being resisted.* " The tide was beginning to turn again, and Hemingway's next novel accelerated the ebb.

Cyril Connolly had reprinted from *The Kenyon Review* Robert Penn Warren's essay on Hemingway in *Horizon* for April 1947 in the series " Novelist-Philosophers, " but even Connolly's loyalty was strained to breaking point by *Across the River and Into the Trees* in 1950. In *The Sunday Times* he announced that it could " *be summed up in one word, lamentable* [...] *The novel fails because it is constructed from a false sense of values. The attitude of Hemingway is romantic and adolescent, a gesture of defiance* [...] *theatrical and sentimental.* " With varying degrees of shrillness other papers took up the refrain : " *an evil book* " said *The Sunday Graphic* " *Mr. Hemingway deserves to be hanged* " ; " *For Whom the Bell Tinkles* " quipped *The Evening Standard*; while Henry Reed in *The Listener* dismissed it as " *false and hollow* " with " *only an affected roughness which suggests a quick-return evasion of all difficult problems.* " The Colonel, to Connolly " *one of the most unlikeable, drink-sodden and maundering old bores* " was for *The Observer* only Mr. Hemingway " *pulling martial faces in a mirror.* " Evelyn Waugh in the Roman Catholic periodical *The Tablet* somewhat unexpectedly stood up for it, but this was rather as a means of attacking the other critics than on reasoned literary grounds : he did not make a strong case for his argument that the critics " *have detected in him something they find quite unforgivable — Decent Feeling,* " and his complaint that " *these reviewers have been telling us for years that we must not judge novels by the amiability of their characters* " ignores the more serious grounds for criticising this novel.

The Times Literary Supplement was the only one seriously out of step as it not infrequently is. From behind its customary anonymity, and in its centre-page review, the critic delivered himself of such unexpected judgments as " *Never has his writing seemed more spontaneous and less laboured [...] for the first time passion is under control. At last Mr. Hemingway knows his own strength;* " *A Farewell to Arms* seemed by comparison " *in retrospect diffuse, formless and wordy.* " Even Tennessee Williams (who called it " *the finest thing that Hemingway has done* ") could not have said more.

The wisest word came once more from Cyril Connolly :

> If Mr. Hemingway is to turn the corner he will have to cease to be a repressed intellectual... The hardest task before any writer awaits Mr. Hemingway, and because he is capable of it, we set it confidently before him. At the age of fifty (which is much younger than he thinks) to take himself to pieces for a few months and then begin again... equipped at last with a comprehensive and adult philosophy in which the mind is recognised as what is most peculiar and wonderful in man.

Once again, in the opinion of many readers, Hemingway was fully to justify Connolly's confidence, for, as *The Times* said in its obituary notice " *His career as a writer seemed about to end in disgrace but he suddenly recovered himself in* The Old Man and the Sea. "

Of all his works none has aroused a more unanimous approval in England than this. Some objected to the opening pages as "*too solemnly simple*" *(The Listener)* or "*almost strangely sentimental*" *(The Observer)*, but the narrative of the battle with the fish won universal applause. Edwin Muir's faith in Hemingway was restored : " *the toughness and the sentimentality are gone and Mr. Hemingway is in the world of free poetic imagination where he is really at home* " because he is " *essentially an imaginative writer, and his imagination has never displayed itself more powerfully than in this simple and tragic story.* " *The Listener* and *The Tablet* both spoke of it as a lyric, while Connolly in *The Sunday Times* saw it as " *a primitive painting, truthful and crystalline* [...] *the best story Hemingway has ever written.* " Once again *The Times Literary Supplement* got off on the wrong foot with a sneer at Hemingway as " *hopelessly muscle-bound* " : " *we turn the pages unable to think about anything but Mr. Hemingway himself. It is all very distressing.* " The tale, it felt, " *does not always escape the precious in its sometimes ponderous simplicity and tendency to imply an inner meaning,* " and it made heavy weather of it as an allegory. But a critic who could wish that " *it might have been alleviated in some degree by a ray of humour* " is too much out of sympathy with the tale to be intelligent about it.

In summary we may say that Hemingway has been appreciated in England as a story-teller and particularly as a teller of war-stories. His narrative powers and his dialogue have been admired, but the evaluation of their importance has been less easy to agree upon. There has been an uncertainty as to how seriously he was to be taken as a man of letters, and the question may have been further complicated by a residuary uneasiness over the case of Kipling. The generation confronted by

Hemingway had rejected Kipling's glorification of simple, heroic virtues of action and battle : this chap looked different, but was he going to turn out the same? It must have occurred to many, long before Evelyn Waugh formulated it in 1950, that Hemingway "*had a Kiplingesque delight in the technicalities of every trade but his own,*" and Hemingway's brand of knowingness did not commend itself more than Kipling's by having an American instead of a Cockney accent. His powerful simplifications looked more salutary in some lights than in others, and Wyndham Lewis summed up this sort of reservation very well in *Blasting and Bombardiering* (1937): "*Every Anglo-Saxon community should have its Hemingway to disinfect it of its inveterate "uplift," and provide a background of insensitiveness and alertness. — And then, of course, you need something else to dekiplingize you afterwards of your Hemingway.*" One rationalisation of this dilemma lies in the suspended judgment so recurrent in Hemingway criticism — the reservations about the achievement to date, coupled with the belief in his power to achieve maturity in a later work. That form of speculation having been now denied us, a more definitive judgment may be expected, but it will probably be on the lines of Savage's verdict. It may be that more favourable judgments would have been formed had Hemingway been personally better known in England. Stephen Spender's and Arturo Barea's descriptions of their acquaintance with him in Spain suggest a personality more attractive and even more genuine than sometimes emerges from the printed page (and the Hemingway myth suffered because it always reached the reader at second — or even third-hand). But Hemingway in Spain and Hemingway in London would have been so different that it might only have aggravated the myth, which has already done his reputation more harm than has his writing.

With the development of the study of American literature as a subject *sui generis* there is every indication that Hemingway is once more coming to be discussed on his own literary merits and not merely castigated as a baleful influence on English writing. The treatment that he is accorded in Marcus Cunliffe's *Literature of the United States* (1954) or in the two special American numbers of *The Times Literary Supplement* (17 September 1954 and 6 November 1959) is more informed and constructive than in many articles discussed above, even if the equivocal and ambiguous note is not entirely absent.

To whatever objections this account of the fluctuations of Hemingway's reputation may be liable, it is at least easier to trace with some accuracy than is the extent of his influence. Stewart Sanderson in his recent book has wisely described that as "*incalculable.*" Any attempt at charting it in even the most general terms must begin by distinguishing between influence and imitation. The shoals of imitators of the Hemingway style, justifiably deplored by so many reviewers, have been less influenced, in any meaningful and constructive way, than many writers whose styles bear no superficial traces of Hemingwayese at all. There are hardly any major English novelists to whose work one may confidently point and say "Here and here is the influence of Hemingway," and yet it is incontrovertible that the English novel would have developed differently had he not written. One of the qualities that won him many of his English admirers was that, as Philip Henderson said in *The Novel Today* (1936), he "*writes with a freshness and vitality unknown to the English novel.*" No elaborate exercise in practical criticism is needed to verify this. Compare the ambulance journey at the end of Chapter 9 of *A Farewell to Arms* with any war-scene from one of the English war narratives published at the same time: Blunden's *Undertones of War*, for example. The ugliness of war reaches the reader through the filter of Blunden's sensibility: nothing is withheld or distorted, and Blunden's relations with the reader are more spontaneous than many, but behind the printed communication lies a common bond of the Decent Feeling that Waugh affected to find in Hemingway. I do not say this disparagingly: the force of Blunden's writing lies in his appeal to this bond through the reticent graces of his careful prose, his felicitous allusions, and his ability to transmit to a particular sort of reader his emotional response to experience. In 1929 this was the English way to present war, and it was not a bad way at all. At the same time it was not Hemingway's, and it is easy to see that to a different sort of reader Hemingway's apparent avoidance of this " filter " technique might seem to result in greater immediacy of effect. There ought, however, to be room for both, and the antithesis that John Atkins sets up between Hemingway and Osbert Sitwell is both false and tasteless in its one-sidedness.

Long before Atkins' book, Cyril Connolly had had second thoughts on the effect of too much Hemingway and it is noteworthy that his own style has never succumbed obviously to that influence. Writing on " Defects of English Novels " in 1935, [10] he complains that

> the English novelist never establishes a respect-worthy relationship with his reader. The American novelists, Hemingway, Hamnett, Faulkner, Fitzgerald, O'Hara, for instance, write instinctively for men of their own age, men who enjoy the same things ; [...] it is an intimacy which at its worst degenerates into dogginess, but which in general brings out everything that is natural, easy and unrepressed in the author... English novels seem always to be written for superiors or inferiors, older or younger people, or for the opposite sex.

Yet by 1938 when Connolly published *Enemies of Promise* he has detected a change in this situation which is not wholly an improvement. In the chapter called *The New Vernacular* he makes an amusing but illuminating experiment by interweaving into a consecutive narrative a number of sentences taken from *To Have and Have Not*, Christopher Isherwood's *Sally Bowles* and George Orwell's *Road to Wigan Pier* : the passages are virtually indistinguishable from each other. Connolly's point is that " *this is the penalty of writing for the masses* " (Wyndham Lewis or D. S. Savage would have called it proletarianization), though he does not claim that it is exclusively the influence of Hemingway (his frequent references to Hemingway throughout this book are extraordinarily balanced in their critical judgment).

Not everyone saw Hemingway as a vital influence on English writing : E. M. Forster, lecturing in 1944 on " English Prose between 1918 and 1939, " [11] mentions him only as having introduced " *A new technique of conversation.* " On the other hand, in 1945, Julian Symons, writing in *Focus One* " Of Crisis and Dismay : a Study of Writing in the Thirties, " isolates Graham Greene, Evelyn Waugh and Christopher Isherwood as typical of the generation ; he sees in their work " *the shadowing presence of Ernest Hemingway,* " and continues :

This American naif of genius was one of the two writers of the twenties (Eliot was the other) whose direct influence upon the succeeding generation was really marked. The brilliant tricks of his dialogue, the understatements by which so much is conveyed, the apparent and sometimes real irrelevancies, above all the casualness and the production of something which gave an impression of " life " obtained by a method altogether opposed to naturalistic realism — all these very personal characteristics of Hemingway's art were noted, assimilated and turned to their own uses by these three young men, who have all great skill in writing dialogue, a dislike for regular or conventional form, a febrile and dispassionate wit.

But even Symons was quick to stress the importance of other influences such as that of Kafka on Greene, and the mass media of communication on all of them. He might have added also the influence of the early Aldous Huxley, to the laconic drynesses of whose style the 'thirties owed as much, perhaps, as to Hemingway.

Of recent years the influence has declined or been dispersed among a host of others. To that extent the *Times* leader was justified in seeing him as an historic figure rather than a living force, and perhaps the best description of him in that role was made by V. S. Pritchett, reviewing *For Whom the Bell Tolls* in 1941 :

No other prose writer since Lawrence has had his influence. It lies partly in his manner of writing, which is a sort of stylisation of vernacular speech, but chiefly in his view of life and character. More than any other writer he has defined for us the personality of our own time [...] I rather think we have to go as far back as Byron and Byronism before we can find a type which has been stamped as vividly as Hemingway's upon a decade [...] What has attracted us to the Hemingway man is his adaptability, the lightness of his luggage, his mobility [...] The Hemingway man has become an expert in de-civilisation. We admire him because he has made terms with his time.

NOTES

1. Robert Penn WARREN, "Hemingway" in *Horizon* XV, April 1947, and Frederick J. HOFFMANN, "No Beginning and No End : Hemingway and Death", in *Essays in Criticism* III, January 1953.
2. *New Writing and Daylight*, London, 1946.
3. *Death in the Afternoon*, 1932, pp. 190 ff. This passage is discussed at length by Cyril CONNOLLY, *Enemies of Promise*, Chapter 8.
4. It is reprinted in *D. H. Lawrence : Selected Literary Criticism*, ed. A. Beal, London, 1955, pp. 427-8.
5. It is reprinted in *Granite and Rainbow*, London, 1958, pp. 85-92.
6. *World Within World*, London, 1951, p. 96.
7. April, 1933, p. 471.
8. In *New Country*, ed. M. Roberts, London, 1933.
9. *Ernest Hemingway : The Man and His Work*, Cleveland, Ohio, 1950, p. 11.
10. It is reprinted in *The Condemned Playground*, London, 1945.
11. *Two Cheers for Democracy*, London, 1951.

The following are the English reviews of Hemingway's works mentioned in the foregoing pages; there were, of course, others not discussed here. The date given against the title of the novel is that of its first English publication.

IN OUR TIME [1926]

Times Literary Supplement 4 November 1926.
Observer 7 November 1926.
Calendar of Modern Letters April 1927.

FIESTA [1927]

Times Literary Supplement 30 June 1927.
Nation and Athenaeum 2 July 1927.

MEN WITHOUT WOMEN [1928]

New Statesman 26 November 1927.

A FAREWELL TO ARMS [1929]

Evening Standard 14 November 1929.
Times 15 November 1929.
Spectator 16 November 1929.
Observer 17 November 1929.
Times Literary Supplement 28 November 1929.
New Statesman 30 November 1929.
Now and Then Winter 1929.

DEATH IN THE AFTERNOON [1932]

Times Literary Supplement 8 December 1932.

THE TORRENTS OF SPRING [1933]

No reviews quoted.

WINNER TAKE NOTHING [1934]

New Statesman and Nation 10 February 1934.
Now and Then Spring 1934.

GREEN HILLS OF AFRICA [1936]

New Statesman and Nation 4 April 1936.
Times Literary Supplement 4 April 1936.
Sunday Times 5 April 1936.
Observer 19 April 1936.

TO HAVE AND HAVE NOT [1937]

Times Literary Supplement 9 October 1937.
New Statesman and Nation 16 October 1937.
Sunday Times 17 October 1937.
Listener 27 October 1937.

FIFTH COLUMN AND FIRST 49 STORIES [1939]

Times Literary Supplement 17 June 1939.
Sunday Times 9 July 1939.
Scrutiny December 1939.

FOR WHOM THE BELL TOLLS [1941]

Times Literary Supplement 8 March 1941.
Observer 9 March 1941.
New Statesman and Nation 15 March 1941.
Sunday Times 16 March 1941.
Horizon May 1941.
Scrutiny June 1941.
Listener 10 July 1941.

ACROSS THE RIVER AND INTO THE TREES [1950]

Observer 3 September 1950.
Sunday Times 3 September 1950.
Tablet 30 September 1950.
Times Literary Supplement 6 October 1950.
Listener 9 November 1950.

THE OLD MAN AND THE SEA [1952]

Observer 7 September 1952.
Sunday Times 7 September 1952.
Times Literary Supplement 12 September 1952.
Listener 18 September 1952.
Tablet 27 September 1952.

Obituary and Leading Article : *Times* 3 July 1961.

FRENCH REACTIONS TO HEMINGWAY'S WORKS BETWEEN THE TWO WORLD WARS

by Roger ASSELINEAU

NOWADAYS no history of contemporary French literature fails to mention Hemingway. His works have been discussed by Gide, [1] Camus and Sartre and his influence can be felt in most French novels written since World War II. But this is no new phenomenon; it is only the result of a slow permeation which began as early as the late 1920's, that is to say, practically, as early as Hemingway's works were published, for there was almost no timelag between the appearance of his first stories in America and in France. This process having lasted so long and having had such far-reaching consequences, it might be interesting to study its origin and development. However, it would be arbitrary and clumsy to limit our investigation to the 1920's, for the French translations of Hemingway's major novels did not appear until the early 1930's and it was only then that French critics became fully aware of all the implications of his works. The first French readers apparently were pleasantly surprised by the novelty of the sensations that his books procured, but did not analyze with sufficient precision what they felt. Studying their inchoate reactions would amount to dissecting buds in order to discover characteristics which are obvious in the full-grown plant. So it is my purpose to study the overall impact of Hemingway's works during the two decades of the inter-war period.

This subject is not new. It has already been explored by Félix Ansermoz-Dubois in his book on *L'Interprétation française de la littérature américaine d'entre-deux-guerres* (Lausanne, Imprimerie de la Concorde, 1944, XVIII + 237 pp.) and more recently by Thelma M. Smith and Ward L. Miner in *Transatlantic Migration ; The Contemporary American Novel in France* (Duke University Press, 1955, IX + 264 pp.). But, in many respects, both books are too ambitious. Their authors, by trying to cover the whole field, have merely skimmed the surface of their subjects, or, to use another image, they have done some very useful spade-work, but have not dug deep enough. Félix Ansermoz-Dubois' book is the better of the two — at least it is better balanced. Thelma M. Smith and Ward L. Miner may seem more thorough, but they have no sense of perspective or proportion. In their book all French critics, whether important and competent or the reverse, are placed on the same level and quoted with the same respect. No distinction is ever made between highbrow and lowbrow readers, between literature and the book-trade, between best-seller lists and real values. Besides, they are primarily specialists of American literature with only a scanty knowledge of French and of French literature, so they never dare venture into literary appreciation ; they prefer to rely on statistics and sales figures and are more interested in the spectacular success of *Gone with the Wind* than in the critical reception of Hemingway's or Faulkner's works. Moreover, they seem to believe that, except for Poe, the French first discovered American literature in 1919, as if Emerson, Thoreau, Whitman, Henry James, Edith Wharton, Mark Twain and others had not been discussed in French reviews, sometimes at great length, as early as the 1870's. [2] Another defect of their book is that they lay stress with evident self-satisfaction on the boom enjoyed by American literature in France in the years immediately following World War II, and neglect its humbler beginnings in the 1920's. For all these reasons, though their book is a mine of precise information, its conclusions cannot be wholly trusted. It is a lopsided, superficial and sometimes naive study of an important, complex and tremendously vast subject. It would probably be wiser and more rewarding to restrict one's investigation to the impact of one author during a more limited period of time, and this is precisely what we are going to attempt.

But, in order to start from a solid basis of facts, let us first of all examine the chronology of the French translations of Hemingway's works during the inter-war period, together with the articles and reviews which they provoked as they came out. Hemingway's first publication in French was a short story, « L'Invincible, » which appeared in an obscure little magazine called *Le Navire d'Argent* in March 1926. The same issue contained Walt Whitman's *Eighteenth Presidency* translated by Sylvia Beach and Adrienne Monnier, with an introduction by Jean Catel who had discovered it in Boston ; also included were fragments of *The Great American Novel* by William Carlos Williams, translated by Auguste Morel, one of the translators of *Ulysses*, " The Advertising Agency " (« L'Agence de publicité »), by Robert Mc Almon [sic], translated by Sylvia Beach and Adrienne Monnier, and " Sipliss, " an extract from *The Enormous Room* by E. E. Cummings, translated by Georges Duplaix. *Le Navire d'Argent* was edited by Adrienne Monnier who, like her friend Sylvia Beach, kept a bookshop in the Rue de l'Odéon but who, above all, tried to mediate between French and English or American authors. Though *Le Navire d'Argent* had a small circulation, Hemingway was lucky to have a story published in it, for the magazine reached a select circle of connoisseurs and writers. Moreover, his name was hardly known at all at this time. Régis Michaud did not even mention it in the series of lectures on the contemporary American novel which he gave at the Sorbonne from February to May 1926 and which was published in book-form later in the same year under the title of *Le Roman Américain d'Aujourd'hui* (Paris, Boivin). But this omission was excusable, for *In Our Time* (capitalized) had come out only some six months earlier, in October 1925, and had caused very little stir. *The Torrents of Spring* was to appear only in May 1926 and his first successful book, *The Sun Also Rises*, in October of the same year. As to the original of « L'Invincible », it had been published only a few weeks before its translation into French in a little magazine called *This Quarter* (vol. I, issue for Autumn-Winter 1925-26). But *The Sun Also Rises* launched Hemingway on both sides of the Atlantic. The clearest proof of his recognition in France was the appearance in the *Nouvelle Revue Française* in May 1927 of a short story entitled « Cinquante mille dollars » ("Fifty Grand"). And this was merely a premonitory sign of the publication by Gallimard in 1928 of a collection of short stories entitled *Cinquante mille dollars*. It was translated by Ott de Weymer and contained the following stories besides "Fifty Grand" which gave its title to the book : "My Old Man" (« Mon vieux »), "The Undefeated" (« L'Invincible »), "The Battler" (« Le Champion »), "Indian Camp" (« Le Village indien ») [3], and "The Killers" (« Les Tueurs »). *Cinquante mille dollars* immediately drew the attention of most critics. Even Henri de Régnier, an aristocratic member of the Académie Française, a refined symbolist poet and an ethereal novelist, thought it necessary briefly to salute the newcomer at the end of his weekly column in *Le Figaro* (Oct. 9, 1928, p. 2) : "*Among the stories translated by M. O. de Weymer, stories of a somewhat brutal realism and written in a much too slangy style, I have above all enjoyed the one which is entitled 'L'Invincible'... Théophile Gautier and Mérimée would have liked this picture à la Goya...*" [4] Raoul Celly in the *Revue Nouvelle* (Oct. 28, pp. 175-176) praised Hemingway for the bold vigour of the matter and manner of his stories. Louis-Jean Finot in the *Revue Mondiale* (Sept. 15, 1928, p. 196) devoted a short but enthusiastic review to Hemingway's book : "*Few novelists are successful short-story writers. And yet what pleasure a well-constructed and well-written tale gives to the reader ! It is precisely this kind of satisfaction that you experience again and again if you read* Cinquante mille dollars... *these stories are exciting and very cleverly told. In short, it is an excellent book.*" [5] A little later Emmanuel Buenzod in the important *Revue de Genève* (Nov. 1928, p. 1416) concluded : "*Here are five stories which the most absent-minded reader will never be able to forget, and their collection, it seems to me, constitutes a masterpiece.*" [6] Victor Llona, a translator of South-American origin, in January 1929, added in the *Nouvelle Revue Française* that it was impossible to do full justice to Hemingway's spare prose in a translation, and cleared him of the charge of being a mere reporter. He is "*a bad reporter,*" Llona wound up, "*but let him get over it, he is worth much more than that.*" [7] *Cinquante mille dollars* thus got an excellent press and the *Nouvelle Revue Française* for six months ran a full page advertisement quoting reviews from various dailies : *L'Intransigeant, L'Avenir, La Gazette de Lausanne* and *Le Figaro*.

By this time, the interest of the public in Hemingway's works was such that a magazine for the general reader, the *Revue Européenne* (March 1928, pp. 322-23), did not hesitate to publish a review of *Men Without Women*, though it had not yet been translated into French. The reviewer was Bernard Faÿ who was to become a few years later Professor of American Civilization at the Collège de France. He gave to Hemingway first place among the young American writers of his generation : "*She* [America] *has her own team of discoverers. The most distinguished and most gifted of them all is Ernest Hemingway whose popularity on the other side of the Atlantic is so great nowadays that he makes up with Cummings and Wescott a sort of glorious and youthful triumvirate.*" [8] Régis Michaud now repaired in his *Panorama de la littérature américaine* (Paris, Kra, 1928, 275 pp.) the omission which he had made two years before in his *Roman américain d'aujourd'hui*. He devoted a paragraph to Ernest Hemmingway [sic] in the last chapter of his new book and praised "*the verbal stenography*" both of *The Sun Also Rises* and *Men Without Women* (pp. 254-255).

In 1929 there came out a French translation of another story by Hemingway : « Les collines sont comme des éléphants blancs » ("Hills like white elephants") which had first been published in *Transition* (the international bilingual review edited by Eugène Jolas) and which now appeared in the third number of *Bifur* (short for *Bifurcation*, i. e. crossroads), edited by Georges Ribemont-Dessaignes. (The translation was the work of Alice Turpin.) As the title indicates, this review was meant to be a meeting-place for French and foreign writers. The assistant-editor in charge of English and American literature was William Carlos Williams.

All this constituted a very good start. But then came a lull. For no apparent reason, though Hemingway went on writing and publishing in America, no one spoke of him any more in France or thought of translating any of his stories. This silence lasted until 1931 when Victor Llona edited an anthology of American stories entitled *Les Romanciers américains* (Paris, Denoël & Steele). It included tales by Sherwood Anderson, Louis Bromfield, James Branch Cabell, John Dos Passos, Ludwig Lewisohn, Jack London, Upton Sinclair, Gertrude Stein and Glenway Wescott. Hemingway was represented by a short story entitled « Je vous salue Marie » which Victor Llona himself had translated ; André Maurois had written an introduction to it (pp. 193-197) in which he showered compliments on the author : " *When I was at Princeton two years ago,* " he began, " *the professors there talked a lot about a novel which one of their former students had just published* [Maurois here must have confused Hemingway with Francis Scott Fitzgerald, but it does not really matter]. *I asked the title : 'The Sun Also Rises'. — And is it good ? — It is quite ruthless and cynical, but extraordinarily true... I bought it. It was excellent.* " [9]

The following year, Hemingway achieved an even greater victory, for Gallimard published a translation of *A Farewell to Arms* done by Maurice-Edgar Coindreau. He was fortunate fot two reasons. First, he was thus becoming one of the authors whose works were regularly published by such an influential and vital firm as Gallimard. This firm had developed around the *Nouvelle Revue Française*, and, under the guidance of such writers as André Gide, Jean Schlumberger and Jacques Rivière, had gathered under its flag all the authors who really counted in France at that time. So it was a great honour for Hemingway to become « un des auteurs de la maison ». Secondly, whereas his works so far had been translated by indifferent translators, he was now in the hands of a most distinguished practitioner. For Maurice-Egdar Coindreau is an extraordinarily gifted and versatile translator who, after specializing in Spanish literature and translating some of Valle-Inclán's works, became interested in American literature, settled at Princeton where he taught French, and embarked on a brilliant career as a translator of American novels. He is endowed with a prodigious agility of expression and should and could write in his own name, but, for some reason, he prefers to express himself by proxy, so to speak, and translate the works of others — not any works, though, only the works of authors to whom he — momentarily — feels a certain affinity, which he thus in a way recreates. This is precisely what he did with *A Farewell to Arms*. Now, an author's reputation and success in a foreign country to a large extent depend on the quality of the translator who has happened to become interested in his works. Poe's apotheosis in France, for instance, was a sheer stroke of luck. Without Baudelaire's mediation he would never have known the same success. Conversely, as Thomas Wolfe has failed to attract a good translator's attention, his works, contrary to what happened in Germany, have remained practically unknown in France.

Hemingway was fortunate for even a third reason : *L'Adieu aux armes* was prefaced by Drieu La Rochelle, a dynamic — though tormented and unstable — young writer of about the same age, who had also been wounded during the war and who since the appearance of *Le Jeune Européen* (1927) was considered one of the spokesmen for his generation. He confided : "*I met Hemingway only once... He is a hefty fellow. I liked him very much... He is one of those guys with whom you must go hunting or fishing...* " And he praised what he called « *le démon d'Hemingway,* » " Hemingway's demon, " " *that of health ; what touches you* [when you read his dialogues], [he went on], *is the very* tone *of his life, of his health, the temperament of a tough guy.* " [10]

Once more French critics were enthusiastic. Denis Marion in particular in the *Nouvelle Revue Française* (October 1933, p. 633) insisted on Hemingway's careful artistry for all his apparent offhandedness. [11]

Then, less than a year after the appearance of *L'Adieu aux armes*, Gallimard published a translation of *The Sun Also Rises*, *Le Soleil se lève aussi*, also done by M. E. Coindreau and with a preface by Jean Prévost, another young writer of the *Nouvelle Revue Française* team, who was both a brilliant intellectual and a good athlete and who was particularly sensitive to the vigour and virility of Hemingway's works.

Hemingway now had three books in print in France, and Philippe Soupault, the novelist and surrealist poet, reviewed them jointly in *Europe* (Sept. 1933, pp. 140-141). He liked above all the peculiar and novel alliance of refined art and complete naturalness which characterizes Hemingway's novels, as well as their warmth and rich humanity. But he complained that they had not yet obtained the success which they deserved. " *Once more, in this domain as in many others, we find this strange apathy, this inability to become interested which seems to be characteristic of the years 1930 to 1933.* " [12] Jean Prévost had made very much the same complaint in his preface to *Le Soleil se lève aussi* : " *Here is a writer who has become famous in his own country, but ours has not yet given him his rightful place.* " [13] He thought he could give an explanation for this. According to him, literary reputations in France are made by women, and French women, he claimed, could not bear the excessive virility of Hemingway's stories ; they found them " *too strong, too brutal,* " they missed in them " *the presence of a feminine sensibility and a tribute to Woman.* "

Thus, Hemingway, though admired, was not pushed by that force which is more powerful in France than all the critics put together : table-talk at tea-time, praises in the mouth of elegant women... Knut Hamsun has been treated with the same injustice : he too depicted man as different from woman... The fame of Hamsun, like the young notoriety of Hemingway, has succeeded in spreading in countries where women, as in France, make literary reputations : in Scandinavia or the United States ; but it is because in those countries which have taught us the beauty of broad shoes, of heavy fabrics and the elegance of pipe-smoking, women approve of a young man who is a young man in the full acceptation of the term. [13]

So, in the late twenties and early thirties, there was undeniably in part of the French public — among general readers at least — a resistance to or revulsion from the more aggressive aspects of Hemingway's "tough guy" attitude. And, strangely enough, it soon affected — or, should I say, infected M. E. Coindreau himself. He had hardly finished translating *A Farewell to Arms* when he published in *Les Cahiers du Sud*, in April 1932 [14] the severest denunciation of Hemingway's art and personality that had — or even has — ever appeared, under the title of « L'Amérique et le roman alcoolique ». It was a venomous attack full of vitriolic personal allusions. Discussing *The Torrents of Spring*, Coindreau said, for instance, that it already contained the whole " *tragedy of Ernest Hemingway* " : " *his obsession with impotence, his tendency to put a few stories end to end in the hope of building up a novel, his anti-social attitude which was the natural consequence of his inferiority complex.* " [15] The whole essay was a diabolically clever mixture of praise and blame. Again and again Coindreau conceded that Hemingway's art was novel and powerful, the better to run down his adversary in the next sentence by showing him up as a fake and a charlatan. Thus he admitted that everything in *The Sun Also Rises* might seem new,

the subject-matter because of its boldness, the style because of its metallic sobriety, the attitude of the author towards his characters, a kind of detachment re-inforced by deliberate cynicism which deceived many readers [including Coindreau himself apparently] and prevented them from becoming aware of the sentimentality which cropped up in every sentence. For, just as some women are not so thin as they look, some men are not so tough as one might think. [16] In *The Sun Also Rises* all the characters are alcoholic cowards... their drunkenness is even emptier than their minds. [17] *A Farewell to Arms* is again a mere story of impotence, cowardice and fear... Hemingway's characters, for all their 'double muscles,' belong to the race of the defeated. They know it and they hide their fear under a mask of cynicism. [18]

And Coindreau went even so far as slyly to suggest that Hemingway himself, like his characters, was nothing but an impotent weakling and a coward : " *Just as shy children sent out to walk in the dark sing in order to screw up their courage, so Hemingway shouts at the top of his voice, plies his gun and his knife. He behaves very much like Tartarin.* " [19] " *He prefers to dress like a Tartarin and hobnob with guys who shout, kill and fornicate, but have been nonetheless doomed to defeat from their birth. And they know it, but they try to deceive themselves by making so much noise. However unpleasant the thought may be, one cannot help suspecting Hemingway, the writer, of being somewhat in the same case...* " [20] One could hardly go further. And this savage indictment was all the more unexpected as it came from the man who had just translated two of Hemingway's novels. It was a strange about-face indeed ! Coindreau was thus publicly burning what he had just been worshipping. He has never given any reason for this sudden reversal of opinion and has persisted in his rejection of Hemingway ever since. In 1932 he published in the *Nouvelle Revue Française* (Nov., pp. 778-781) a severe review of *Death in the Afternoon*. In March 1938 he wrote an even harsher one of *To Have and Have Not* (pp. 501-503) ; " *He* [Hemingway] *has just proved beyond doubt that his conception of society in general and of the individual in particular is that of a twelve-year-old schoolboy who pretends he is a man and worships such heroes as d'Artagnan, Buffalo Bill or Jack Dempsey.* " (p. 501). And his first denunciation, « L'Amérique et le roman alcoolique » was reprinted in 1946 in his *Aperçus de littérature américaine* (Paris, Gallimard) with hardly any changes at all in the chapter entitled « Romans alcooliques et exaltation de la brutalité » (pp. 70-94).

Coindreau's subsequent career, however, has shown that

he is given to such sudden changes. Unlike those virtuosos who keep interpreting the same composer all their lives, he is temperamental and fickle-minded. He rapidly gets tired of the authors he has translated. After renouncing Hemingway, he similarly repudiated in rapid succession Faulkner, Caldwell, Truman Capote and William Goyen, and finally, rejecting all American writers, returned to his first love and set about translating the works of young Spanish novelists. Sooner or later his literary loves disappoint him and he jilts them, claiming an incompatibility of temper. Hemingway apparently both attracted and repelled him. He admired the artist, but could not stand the man or rather what he called the " Hemingway-myth, " Hemingway posing as a tough guy. This twofold reaction is again and again described in his reviews : " *One yields to the charm of this somewhat dry and brittle prose as sharp as the edge of a diamond,* " he will write for instance, " *but suddenly the Hemingway-myth reappears with its affectations of depravity and the spell is broken.* " [21] " *You shut the book somewhat sickened, disappointed and above all angry with such a fine writer who keeps so badly the promises which he had made. Why is not Hemingway content to be himself?* " [22]

Coindreau's attacks must have had a sobering effect on French critics, for in the next few years little interest was shown in Hemingway's works except among academic critics, who are less susceptible to the changes of fashion. In the *Revue Anglo-Américaine* for April 1933, Professor Charles Cestre reviewed favourably, but very briefly, both *In Our Time* and *The Torrents Of Spring* and in April-June 1938 Professor Jean-Jacques Mayoux boldly proclaimed his admiration for *To Have and Have Not* which had just been cut up by Coindreau in the *Nouvelle Revue Française* : " ... *each of Hemingway's books renews in me the same admiration... never before this book has the type — man of adventure — been given such human significance...* " Yet the translation of *Green Hills of Africa, Les Vertes collines d'Afrique* (Paris, Gallimard, 1937) was received with general indifference. Henri Hertz devoted only a few lukewarm lines to it in *Europe* (Nov.

15, 1937, pp. 402-403) and Louis Pacteau in *Études Anglaises* (Oct.-Dec. 1938, p. 441) declared : " *This story told by a self-complacent and conceited hunter reads well, but will not add anything to the reputation of Hemingway.* " [23] In *Les Nouvelles Littéraires*, Georges Charensol, in spite of his friendship for the translator, Jeanine Delpech, was obliged to admit that : " *One regrets that such a considerable talent as that of Hemingway should be wasted on such trifles.* " [24] Another reason for the failure of the book must have been the poor quality of the translation which was marred by innumerable anglicisms, as Louis Pacteau pointed out in his *Études Anglaises* review.

Gallimard was not discouraged, however, and remained loyal to Hemingway. In May 1938, they published a translation of *Death in the Afternoon, Mort dans l'après-midi*, by René Daumal who, being a good writer in his own right, did a much better job than Jeanine Delpech. Yet the book was not a success, probably because the French public had already read better books on the same subject from *Arènes Sanglantes* by Blasco Ibañez to *Les Bestiaires* by Montherlant and Gabriel Peyré's *Sang et lumière* and *De cape et d'épée*. Marcelle Auclair (Jean Prévost's wife) was enthusiastic over it, though, in *Les Nouvelles Littéraires* (Sept. 3,1938) [25], but all that Pierre Leyris found to praise in the *Nouvelle Revue Française* (June 1939) was " *the human quality* " of the book.

So, when World War II broke out, Hemingway's reputation was petering out in France. The blaze of enthusiasm with which his works had been welcomed from 1928 to 1932 may thus seem strange, but it will become comprehensible if we refer to the French literary context of those years.

First of all, it should be noted that after World War I the novel enjoyed in France a period of extraordinary prosperity, « une vogue extraordinaire », as the phrase was. People wanted to read, to be diverted, to forget the horrors through which they had been, or to recollect in tranquillity the emotions they had experienced. There was both an infinite craving for diversion and escape, and a passionate desire to understand what had happened (and why it had happened) during the nightmarish years of the Great War. All this encouraged fiction-writing, more particularly in the direction of the novel of action, or of adventure.

There was at the same time a marked desire for a change, if not of subject-matter at least of tone. The younger generation, naturally, felt bitter about the war into which it had been thrown whether it liked it or not. It boldy criticized its elders whom it held responsible for all that had happened, it called the older generation a failure and loudly asserted the claims of youth. It was the age of the « moins de trente ans ».

It was also a period of unprecedented economic prosperity, and the publishing trade had its share of the post-war boom. More and more novels were published, and they sold well — in tens or sometimes hundreds of thousands.

After the chaos of the war which had disrupted so many traditions and well-established customs, people felt restless and wanted to travel. The word "tourist" became a household word. Those who could not travel read books. Hence the success of books of travel or of adventures in distant lands. Exoticism became the fashion. [26] One of the most popular authors was Paul Morand with books like *Ouvert la nuit* (1922), *Fermé la nuit* (1923), *L'Europe galante* (1925), *Bouddha vivant* (1927), *Magie noire* (1928), *Paris-Tombouctou* (1928), *New York*, (1930), *Londres* (1933). The very titles speak for themselves. He took his readers all over the world. Roland Dorgelès, Maurice Bedel, Luc Durtain, Louis and Marc Chadourne and many others supplied the general public with similar products.

Another favourite of the post-war years was Pierre Benoit, a clever writer of thrilling and nostalgic books of adventure like *Koenigsmark* and *L'Atlantide* (1919).

A more serious aspect of this widespread desire for escape and exoticism was an intense intellectual curiosity for what was going on in other countries. The war, by bringing so many nationalities into contact, broadened the horizon of the French reading public. It was at this time that reviews with such significant titles as *Europe* (1923) and *Revue Européenne* (1923) were founded, and translations of foreign books became more and more numerous. The quarterly *Commerce* (1924-1932), under the joint-editorship of Paul Valéry, Léon-Paul Fargue and Valery Larbaud, regularly published translations from half a dozen foreign literatures, and Valery Larbaud exalted the part played by translators : " ... *the translator,* " he claimed, " *plays in literary history a part incomparably more active and important than the critic or the scholar who supplies the readers of his country with information about the literary movements of a foreign country.* " [27]

Some of the writers of this period, however, refused or failed to escape into exoticism and romance ; they preferred to indulge in their spleen and express what Marcel Arland called « le nouveau mal du siècle » in his *Essais critiques* because it somewhat resembled « le mal du siècle » of the generation which came of age at the end of the Napoleonic wars — « le cafard, » as it was lugubriously named by some of its addicts. Francis Carco was probably the best interpreter of this mysterious melancholy and unaccountable *taedium vitae*. The irresistible sadness of long rainy days in winter pervades all his books, the same sadness that darkens the closing chapters of *A Farewell to Arms*. In the same key Pierre Mac Orlan created romantic heroes doomed to tragic failure from their birth and full of an incurable sadness and stoic despair like some of Hemingway's characters. [28]

Other writers of this generation tried to find a way out of this morass of spleen. They entertained no illusions about life. They knew that it was sad, often repulsive, absurd and meaningless, but, instead of despairing, they tried to give a meaning to it, to invest it with nobility. Their works exalted energy and heroism and virility in a world of men without women. Thus André Malraux's novels from *La Voie royale* (1930) to *L'Espoir* (1938) by way of *La Condition humaine* (1933) were an effort to find a new faith in man and resist the temptation of nihilism. As to Montherlant's books, they were mostly portraits of the artist as a hero and a misogynist. In this group we also find two authors who wrote prefaces for two of Hemingway's novels :

Drieu La Rochelle and Jean Prévost. The coincidence is significant. Drieu La Rochelle in *État civil* (1921) expressed the despair of a young veteran, but as early as 1932 *Mesure de la France* already proposed remedies and reasons for hope. Jean Prévost (born in 1901) had not taken part in the war, but he was also torn between disgust (*Tentative de solitude*, 1925) and hope, and one of the solutions he found was the practice and exaltation of athleticism (*Plaisir des sports*).

Such was the background against which the French translations of Hemingway's works developed. In many respects the circumstances were favourable, World War I having had the same effects on his French fellow-writers and on his prospective readers as on himself. There was thus a sort of pre-established harmony between his public and his works. But this parallelism is not a sufficient explanation of his popularity in the late 1920's and early 1930's. It can be accounted for by a number of specific causes which we must now try to define.

First of all, there were topical causes. Hemingway lived in Paris as an expatriate after World War I. Thanks to Adrienne Monnier and Sylvia Beach, as we have seen, he came to know a number of French writers who became interested in American literature in general and in his works in particular. Besides, he was able to publish some of his stories either in translation in such little magazines as *Le Navire d'Argent* and *Bifur*, or in the original in international magazines like *The Boulevardier, the transatlantic review, This Quarter* and *Transition*, which, being published in Paris, were read by French connoisseurs of English and American literature. He was thus known to a number of French critics even before he became famous in America and this certainly helped the spread of his reputation in France. But this circumstance was merely an accidental factor. [29]

There were also political causes. After World War I in which the United States had played such a decisive role, the French public wanted to know more about that remote country which had suddenly become one of the Great Powers. French people often had seen American soldiers or even had come into contact with "Sammies" and they were now anxious to know what made them tick, so to speak. It was to meet these needs that chairs in American literature and civilisation were precisely at this time created in two French universities, in Paris and Lyon. As Julien Gracq put it : " *The public is becoming more and more aware of the fact that France weighs less and less on the political plane. It is thus brought to think that the countries which nowadays 'lead the world' probably also have something to say which in all likelihood is important. This newly opened window in a room which seemed too close has become wider and wider open since 1919 ; it will never be closed again.* " [30]

On the other hand, French intellectuals soon realized that a new civilization was developing in the United States, a civilization founded on technology and resulting in mass-production and standardization. They distrusted it. They feared lest it should eventually lead to the enslavement of the individual by the machines which originally were supposed to liberate him. Georges Duhamel expressed these fears in 1930 in *Scènes de la vie future* which was less an indictment of the United States than of industrial civilization in general. French intellectuals therefore watched with great sympathy and interest the revolt of some young American writers against the technological civilization in which they were caught. As early as 1928, Bernard Faÿ wrote in *La Revue Hebdomadaire* (May 12) :

America, which has carried standardization and democracy farther than any other nation, observes with astonishment and a forbearance tinged with indignation those of her artists — and there are many of them to tell the truth — who want to save their personality and refuse to write best-sellers... One sees the [American] artist making violent efforts in order not to be caught in the vice — these efforts may seem comic or tragic according to your character, but the conservatives should not despise them, for this effort is similar to the one which they are making in order to save an old tradition of mankind, namely human personality, and the revolutionists should not be contemptuous, for it is an attempt to safeguard a principle in the name of which they have started most of their revolutions, namely human individuality. [31]

And Faÿ mentioned Hemingway among the artists in revolt against industrial standardization. [32]

These considerations lead us to another set of causes of a moral or metaphysical nature. What attracted some French readers to the works of the Lost Generation in general and of Hemingway in particular was the fact that they revealed an acute consciousness of the tragedy of the human condition in the modern world, an awareness made all the keener by the war and also by the excesses of an industrial civilization which had been pushed farther in the United States than in Europe. American writers, in a way, found themselves in a privileged position on account of the magnifying power of American civilization. French intellectuals sympathized with their revolt and appreciated the quality of their lucid pessimism. Drieu La Rochelle thus wrote :

This youth or health [*of Hemingway's*] does not exclude pessimism. There is pessimism in Hemingway, a d—d vigorous pessimism. I remember an old American lady who once told me : 'Why are European literatures so sad ?' I answered her : 'You have never looked at yourself in a glass.' I was thinking of Whitmann [*sic*], of Thoreau and of Poe. [*He could easily have found better examples.*] Pessimism is the privilege of strength and youth... [33]

Raoul Celly had already pointed out in 1928 that Hemingway's was " *a form of pessimism checked by a sort of fatalistic resignation. When you cannot alter the course of events, you bow your head...* " [34] And André Maurois also noted : " *... if he is a realist, he is quite different from the realists of the French school of 1880... His picture of life is as dark as theirs, but it is less pessimistic. The final impression is one of vigour and courage.* " [35]

Thus the mood of stoic despair which was to make the novels of Hemingway and Faulkner so popular with the existentialists in the 1940's was already very much appreciated in the interwar period, though critics did not then insist on it as much as they would later.

The French readers of the 1920's and 1930's were above all attuned to the mood of disillusionment and nihilistic revolt expressed by Hemingway's works. Régis Michaud thus wrote in 1928 in his *Panorama de la littérature américaine* :

> As in Ben Hecht's novels you can hear at every page an echo of Hamlet's pessimism : 'What is life good for ?' A war to save Right, Civilization, the dollar, flirting and machines ? And then what ? Drinking, gambling, debauchery, suicide, or for the luckier ones some sort of escape — such is the conclusion of these calm and despairing self-examinations. The young American no longer believes in America. On the same day he lost his faith both in himself and in his country. In revolt against his parents and his masters, he does not find any outlet for his energy. He regrets and curses, and for want of something better wallows in bohemia and dilettantism — only too happy if he can write or paint in order to forget. (See ... *In Our Time* by Ernest Hemingway). ...The fine enthusiasm for entering the war, as it can be found in Willa Cather's *One of Ours*, did not last long. Robert McAlmon's new recruits are even more pessimistic than those of Barbusse... [36]

Philippe Soupault later concluded in *Europe* :

> ... American writers are above all rebels. Their revolt against 'all the lies that stifle us' (Dos Passos dixit) have found an echo in the various European literatures of the post-war years. Properly speaking, one cannot claim that there was any real and profound influence. It was rather an identity of views which confirmed young American writers in their tendencies and attitudes. [37]

The image of the United States as a land of crass materialism and intolerant philistinism became a cliché among left-wing reviewers, for these critical reactions sometimes had political undertones and were the corollaries of an anti-capitalistic attitude. Thus René Lalou wrote in *Les Nouvelles Littéraires* in 1927 : " ... *will hypocrisy remain there as an institution, reducing art, whether realistic or in revolt, to the status of a by-product ?...* " — and he spoke of the tragedy of a society which imprisons God in a wad of dollar-notes and Satan in a bottle of whisky. [38]

As early as 1925, in an article devoted to Sinclair Lewis, Dreiser, Sandburg and Mencken, Firmin Roz had detected — and praised — the new spirit of revolt against American society which characterized these writers :

No novelist until recently had called to account these very principles, had denounced the fundamental conceptions on which the life of their country is resting. It was because these principles, these conceptions daunted American writers on account of their very efficiency. Nowadays American writers have a different purpose which precisely seems to be, as it were, to scandalize and so wake up the dormant and self-satisfied consciousness of their fellow-countrymen. There is among the writers of the new school a feeling of exasperation and revolt against the inertia of a society which they reproach with having made its essential characteristics empty of their contents... Puritanism is no longer anything but a conventional attitude in a society where comfort has become more important and wealth is more highly prized than in any other country. [39]

This shows the fascination wrought on French intellectuals by the new non-conformist trends of American literature and how ready they were to welcome Hemingway's novels even before they were published at all.

An aspect of this revolt against puritanism which was particularly popular among French readers — at least at the beginning — was the aggressive frankness of the new writers as regards sexual matters. Reviewing *Death in the Afternoon* in 1932, M. E. Coindreau praised this form of realism:

Ernest Hemingway has just published a novel which will have about the same effect on the American public as *Corydon* had on the readers of André Gide... Mr. Hemingway cannot forget that he is a member of that band of 'enfants terribles', those post-war writers who, in order to react against the puritanism of their country, adopted the 'tough guy' type. Their influence was excellent and they have certainly contributed to rid American literature of the sentimental insipidities which rendered it anaemic.

But he added:

One, however, should leave well alone... It is not enough to strike hard, the blows must also be well aimed, and in the course of the last few years the mentality of the American public has changed to such an extent that it soon won't be necessary to strike at all. [40]

The same thing, after a time, might have been said of the French public, which also got tired of sexual realism, or at least ceased to be surprised by it. Besides, this realism had been practised with even more boldness by D. H. Lawrence and James Joyce. There were other — and more powerful — reasons for the interest of the French public in Hemingway's work. Its greatest novelty and most striking originality for a French reader was its directness and complete lack of intellectuality. Hemingway's novels gave an impression of energy and irrepressible vitality which was often lacking in the overintellectual disquisitions of French novelists. Buenzod noted as early as 1928 in his review of *Cinquante mille dollars* :

A few characters, always the same, but standing out with an extraordinary relief obtained by a truly startling minimum of means. And this is the very essence of American genius. This direct way of imposing oneself, of reaching the first rank by powerfully jostling one's way to the front... this method may produce brutes, but once in a million this brute happens to go to the pains of seeing and describing and the result is a prodigious story-teller. [41]

Jean Prévost also admired in *Cinquante mille dollars* — " *the dramatic power, the concise and vigorous way of seeing and describing... One cannot say,* " he added, " *that too much refinement or too much intellectual complexity make of him the novelist of an élite. Each of the truths which he notes down at a gallop gives the reader,* any reader, *a sort of fleshly thrill.* " [42] What struck Maurois when he first read Hemingway's novels was that his characters did not analyze themselves, were content to live and be. No introspection as in French novels : " *... Hemingway's characters* lived, *they did not unravel* (« délabrynther ») *their feelings, they ordered drinks, dinners, they cursed, they laughed, nothing more, but one knew them as intimately as Odette Swann or Charlus or Legrandin* " (in Proust's novels). [43] Raoul Celly wrote in the *Revue Nouvelle* in 1928 : " *Ernest Hemingway is one of those writers who want to have a vision of the world and of men other than can be got in libraries. It is essential to live ; it is necessary to come into close contact with the most diverse and opposite activities of man.* " [44] And that is why Soupault praised the human quality of Hemingway's novels : "*For my part, what I prefer in Hemingway's books is their human quality. His characters are in no way literary.*" [45] Drieu La Rochelle compared him to "*a joyful rhinoceros who has bathed early in the morning and rushes to breakfast.*" [46] For, as Maurois pointed out, "*there is in Hemingway's stories an almost physical force.*" [47]

French readers, however, were not taken in by deceptive appearances; they realized that this directness and closeness to life was the effect of a subtle art and their admiration for Hemingway's art was also due to aesthetic and literary reasons. Victor Llona thus asserted in the *Nouvelle Revue Française* in 1929 :

> Superficial persons have said of these bare stories (in *Fifty Grand*) that they were mere reporting. How absurd! As if reporters did anything but dilute and prettify their prose in order to seduce the public. 'Take eloquence and wring its neck,' Verlaine said... With his strong hands, the strong hands of a boy from the Middle-West, Hemingway has obeyed him thoroughly and uncompromisingly. Neglecting vain embellishments, he goes straight to his goal like a sprinter who rushes forward with his elbows stuck to his body... [48]

Jean Prévost, though fascinated by Hemingway's vigour, declared : "*Any writer who knows his trade will praise the dialogue, the progression of his effects, the absence of rhetoric and facile effects, — in short, an art impeccable in its roughness.*" [49] André Maurois defined the qualities of Hemingway's style with his usual skill in *Les Romanciers américains* (1931) : "*His style is made of wellcut metallic elements. It calls to mind certain modern buildings : girders and concrete. Elegance is obtained by shrinking from elegance. There are on Hemingway's façades neither Corinthian capitals nor mass-produced naked women...*" [50] This preoccupation with style explains why Hemingway was always more popular in France than the writers of the preceding generation. For, as Lloyd Morris pointed out as early as 1925, in *Vient de paraître* :

The generation of American writers now in their middle age has given us a vigorous criticism of its environment, but it has failed to give it an aesthetic expression. A sharp difference appears when one passes from the works of this generation of writers to those of its successors... They are less preoccupied than their elders with the defects and weaknesses of the civilization which surrounds them... They replace the negative hostility to life of moralists by the positive joy of artists... They consider a story as a form of art rather than as a vehicle for moralistic propaganda... What distinguishes them from their older contemporaries is not the discovery of new materials, but the discovery of new ways of using them. [51]

French critics were thus, in general, fascinated by Hemingway's technique and, above all, by his handling of dialogue. Bernard Faÿ, for instance, noted : "*His descriptions are not always clear or powerful, his stories are sometimes lacking in strength or clarity, but, as soon as his characters start speaking, they become alive, irrefutable and invincible... One might say that his characters do not talk, that they do not speak. The noise which they make is rather a sort of breathing.*" [52] Denis Marion reviewing *L'Adieu aux armes* in the *Nouvelle Revue Française* in October 1933 wrote : "*As usual the dialogues are extraordinary. One might think that they are strictly phonographic. Yet they are composed with an extreme precision which gives them a meaning that transcends their mere contents.*" [53]

The acuteness of this last remark, though, is exceptional. For all their interest in Hemingway's new techniques, the French critics of the inter-war years did not carry their analyses very far and failed for instance to grasp the importance of the behaviouristic objectivity of Hemingway's descriptions. Only Philippe Soupault had an inkling of it : "*He accepts what his characters tell him and reproduces the spectacle of their comings and goings. It does not matter to him whether they are unexpected, contradictory, absurd or, on the contrary, natural.*" [54] This certainly lacks the clarity and acumen of Camus's comments on the same subject :

Its technique consists in describing men externally in their most unimportant gestures, in reproducing their speech without commentary even to its repetitions, in acting as if men were entirely defined by their everyday automatisms... This technique is called realist only through a misunderstanding... it is clear that the world of the American novel does not aim at the pure and simple reproduction of reality ; it aims at the most arbitrary kind of stylisation. [55]

There was one thing, though, of which some French critics of the inter-war years were fully aware and that was the fact that all Hemingway's so-called new techniques were merely the systematization of methods which had already been used in the past by French writers. French readers thought that they discovered America when they read Hemingway's novels, whereas they were only re-discovering French techniques transplanted in America. Hemingway was not really a Redskin, to use Philip Rahv's terminology, but rather a European masquerading in American dress. Thus Maurois noted that Hemingway's manner to some extent recalled that of Mérimée or that of Kipling. [56] Drieu La Rochelle compared Hemingway to Maupassant [57] and Jean Prévost to Stendhal [58] on whose works he was later to write a penetrating critical study. [59] These resemblances — which were not all mere coincidences — certainly made Hemingway easier of access for the general public, and thus to some extent account for his success in France.

Such were the reactions of French critics between the two World Wars. During all this period, they wrote only short and fairly superficial articles or reviews. But, though they showed discrimination and raised some objections, they were all agreed that Hemingway was a great writer of the very first class and no one contested it between 1928 and 1932. When M. E. Coindreau, his best translator, who had done so much to acclimatize his works in France, suddenly disowned him, his reputation to some extent underwent an eclipse, but, in spite of this, as Jean-Paul Sartre pointed out on the eve of World War II in a special issue of *Les Cahiers de Paris* on the contemporary American novel :

The greatest literary development in France between 1929 and 1939 was the discovery of Faulkner, Dos Passos, Hemingway, Caldwell, Steinbeck... These authors have not had in France a popular success comparable to that of Sinclair Lewis. Their influence was far more restricted, but infinitely more profound... To writers of my generation, the publication of *The 42nd Parallel, Light in August, A Farewell to Arms* evoked a revolution similar to the one produced fifteen years earlier in Europe by the *Ulysses* of James Joyce. [60]

To the name of Sinclair Lewis he might have added those of Pearl Buck and of lesser writers and he might have gone even farther for, between the two groups of authors, there was not only a difference in degree, as he suggested, but a difference in kind. Neither Sinclair Lewis nor Pearl Buck had a new style to offer, they created no new form of sensibility and had no new *Weltanschauung* to express. On the contrary, Hemingway had evolved a new technique which exerted a strong influence on Sartre himself and on Camus among others. The attitudes he struck in his books were also widely imitated. He was responsible for a new Byronism made up of disenchantment and tough guy nihilism, traces of which can be found in the works of writers as different as Montherlant and Jean Prévost. And, finally, without in the least philosophizing, he gave a striking picture of the crisis of man in our war-torn, overindustrialized world, and his French readers recognized their own predicament in that of his heroes.

This was only the beginning. For, after World War II, his influence in France became even more widespread and profound and eventually led to the development of the so-called new French novel with Michel Butor, Nathalie Sarraute, etc. The common aim of all these writers is to dissolve the boundary line between the objective and subjective worlds and, in order to obtain this result, in Nathalie Sarraute's own words, they have " *to post another consciousness on the outer boundaries of the character's consciousness, one that is more clearseeing than his own, and which records these movements as they develop, more or less in the manner of a movie camera* " — or of Hemingway.

But this is another story.

It is still too early to tell it, since the last two decades cannot yet be seen in the proper perspective. But it is possible to sketch briefly the growth of Hemingway's reputation in France after World War II.

It should first of all be noted that, though Hemingway never was such a Protean artist as Picasso, for instance, one may speak of at least two distinct " periods " in his production : a dark, or nihilistic period which extends from his first works to, but not including, *For Whom the Bell Tolls* and a whitish or rosy, or idealistic period from *For Whom the Bell Tolls* to his death. Now this break in his career also corresponds to a break in the story of his reputation as far as France is concerned, for the first French translation of *For Whom the Bell Tolls* reached the French public only in 1944 after the interruption of World War II and the German Occupation. Though this translation, which had been hastily done in England by Denise V. Ayme and published by a British publisher, Heinemann and Zsolnay, was very poor in quality, the book had a fantastic success. By 1948 over 100,000 copies had been sold. [61] Then Denise Van Moppès revised her war-time translation and *Pour qui sonne le glas* now taken over by Gallimard, pursued its triumphant career as a best-seller. In 1950 a 5,000-copy edition of the book was sold out in three days, so that another had to be printed which sold almost as quickly. [62] Thus, after World War II Hemingway ceased to be the exclusive property of a discerning minority and became the idol of the general public. Everybody loved this romantic story, which instead of debunking war gave a meaning to it, and instead of expressing disillusioned views about love exalted it. Instead of describing wholesale slaughter like *Le Feu* or even *A Farewell to Arms*, it recounted thrilling adventures with relatively little bloodshed. The hero was attractive and so was his partner. The end was sad, but so noble and moving that the readers forgave the author. And, when *Pour qui sonne le glas* became the book of an excellent film, its popularity further increased. Moreover, this popularity was enhanced by the new Hemingway myth which showed Hemingway no longer as a cynical tough guy, but as The Happy Warrior who had taken an active part in the Liberation of France. This image was spread by the popular magazines and the newspapers with a generous accompaniment of picturesque photographs. No one could resist it. For once, the highbrow critics ratified the judgment of the general public. Reviewers were unanimous in praising the book [63] and compared it favourably with *L'Espoir*. [64]

On the contrary, the translation of *To Have and Have Not*, *En avoir ou pas* (1945), though it was the work of M. E. Coindreau, was received with complete indifference, and so was *Dix indiens* (1946), a collection of short stories translated by Marcel Duhamel, because both books belonged to the nihilistic period of Hemingway. As for *Across the River and Into the Trees*, it was not even translated into French. Apparently Hemingway refused to sell the translation rights for fear of being as savagely cut up in France as he had been in America.

But, when *Le Vieil homme et la mer* appeared in 1952 almost simultaneously with the original, there was once more a chorus of praise. [65] The translation was excellent; it was the work of Jean Dutourd, a brilliant young novelist in his own right. Jean Guéhenno [66] and two young novelists, Michel Mohrt [67] and Romain Gary [68], were especially loud in their praises and extolled to the skies the beauty both of the matter and the manner. It was a sort of pre-apotheosis before the official apotheosis of the Nobel Prize in 1954.

On the other hand, more and more serious studies of Hemingway's art appeared in France : Raymond Las Vergnas's essay in *Cahiers des Langues Modernes* (1946), Claude-Edmonde Magny's chapter on " Hemingway, ou l'exaltation de l'instant " in her book on *L'Age du roman américain* (1948) and finally G. A. Astre's excellent little critical biography in 1961. [69]

So, when Hemingway died in 1961, his reputation both as a popular novelist and a great writer was well established in France. And that is why François Mauriac, though he is in many ways the very opposite of Hemingway, felt obliged to conclude :

Hemingway is synonymous with triumphant physical strength, war when you are twenty, big game hunting, love (four legitimate wives, all loved with passion, and many others besides, I suppose), liquor galore... But this boxer, this trapper, this big game hunter has written great works and done more than merely write them; he lived them side by side with that Spanish people up in arms which he loved so much.

As a Christian, Mauriac made one reservation, however : *" ... I think that Hemingway was wrong : truth cannot correspond to only one period of life; it cannot belong only to young males intoxicated with their strength, for this does not last; it must also suit weak and mild natures... "* [70]

All this is true. Taking only surfaces into account, Hemingway achieved popularity because his works extolled a new style of living, tougher, more daring, more heroic, more idealistic than those which are commonly accepted, and because at their best his novels implied a stoic awareness of the " human condition ". But he never really had a valid message to communicate and, compared to such writers as Stendhal and Malraux who touched upon the same subjects, he looks almost immature. So the main reason for his lasting success with the more discerning critics and writers lies elsewhere. True, he had little to say, but he said it wonderfully. What so many French novelists admire and envy is his style, that wonderful style with punch in it, that extraordinary style which, taking the vernacular as its instrument, manages to make it express everything and anything and to create a fourth and even a fifth dimension. [71] For all his immaturity, our overcultured authors cannot help being fascinated by the mastery and vigour of this self-taught writer,

" Fond of his sweetheart, relishing well his steak...
Preferring scars and the beard and faces pitted with small pox over all latherers,
And those well-tann'd to those that keep out of the sun. " [72]

NOTES

1. It is to be noted however that there is not a single reference to Hemingway in Gide's *Journal* before 1943. He was a writer of another school.
2. See Cyrille ARNAVON, *Les Lettres américaines devant la critique française, 1887-1917*, Paris, Belles Lettres, 1951, 153 pp. and Roger ASSELINEAU, *The Literary Reputation of Mark Twain from 1910 to 1950*, Paris, Didier, 1954, 241 pp.
3. Also published in *Nouvelle Revue Française*, June 1928, pp. 736-741.
4. « De ces récits traduits de l'anglais par M. O. de Weymer, récits d'un réalisme quelque peu brutal et d'un style par trop argotique, j'ai surtout goûté celui qui a pour titre « L'Invincible »... Théophile Gautier et Mérimée eussent aimé cette planche à la Goya... »
5. « Peu de romanciers réussissent dans l'art de la nouvelle... Et pourtant, quel plaisir un conte bien construit et bien écrit n'offre-t-il pas au lecteur. C'est une satisfaction que vous éprouverez à plusieurs reprises si vous lisez Cinquante mille dollars, *recueil d'une dizaine de nouvelles d'Ernest Hemingway...* elles sont passionnantes et prestement enlevées. Un excellent volume, en un mot. »
6. « ... cinq nouvelles que le lecteur le plus distrait ne saura plus oublier et dont l'ensemble forme, je crois bien, un chef-d'œuvre. »
7. « Autrement dit, Hemingway est un mauvais reporter. Qu'il s'en console, il vaut beaucoup mieux que cela. »
8. « Elle a son équipe de découvreurs. Le plus distingué, le plus doué est Ernest Hemingway, dont la popularité aujourd'hui outre-mer est si grande qu'il forme avec Cummings et Wescott une sorte de triumvirat glorieux et juvénile. »
9. « Quand j'étais, il y a deux ans, à l'Université de Princeton, les professeurs parlaient beaucoup d'un roman que venait de publier un de leurs anciens élèves : Hemingway. Je demandai le titre : The Sun Also Rises. — Et c'est bien ?, — C'est très dur, cynique, mais extraordinairement vrai... Je l'achetai. C'était excellent. »
10. « J'ai rencontré Hemingway une seule fois... Il est très costaud. Il m'a beaucoup plu. C'est un type avec qui il faut chasser ou pêcher.
« ... il y a surtout le démon d'Hemingway... celui de la santé ; ce qui vous touche là c'est le ton même d'une vie, d'une santé, c'est le tempérament d'un gaillard. »
11. « ... la sécheresse et la désinvolture qui caractérisent sa manière. Comme toujours les dialogues sont excellents. »
12. « Une fois de plus, dans ce domaine, comme dans beaucoup d'autre nous retrouvons cette apathie, cette impossibilité de s'intéresser qui semblent être caractéristiques des années *1930 à 1933*. »

13. « *Voici un écrivain, déjà illustre dans son pays et que le nôtre n'a pas encore mis à sa place.* »
« *Mais la lectrice, il lui arrive de trouver cela trop fort, trop dur... il y manquera la présence d'une sensibilité féminine, et un hommage à la femme. Ainsi Hemingway, admiré, n'était pas poussé par cette force plus puissante chez nous que toute critique : les conversations autour du thé, l'éloge d'une bouche élégante... Knut Hamsun a subi chez nous la même injustice : lui aussi nous apportait l'homme différent de la femme... La gloire d'Hamsun, comme la jeune renommée d'Hemingway, a pu sans doute se répandre en des pays où les femmes créent comme chez nous la renommée littéraire : pays du Nord ou États-Unis ; mais parce que, dans ces pays qui nous ont enseigné la beauté des souliers larges, des étoffes lourdes et la coquetterie de la pipe, les femmes savent approuver d'un garçon qu'il soit tout à fait garçon.* »

14. F. Ansermoz-Dubois erroneously ascribes the date of 1922 to this article (p. 154).

15. « *Déjà, nous y trouvons son obsession de l'impuissance, sa tendance à ajouter des contes dans l'espoir qu'il en sortira un roman, son attitude anti-sociale, conséquence naturelle du complexe d'infériorité.* » (p. 77).

16. « *Tout dans ce roman sembla nouveau : le sujet dans son audace, le style dans sa sobriété métallique, l'attitude de l'auteur en face de ses personnages, sorte de détachement soutenu par un parti-pris de cynisme qui trompa bien des lecteurs et les empêcha de percevoir la sentimentalité qui affleurait à chaque instant. Car, de même qu'il y a de fausses maigres, il existe de faux costauds.* » (p. 79).

17. « *Dans* The Sun Also Rises *tous les personnages sont des aboutiques et des lâches.* » (p. 80).

18. « *... A* Farewell to Arms *est encore un roman d'impuissance, de lâcheté et de peur. Les personnages d'Hemingway, malgré leurs 'doubles muscles', appartiennent à la race des vaincus.* » (p. 83).

19. « *Comme les enfants timides qu'on envoie se promener dans le noir chantent pour se donner du courage, Hemingway tonitrue, joue du fusil et du couteau. Il y a en lui beaucoup de Tartarin.* » (p. 93).

20. « *Il préfère s'habiller en Teur et trinquer avec des gars qui gueulent, qui tuent, qui forniquent, mais n'en sont pas moins nés vaincus. Et ils le savent et ils essaient de se donner le change en faisant tant de bruit. Si pénible qu'en soit la pensée, on ne peut se défendre de soupçonner que M. Hemingway, écrivain, se trouve un peu dans le même cas.* » (p. 94). Exactly the same sentence occurs at the end of his review of *To Have and Have Not* in 1938.

21. « *On se laisse aller au charme de cette prose un peu sèche, cassante, nette comme une arête de diamant, mais brusquement Hemingway-mythe réapparaît avec ses mines de polisson et l'enchantement est rompu.* »

22. « *Et l'on ferme le livre un peu écœuré, déçu, et irrité surtout contre un bel écrivain qui tient si mal les promesses qu'il avait données.* »

23. « *Ce récit d'un chasseur complaisamment vaniteux est d'une lecture agréable, mais n'ajoutera guère à la réputation de Hemingway.* » See also the review of *The Sun Also Rises* by Professor M. Le Breton in *Études Anglaises*, Sept. 1937, p. 480 : « *Petit roman à lire en vacances. Peut-être était-il superflu de consacrer tant de pages aux menus faits et gestes de cinq ou six Américains en joyeuse tournée à Biarritz...* »

24. « *On regrette un peu qu'un immense talent comme celui de Hemingway s'attarde à ces fantaisies...* »

25. « *De Cape et d'épée est un recueil de nouvelles très prenantes mais* Mort dans l'après-midi *restera comme un classique.* »

26. « *Au lendemain de 1918, le roman a connu une vogue extraordinaire. Le besoin de distractions et de lecture, créé par les longues absences et les exils de la guerre ; l'attrait des nombreux prix créés pour venir en aide aux romanciers, une sorte de vulgarisation et de divulgation des procédés techniques... la bienveillance d'une presse particulièrement avide d'aspects nouveaux et d'une rare curiosité à l'égard des nouveaux venus, enfin, ce prestige de la jeunesse qui suit toujours les catastrophes et qui fait croire qu'elle seule tirera le monde d'affaire... tout cela donne à la narration une exceptionnelle saveur. Les premiers succès, dès 1919, allèrent au roman d'aventures.* »

27. « *Ainsi le traducteur joue dans l'histoire littéraire un rôle incomparablement plus actif et plus marquant que le critique ou l'érudit qui renseigne les lecteurs de son pays sur les mouvements littéraires d'un pays étranger.* » Quoted by ANSERMOZ-DUBOIS, p. 97.

28. See also the works of Ribemont-Dessaignes and René Crevel ; in particular the latter's *La Mort difficile* (i.e. life.)

29. On these encounters of French, English and American writers in the 1920's in Paris, see *Les Années vingt — Les écrivains américains à Paris et leurs amis*, Paris, 1959, which is the catalogue of an exhibition set up in Paris in 1959 by Sylvia Beach. See also her book, *Shakespeare and Company*, 1959.

30. « *Le public est profondément sensible au fait que sur le plan mondial la France pèse de moins en moins lourd. Il est conduit à penser que les pays qui maintenant 'mènent le monde' ont sans doute 'quelque chose à dire' qui risque de compter particulièrement. Cette fenêtre ouverte sur l'air du large dans une pièce qui paraît trop confinée s'est faite de plus en plus béante depuis 1919 ; on ne la refermera plus.* » Julien Gracq is not only a surrealist, but also a teacher of history and geography.

31. « *L'Amérique qui a poussé la standardisation et la démocratie plus loin que tout autre peuple, contemple avec étonnement et une tolérance mêlée d'indignation ceux de ses artistes nombreux à la vérité, qui cherchent à sauver leur personnalité, à ne point simplement se vendre comme 'best-sellers'... Aussi voit-on, pour échapper à l'étau, l'artiste se livrer à des efforts violents, que l'on peut trouver comiques ou tragiques selon les dispositions de son caractère, mais que les conservateurs ne devraient point mépriser, car cela est un effort analogue au leur pour sauver une vieille tradition de l'humanité, la personne humaine, et que les révolutionnaires ne devraient point insulter, car c'est une tentative pour sauvegarder un principe au nom duquel ils firent la plupart de leurs révolutions : la personnalité humaine.* »

32. « *... Mrs. Wharton... après de longues années fut enfin reconnue par la presse et l'opinion de son pays. Hemingway et Wescott sont en train de se voir conférer le même honneur, car leurs livres se sont imposés aux États-Unis.* »

33. « *Cette jeunesse ou cette santé n'excluent pas le pessimisme. Il y a du pessimisme dans Hemingway. Je me rappelle une vieille dame américaine qui me disait : 'Pourquoi les littératures européennes sont-elles si tristes ?' Je lui répondis : 'Vous ne vous êtes pas regardés.' Je songeais à Whitmann [sic], à Thoreau, à*

Poe... Le pessimisme est l'apanage de la force et de la jeunesse... » Introduction to *L'Adieu aux Armes*, p. 11.

34. « *Pessimisme tempéré par une sorte de résignation fataliste. Quand on ne peut rien changer au cours des événements, on courbe la tête.* » *Revue Nouvelle*, Oct. 1928, p. 175.

35. « *... s'il est un réaliste, il est très différent des réalistes de l'école française de 1880. Il est loin d'eux par sa philosophie. Son image de la vie aussi sombre que la leur, est moins pessimiste... L'impression finale est de vigueur et de courage.* » *Les Romanciers américains*, p. 196.

36. « *Comme dans les romans de Ben Hecht, on y entend à chaque page l'écho du pessimisme de Hamlet : 'A quoi la vie est-elle bonne?' La guerre pour le droit et la civilisation, les dollars, le flirt et les machines? Et puis? et qu'importe? L'alcool, le jeu, la débauche, le suicide ou, pour les plus chanceux, l'évasion, telle est la conclusion de ces examens de conscience calmes et désespérés. Le jeune Américain ne croit plus à l'Amérique. Il a perdu le même jour la foi en lui-même et en son pays. Révolté contre ses parents et ses maîtres, il ne trouve pas autour de lui de quoi assouvir ses énergies. Il regrette et maudit, ou, faute de mieux, se jette dans la bohème et le dilettantisme — trop heureux s'il peut manier une plume ou des pinceaux pour s'étourdir. (Voyez... De notre temps par Ernest Hemingway)... Le bel enthousiasme pour l'entrée en guerre, tel qu'on le trouve dans* L'un des nôtres *de Willa Cather n'a pas fait long feu. Les conscrits de Robert Mc Almon* [sic] *sont encore plus pessimistes que ceux de Barbusse.* » (pp. 246-247).

37. « *... les écrivains américains sont avant tout des révoltés. Cette révolte contre 'tous les mensonges qui nous étouffent' (Dos Passos dixit) trouvait en outre un écho dans la littérature européenne d'après-guerre... A proprement parler, on ne saurait prétendre qu'une influence réelle, profonde se soit faite jour. Il s'agit plutot d'une identité de vues qui confirma les jeunes américains dans leurs tendances et dans leurs manières.* » *Europe*, 15 oct. 1934, p. 274.

38. « *... l'hypocrisie demeurera-t-elle là-bas une institution, réduisant l'art, qu'il soit réaliste ou révolté, à une valeur de sous-produit?... une société qui emprisonne Dieu dans une liasse de dollars et Satan dans une bouteille de whisky.* » *Nouvelle Revue Française*, août 1927, p. 270.

39. « *Aucun romancier jusqu'à ces dernières années n'avait mis en cause cet esprit lui-même, n'avait dénoncé les conceptions fondamentales sur lesquelles reposent la vie du pays. C'est que cet esprit, ces conceptions dominaient, par leur efficacité même, les écrivains américains. Ils ont aujourd'hui un dessein, qui semble être précisément de scandaliser en quelque mesure, c'est-à-dire de surprendre et de réveiller par un choc la conscience nationale endormie et satisfaite. Il y a chez les écrivains — très différents d'ailleurs, — de la nouvelle école, une irritation et une révolte contre l'inertie d'une société à laquelle ils reprochent d'avoir vidé de leur contenu ses caractères essentiels et de s'immobiliser aujourd'hui dans le contentement d'elle-même. Le puritanisme n'est plus qu'une attitude conventionnelle, dans un milieu où le bien-être a pris plus d'importance et où la richesse est plus appréciée que partout ailleurs.* » *Revue des Deux Mondes*, 15 oct. 1925, p. 879.

40. « *Ernest Hemingway vient de publier un volume qui, sur le public américain, produira un effet à peu près semblable à celui que produisit Corydon sur le lecteur de M. André Gide... M. Hemingway ne parvient pas à oublier qu'il a fait partie de la bande des 'enfants terribles', ces écrivains d'après-guerre qui, pour réagir contre le puritanisme désuet de leur pays adoptèrent le genre 'fort en gueule'. Leur*

influence fut excellente et ils contribuèrent certainement à débarrasser la littérature américaine des fadeurs sentimentales qui l'anémiaient. Mais le mieux est l'ennemi du bien. Ce n'est pas tout de frapper fort, encore faut-il frapper juste et, depuis quelques années, la mentalité du public américain s'est à ce point transformée qu'il ne sera bientôt plus besoin de frapper du tout. » Nouvelle Revue Française, Nov. 1932, pp. 778-779.

41. « Quelques types, presque toujours les mêmes, mais 'sortis' avec un relief incroyable, par un minimum de moyens vraiment prodigieux. On touche là du doigt l'essence du génie américain. Cette façon directe de s'imposer, d'atteindre le premier rang en jouant puissamment des coudes... cette façon-là produit des brutes, mais il arrive, une fois sur un million, que la brute se donne la peine de voir, de décrire, et alors cela fait un conteur prodigieux. » Revue de Genève, Nov. 1928, p. 1416.

42. « Personne ne songe à en nier la puissance dramatique, la manière brève et forte de voir et de peindre... Tout écrivain qui connaît son métier en louera les dialogues, la progression d'effet, l'absence de rhétorique et d'effets faciles tout un art impeccable dans sa rudesse. D'autre part, on ne peut pas dire de lui que trop de raffinements ou de complexités intellectuelles le réservent à une élite. Chaque vérité qu'il note au galop frappe le lecteur, n'importe quel lecteur, d'une sorte de saisissement charnel. » Introduction to Le Soleil se lève aussi, p. VII.

43. « ... les personnages de Hemingway vivaient. Ils ne parlaient pas de leur âme, ils ne 'délabyrinthaient' pas leurs sentiments, ils commandaient des boissons, des dîners, ils juraient, ils riaient, rien de plus, mais on les connaissait aussi bien qu'Odette Swann, ou Charlus, ou Legrandin. » Les Romanciers américains, p. 193.

44. « Ernest Hemingway est de la race de ces écrivains qui ont voulu avoir de la terre et des hommes une autre vision que celle que l'on puise dans les bibliothèques. Il est essentiel de vivre ; il faut entrer en contact étroit avec les manifestations les plus diverses et les plus opposées de l'activité humaine. » Revue Nouvelle, Oct. 1928, p. 175.

45. « Pour ma part, ce que je préfère dans les livres de Hemingway, c'est leur humanité. Les personnages de Hemingway n'ont rien de littéraire. » Europe, 15 Sept. 1933, p. 140.

Michel Leiris came to the same conclusion in 1939 ; « D'un point de vue littéraire, le ton du livre [...] est empreint de cette qualité que, faute d'autre mot, l'on baptisera 'humaine', qualité sur quoi repose la valeur particulière de tant d'ouvrages émanés d'auteurs américains, et, très précisément, de la plupart des contes et romans de Hemingway. » Review of Mort dans l'après-midi in Nouvelle Revue Française, juin 1939, p. 1063.

46. « ... un joyeux rhinocéros qui a pris son bain de petit matin et se rue vers son premier déjeuner. » Introduction to L'Adieu aux armes, p. 11.

47. « ... il y a dans les contes de Hemingway une force presque physique... » Les Romanciers américains, p. 196.

48. « Des pense-vite ont dit de ces contes dépouillés jusqu'à l'os, qu'ils étaient du reportage. Quel non-sens ! Comme si les reporters faisaient autre chose que tirer à la ligne et enjoliver leur prose pour séduire le public ! 'Prends l'éloquence et tords-lui son cou', a dit Verlaine... Avec ses fortes mains de gars du Middle-West, Hemingway, lui a obéi, intégralement et sans compromission. Négligeant

les vaines fioritures, il va droit au but, comme un sprinter qui fonce, les coudes au corps. » *Nouvelle Revue Française,* janv. 1929, p. 123.
49. See n. 42.
50. « *Le style est fait d'éléments bien découpés, métalliques. On pense à certains édifices modernes : poutrelles et béton armé. L'élégance y est obtenue par l'horreur de l'élégance. Il n'y a sur les façades de Hemingway ni chapiteaux corinthiens, ni femmes nues sculptées en série...* » *Les Romanciers américains,* pp. 196-197.
51. « *La génération des écrivains américains, aujourd'hui d'âge mûr, nous a donné une critique vigoureuse de son milieu, mais elle n'a pas su y puiser la matière de son expression esthétique. Une transition bien nette devient évidente quand on passe des œuvres de cette génération à celles de leurs successeurs... Ils sont moins préoccupés que leurs aînés des défauts et des faiblesses de la civilisation qui les entoure... Ils remplacent l'hostilité des moralistes envers la vie, par la joie affirmative des artistes... Ils considèrent le récit plutôt comme une forme artistique qu'un véhicule pour la propagande moralisatrice... ce qui les distingue de leurs contemporains plus âgés, ce n'est pas la découverte de matériaux nouveaux, mais la découverte de nouveaux moyens de s'en servir.* » *Vient de paraître,* Nov. 1925, p. 575.
52. « *Ses descriptions ne sont pas toujours claires ni puissantes, ses récits manquent parfois de force ou de clarté, mais dès que ses personnages se mettent à parler ils sont vivants, irréfutables et invincibles... On pourrait dire que ses personnages ne causent pas, qu'ils ne parlent pas. Le bruit qu'ils font, est plutôt comme une sorte de respiration.* » *Revue Européenne,* mars 1928, p. 322.
53. « *Comme toujours les dialogues sont extraordinaires. Volontiers, on les croirait strictement phonographiques. Ils sont pourtant composés avec une extrême précision qui leur donne un sens différent de la portée immédiate des répliques.* » *Nouvelle Revue Française,* Oct. 1933, p. 633.
Coindreau, on the contrary, criticized Hemingway's handling of dialogue rather ineptly in his essay on « le roman alcoolique » : « *Pourquoi fallut-il que Lawrence Stallings s'avisât un beau jour de porter* A Farewell to Arms *à la scène dans une adaptation, si près du texte que les acteurs se virent contraints de réciter tous les dialogues du livre mis en quelque sorte bout à bout ? Le résultat fut désastreux. On eût dit des employés des P.T.T. se débitant leurs télégrammes et les plus fervents durent admettre que les conversations de Hemingway n'étaient que des stylisations habiles sans aucune réalité...* » *Aperçus de littérature américaine,* p. 84.
54. « *Il accepte ce que ses personnages lui confient et reproduit le spectacle de leurs allées et venues. Peu importe qu'elles soient inattendues, contradictoires, insensées ou naturelles.* » Europe, 15 Sept. 1933, p. 141.
55. *Partisan Review,* May-June 1952, p. 279.
56. *Les Romanciers américains,* p. 195.
57. Introduction to *L'Adieu aux armes,* p. 10.
58. Introduction to *Le Soleil se lève aussi,* p. IX.
59. *La Création chez Stendhal,* 1942.
60. Quoted by Thelma M. SMITH and Ward L. MINER, *op. cit.,* p. 20.
61. Figures given by SMITH and MINER, p. 30.
62. A new " popular " edition was published by Gallimard in 1961.
63. e.g. P. GRENAUD, *Europe,* pp. 107-180, Sept. 1946 ; G. JARLOT, *Fon-*

taine, pp. 845-849, May 1946 ; Y. Lévy, *Paru*, pp. 41-46, April 1946 ; Claude-Edmonde Magny, *Gavroche*, p. 4, Aug. 16, 1945 ; Claude Mauriac, *La Nef*, pp. 133-134, Feb. 1946.

64. P. Grenaud for instance wrote : « *Ce qui nous intéresse dans cette action, c'est que chacun des personnages s'arrache à l'emprise des passions pour retrouver la sérénité. Dans ce cas, l'œuvre de Heminway rejoint celle de Malraux, plus par sa morale que par le climat et l'architecture où se fondent leurs thèmes.* » *Europe*, p. 108, Sept. 1946.

65. Jean Blanzat, *Figaro Littéraire*, p. 9, Jan. 3, 1953 ; M. Cournot, *Nouvelle Revue Française*, pp. 351-353, Feb. 1953 ; René Lalou, *Nouvelles Littéraires*, p. 3, Dec. 18, 1952 ; Jacques Vallette, *Mercure de France*, pp. 151-156, Jan. 1953, etc.

66. *Figaro*, p. 1, Jan. 3, 1953 : « *C'est une grande image qui finit par vous remplir l'esprit et vous ouvrir tous les rêves.* »

67. Michel Mohrt, *France-U.S.A.*, p.3, Jan. 1953, reprinted in *Le Nouveau roman américain*, Paris, 1955, pp. 61-70.

68. Romain Gary, « Le retour du champion », *Nouvelles Littéraires*, p. 1, Sept. 11, 1952 : « *La lecture de ce court récit est un de ces très rares moments de perfection qui vous donnent l'impression d'un triomphe personnel, d'un triomphe de l'homme sur l'adversité.* »

69. G.-A. Astre, *Hemingway par lui-même*, Paris, Le Seuil, 19-61, 189 pp.

70. « *Hemingway, c'est la force physique triomphante, la guerre à vingt ans, la chasse aux grands fauves, l'amour (quatre femmes légitimes toutes adorées, sans compter beaucoup d'autres, j'imagine), l'alcool à flots... Mais ce boxeur, ce trappeur, ce tueur de fauves, aura écrit de grands livres et il aura fait plus que les écrire, il les aura vécus aux côtés de ce peuple espagnol en armes qu'il a tant aimé... je crois qu'Hemingway s'est trompé : la vérité ne peut pas être celle d'un moment de la vie ; elle ne peut pas convenir aux seuls jeunes mâles ivres de leur force et qui, d'ailleurs, ne le sont que peu de temps, mais aussi aux êtres faibles et doux.* « Les hasards de la fourchette : Du côté de Hemingway », *Figaro Littéraire*, Dec. 23, 1961.

71. In *Green Hills of Africa* Hemingway himself declared : " *There is a fourth and fifth dimension that can be gotten.* "

72. Walt Whitman, *Leaves of Grass*, " Song of Myself ", § 47, 11. 6, 9-10.

THE CRITICAL RECEPTION OF HEMINGWAY'S WORKS IN GERMANY SINCE 1920

by Helmut PAPAJEWSKI

I SHALL deal with my subject under three main headings : the first covering the period from the First World War up to 1945, [1] the second dealing with the time from 1945 to 1960 in Western Germany, and the third treating the same time in Eastern Germany.

After the military collapse of Germany in 1918, the country's literary output — which could not fail to be affected by political events — was divided roughly into two main movements.

The conservative, nationalistic movement believed that Germany's failure in the First World War was in part due to a lack of emphasis on national themes in literature and to a faulty understanding of those factors which essentially constitute patriotic feeling. But the writers of this trend endeavoured to strengthen the sense of historical, popular, and in some extreme cases, of racial tradition.

The opposite movement thought that the German tragedy was the result of a lack of understanding of other peoples and tried to broaden the reading public's knowledge of foreign literature. They saw literature as the expression of the social development of other countries — countries which had a political structure quite different from Germany. Considered in this light the knowledge of the literatures of the Western nations also meant a kind of indirect contact with their political ways of life. Frequently, however, politics in the West were merely seen as a factor which enabled human feeling to express itself with greater freedom.

It is very understandable that this second movement consciously or unconsciously was striving towards what today would be branded as an a-historical approach. When modern American literature became known in Germany in the middle twenties this tendency became apparent and the hopes which were pinned on the new writing also indicated this subconscious desire. The abundance of periodical literature and the spacious and well-developed literary critical sections of German newspapers in the twenties and thirties helped to acquaint readers with American literature. Hemingway also first became known through these literary periodicals.

The avant-garde periodical *Der Querschnitt* (ed. by Wedderkop) published a number of his poems which had not appeared in America. Shortly after this, one of his boxing stories, translated by Erich Franzen, appeared in another periodical and in 1928 *The Sun also Rises* was finally published by Rowohlt, Berlin.

This, the first novel of Hemingway's to be translated, received a very mixed critical reception. For example, those critics who were very bourgeois and conservative in their attitude, [2] together with strictly Catholic critics, rejected it in no uncertain fashion. Their main point of attack was centered on the characters in the novel whose useless and apparently amoral lives seemed, they thought, to make the translation of the novel altogether quite unjustifiable.

But it was with *A Farewell to Arms* that a larger public became acquainted with Hemingway's work. The pacifistic beliefs of many individuals — so very widespread in Germany after the First World War — were of course a fertile ground for the message of the novel. The moral of the story was readily accepted by the general reading public. Now for the first time, Hemingway's narrative skill was emphasized and praised by the critics. Even a periodical such as the *Gral* (a publication of strict denominational principles) now made a distinction between the artistic and the ethical elements of Hemingway's writing. Although a number of critics still complained of the disregard of the ethical norms in the novel, there was great recognition of Hemingway's remarkable narrative technique. The critics were a little disconcerted and at a loss to find a quite satisfactory interpretation of this new technique. Attempts were made to compare details in Hemingway with those in Hamsun [3] and the apparent "directness" of expression was emphasized. It was also pointed out that some elements of the technique were borrowed from the film, as e.g. the loose sequence of scenes. [4]

Yet the generation between 1920 and 1930 was not so much interested in Hemingway's structural, technical and linguistic methods in the narrowest sense (although, it is true, one critic had already recognized the "*art of omission* [3]"); they were rather interested in the affinity between Hemingway's characters and their own generation.

They were particularly interested in the concept of a lost generation, a notion which was introduced not by a German but by an American critic. An article by Clifton Fadiman [5] on this subject in the *Nation* was translated into German and published in the *Querschnitt*. Fadiman, however, emphasized that the problem of the lost generation was not altogether new in literary history and that similar frustrations were to be found in *Werther*, and Turgeniev's *Fathers and Sons*, and Wilde's *Dorian Gray*. Yet the validity of these strange parallels were not further discussed as the events of 1933 brought an abrupt change into the literary scene.

The idea of a lost generation was not entirely new to German intellectuals. They had realized that State Feudalism under the Kaiser's rule had involved the individual in an unparalleled political tragedy without asking his opinion or arousing in him any desire to take a personal political decision. Those who had come to understand and express this now emphasized the sphere of the personal and private life which attracted them in

Hemingway's writings; and for this reason his earlier works were given due recognition. [4]

The more the impending political change threatened to usher in another period of disregard for personal values, the more their defenders turned to Hemingway's works for solace.

In this context, it is interesting to note that Hemingway was not in the first place regarded so much as an American but as an artist. Individual values seemed threatened in Russia and in the USA : in Russia because of her authoritarian regime, in the USA through "*publicity*."[6] Bearing this development in mind, critics could easily overlook his American nationality and instead herald him as the champion of the protesting individual, as a writer whose realism and contempt for the bombastic and the highflown were signs that pointed to a new, humanistically orientated literature.

After 1933 two events made it impossible for Hemingway's work to exert a wider influence. The one was the beginning of the Second World War. English and American authors were not altogether forbidden in Germany but modern authors in general were regarded as suspect. Above all, however, the Nazis favoured all those authors who were critical towards their own countries or towards the countries of the Allies, as the case may have been. Thus, Eric Linklater's book, *Juan in America*, achieved a great, if unfounded, literary renown in Germany.

The second detrimental event was the closing down of the Rowohlt publishing house, which had hitherto published Hemingway's works.

In 1940 the political situation in Germany might have allowed a work of Hemingway's to be translated, as at this time the United States had not yet declared war on Germany. But the book which appeared at this juncture was *For Whom the Bell Tolls*, which naturally, on account of Hemingway's own participation in the Spanish War and his treatment of it, could not be published in Germany.

The first German edition of *For Whom the Bell Tolls* did

appear as early as 1941 but it was published by the Fischer Verlag, which had emigrated to Stockholm. The novel first appeared in Germany after the war when it could be read both in the Swedish edition and in one prepared and issued by the American occupation authorities in Germany. After the war Hemingway's literary fame increased comparatively quickly — especially with young people. During the last fifteen years Hemingway has remained the most popular American author, followed by Wilder, Steinbeck, O'Neill, Faulkner, and Dos Passos. One has to remember though that in the first postwar years many public libraries were still in a deplorable state and that printing facilities in Germany up till 1949 were insufficient — so that only a limited number of texts could be brought out.

The first novel of Hemingway's to be re-issued in Germany was *A Farewell to Arms*, published on newspaper print by the Rowohlt Verlag. This crude edition had an introduction by the author of *Götter, Gräber und Gelehrte*, who then had not yet assumed the pen name of Ceram, but was still writing under his true name of Marek. The book was generally acclaimed by readers of all ages which is not surprising when one remembers the way in which the story ends. This does not mean that the book was liked only for its political aspects; in fact, many readers were captivated by the love story alone. The tragic ending at a moment when the hero has extricated himself from military involvement and is on the point of withdrawing into a personal and private life is too impressive for readers to remain unaffected.

A more thorough and closely reasoned appreciation of Hemingway was not possible until after 1949 when the general stabilizing of German industry had also put the printing industry back on its feet, so that practically all of Hemingway's works were made available to the reading public. Furthermore, the introduction of pocket books into Germany brought his works within the reach of ever-widening circles of readers. He was thus a formative element in the spiritual orientation of post-war Germany with its two main streams : the specifically religious and the literary-secular.

Hemingway's great success in Germany, both with the reading public and the critics, is actually a very curious phenomenon, because it certainly is not clear why an author who is so preoccupied with violence should have had such a favorable reception in a country that had suffered so much from violence during the previous twelve years of its history.

In trying to solve this enigma, as has been attempted by various writers — Friedrich Sieburg for one — it must be remembered that a literature of violence had existed in the Germany of the twenties and had become widely accepted during the thirties. The impact of the defeat of Germany in the First World War on the minds of right-wing writers like Ernst Jünger or Beumelburg — to name only two — had resulted in a glorification of violence which raised it to an almost mythological significance. After the Second World War when this type of violence had been discredited, it was replaced with a literary treatment of violence in a form entirely different from that of crude nationalism.

In the new and detailed appreciation of his work and especially in the analysis of his ideas, Hemingway's affinity to Existentialist philosophy became apparent. Existentialist philosophers and their students already had analysed individual German works and they now proceeded to approach Hemingway's work armed with Existentialist categories. After the First World War German readers and critics had mainly been interested in the discussion of social problems in American literature and they had found an abundance of material in authors such as Sinclair Lewis. Now their interest centred on the states of the individual soul. It is true, there were still numerous readers who deplored the gradual disappearance from belles-lettres of a type of book calculated to give a picture of a country's social and sociological structure. After a war there is always this strong desire to come to know what has been no-man's-land for so long — especially through the medium of literature. The desire, however, is naturally only rarely fulfilled by great literature, but rather by the average run of descriptive story-tellers. This is the reason for the popularity with German readers of Warwick Deeping and also Galsworthy — to name only two examples from English Literature.

What so surprised German readers of Hemingway and the other authors of the " Lost Generation " was to find two of the important elements of Existentialist philosophy, fear and *Angst*, also playing such an important role in contemporary literature, in a country which they had supposed to be rejoicing in its feeling of security. Karl Jaspers has coined the word " Geworfensein, " meaning man being flung helplessly into a largely hostile world, and readers immediately connected the people in Hemingway's stories with this state of " Geworfensein. " [7]

Critics further emphasized the great passivity [8] of Hemingway's characters — a passivity that even influences their way of speaking. Similarly it was noticed at an early critical stage that these people seemed to be driven by their impulses into actions for which there was no rational explanation. For readers with a knowledge of Existentialist philosophy it was interesting to find in Hemingway the other Existentialistic characteristics : boredom and the sense of banality. Kierkegaard has given an exhaustive discussion of boredom ; Hemingway seemed to provide a modern illustration of this phenomenon — for it is through the experience of boredom that many of Hemingway's heroes become aware of their own existence in an extremely painful way.

Hemingway's conception of his protagonists or " heroes " in his novels and short-stories was a source of great difficulty. The entirely artificial hero of Nazi times was now confronted with a hero altogether different. The ideal of the hero had already been a bone of contention, especially as a consequence of some of Bernard Shaw's dramas which had been rejected by conservative circles and had occasioned a strange rift in literary judgements resulting in judgements on political grounds. Thus every new drama by Shaw was automatically rejected by right-wing critics and quite as automatically acclaimed by the left-wingers. In the Nazi period Shaw's works were not banned — partly because of his expressly socialist attitude and partly because of his partially approving remarks about the Nazi regime, so that every now and then a play of his would appear on a German stage. His anti-heroic utterances may have made a few Germans doubt the validity of their national hero-conception — but these single instances were definitely without widespread or essential effect.

As for Hemingway's hero, he could at first be understood only partially, the difficulty being that certain parts of his heroes' lives are autobiographical and German critics were more or less ignorant about Hemingway's life. Thus only very few people realized that the Nick Adams stories in *In Our Time* have an inner unity which is continued and resumed in *The Killers*. Of course, Hemingway's heroes were by no means of a type conducive to a new hero-cult of the conventional kind, for this hero was conspicuously lacking in what was formerly called "*positive achievement.*" Rather was he characterized by his ability to survive [9] — survive as an integrated personality in a time when the vulnerability of the individual had become all too apparent.

In dealing with the "*terrors of existence*" [10] in Hemingway's work, existentialist analysis had also revealed another characteristic : the isolation of the individual [11] — which Hemingway seemed to have felt to an almost obsessional degree — so much so that even love between the sexes appears incapable of breaking down the barriers between human beings. [9] Wherever love manages to penetrate isolation as in *A Farewell to Arms* and *For Whom the Bell Tolls* it is, after a period of beautiful fulfilment, doomed to destruction. Apart from the actual plots of the novels this conception is also barred by Hemingway's remarks that a great and fulfilled love would be turned into an even greater tragedy by the early death of one of the partners — which in our context is to be equated with greater isolation.

In his determination to "survive" morally the hero had to regulate his own behaviour by a code. The meaning of this code for Hemingway had already been clearly understood, namely : that life, basically disturbed as it is by many traumatic experiences, would be altogether impossible if it could not at least be made tolerable by a certain dignity which only a code of living could provide. This code may not be the final means of overcoming the individual's isolation but it affords a possibility of living within a circle of similarly minded fellow-beings. Thus a common denominator, so to speak, for life in a chaotic time had been found. [12]

It must appear rather strange that in the first years after the war Hemingway's bullfighter stories should have been so successful in Germany. It may be accounted for by the fact that bullfighting may be regarded as the extreme form of the heroic code. The most dangerous form of sport which demanded the strongest will to survival had thus developed a strongly formative element. Another facet of Hemingway's work — his lack of intellectualism and the omission of a cultural background in his work [13] — might have deluded German readers of the depressing post-war period into a kind of negation of culture, as did actually happen with a section of the younger readers. The catch-word of the " skeptical generation, " a term coined soon after 1945 and referring to the scepticism of the war generation with regard to former cultural values — is indicative of this negative attitude to culture. Serious literary critics realized, however, that Hemingway in simplifying his characters had also given them a new depth, a depth which, in the last analysis, was often only to be achieved by the repetition of the traumatic experience. [14]

In talking about Hemingway's simplification critics sometimes overshot their mark : one single instance may serve as an example. The basic elements in *The Old Man and the Sea* have been overhastily connected with Jung's system of archetypes. [15] Others subjected his work to a psycho-analytical examination. It ought to have been clear that this was the wrong approach from Hemingway's own ironical and negative comments on psychoanalysis.

Critics analysing the simplicity of the conception and structure of Hemingway's stories had come to two basically different ways of understanding his writing. The one had drawn upon the existentialism of Kierkegaard for enlightenment. It used phrases like " Nullpunktexistenz " — " life at zero " — meaning the conscious reduction of life to its most elemental forms. This deliberate simplification arose from the impact of great catastrophes upon the human mind. These " natural shocks " diverted man's consciousness from his own overcomplex and artificial world and led him back to a realization of the great elemental forces at work in life and thus to a true understanding of his own real existence.

To other critics Hemingway's construction of his stories seemed in keeping with classical tradition. Epithets like " related to classical tragedy " or " Homeric " were applied, especially to *The Old Man and the Sea*. [16] Pongs speaks in this context even of " *archaic dignity*. " [17] Naturally such concepts are not really applicable to this particular genre and have to be taken with a grain of salt. They are intended to indicate on the one hand the " simplicity " of Hemingway's world, on the other hand the sense of tragic doom which broods over his characters.

Hemingway's style, in the narrower sense, had impressed German critics very deeply. His paratactic language met with a very favourable reception, although the intellectual novels of Thomas Mann and Hermann Broch had accustomed readers to a style hypotactic in the extreme. Thomas Mann himself commented very favourably on a novel like *A Farewell to Arms* without allowing himself to be drawn into a discussion of the controversial style.

The influence of Hemingway's style [18] on other writers dates back to before the Second World War, when only a small group of German writers knew Hemingway's work in detail. These, however, were greatly impressed by Hemingway's paratactic style with its technique of " closing in " — impressed to such an extent that Erich Kästner predicted the danger of a host of Hemingway imitators determining the future style of modern German literature. In the course of three decades during which Hemingway has been known in Germany a considerable group of writers have attempted either to imitate him directly or to develop their individual forms of his simplified style, — without, however, following the Master's stylistic precepts too closely. Wolfgang Borchert, Heinrich Böll, Gerd Gaiser, Bastian Müller, and Siegfried Sommer belong to this group. It must also be mentioned that this imitation hardly ever proceeded from the original English version but mostly from the translations of Annemarie Horschitz-Horst.

In considering the merits of these imitations — whether of the direct or indirect type — the critic is almost inevitably drawn into a reappraisal of Hemingway's realism. His specific form of understatement [19] was difficult to imitate and has in some cases resulted in a mistaken objectivity of style that merely presents things, actions and characters, without lending them any deeper significance. Certain other traits, such as the apparent absence of the " inner monologue, " were also regarded as artistic consequences of Hemingway's special branch of objectivity. In his book *Urmensch und Spätkultur* [20] Arnold Gehlen criticizes Hemingway's presentation of the fisherman's soul in *The Old Man and the Sea* as pseudo-objectivity which was in reality subjective to a very high degree.

It was further noted that the author remains anonymous behind his characters, but the exact extent and meaning of this phenomenon was not further discussed. It was only stressed in this context that the author allows the external world of appearances to speak for itself but the relation of these appearances to the author was left out of account. [21]

Hemingway's own theories on style were relatively little discussed. Speyer had at an early point spoken of his " art of omission, " but this was deduced from a critical examination of his technique and not from the author's own theoretical remarks. A thorough-going analysis, for instance, of the "iceberg theory," i.e. that only one-eighth of the full meaning is directly expressed, would probably have brought greater clarity into this critical field.

One of the recent marked trends in German literary criticism is intensive research into symbolism, a trend that has received a powerful stimulus from Wilhelm Emrich's book on the symbolism in the second part of *Faust*. During the last years of the Nazi regime writers like Jünger experimented with an often half concealed symbolism, and in the post-war novels symbolism was sometimes very extensively used indeed, so that criticism generally was awakened to a new awareness of this artistic means of expression. It is therefore hardly surprising that critics also tried to find evidence of symbolism in Hemingway's work. One school of critics flatly denied the presence of symbols, another school accorded him a kind of "*symbolic realism*" without, however, exactly defining its extent and meaning. The impressive and yet somewhat questionable symbols which had already been found by American scholars, such as the symbol of the bridge were not critically examined in Germany.

Hemingway's reception in the Soviet Zone of occupation must be dealt with separately because conditions there differed from those obtaining in the Zones occupied by England, France, and America after 1945. The first concern of the Western occupation authorities was to clear the way for their literary products on as wide a scale as possible — partly also with a view to the political re-education of Germany — for which latter purpose an edition of *For Whom the Bell Tolls* was brought out immediately. The literary taste of the West German public was largely determined by the critical criteria of traditional Western bourgeois society.

The case was different in the Eastern Zone, although in the beginning literary judgements there were not yet required to conform slavishly to proletarian dogmatism. I shall first give a short survey of the most important stages in this development and then treat in greater detail the more prominent features of

East German criticism. Hemingway was first officially heard of in East Germany on his fiftieth birthday, on the 21st of July 1948, with the publication of *The Old Man and the Sea*. He also was heard of later with his nomination for the Nobel Prize in 1954. In 1948 critical assessment was still largely positive. Certain reservations were nevertheless made which appeared in the form of a somewhat cheap and schematic Hegelianism : " *Hemingway is a dialectical writer — whose antitheses, however, do not lead to a synthesis — and this is where he is in danger of falling prey to despair.* " [22] By and large this is also the tenor of Soviet criticism of Hemingway. We cannot and need not here deal extensively with the earlier critical development in the Soviet Union. Hemingway was not treated in the large *Literary Encyclopaedia of Soviet Russia* — because this work was forbidden on account of its " *vulgar sociological basis* " (alias Trotzkyism) before the volume containing the article on Hemingway appeared. In the *Soviet Encyclopaedia*, however, we do find an article on Hemingway, which is partly approving, partly critical. It says that Hemingway was well aware of the faults of bourgeois society but that he nevertheless lacked a constructive synthesis which should have resulted from the thesis of the bourgeois world and the antithesis of the criticism of this world.

The programme of " Socialist realism, " first formulated in 1934 and largely implemented by Zdanov in the following years, requires a so-called positive hero, bound by party loyalties, and it contains a marked rejection of the decadent hero who does not strive for positive achievement but is tormented by his fear of death. Hemingway's literary work was of course difficult to bring into line with such a programme. There were also other difficulties which arose from the ideology of the positive hero. Robert Jordan does fight against fascism, but was he trying to bring about a socialist reconstruction of the World ? And *The Fifth Column* must have caused even greater embarrassment, for it does not describe only the " *white terror.* " [23]

Hemingway's artistic achievement at least was to some extent acknowledged. From 1953 however, the situation became increasingly critical. The official *Literaturnaja Gazeta* — which began to appear in 1955 — did not at first enter into a discussion of Hemingway's work. The first attack, in May 1953, appeared in the *Neue Deutsche Literatur* in the Eastern Zone, beginning typically with the following sentences: "*If one were good-natured enough to shut one's right eye — then one could perhaps have believed a long time ago that the writer Ernest Hemingway was a man of the left. In the meantime even the kind-hearted have had their eyes opened to the fact that that was no more than a pose on Hemingway's part.*" [24]

The title of the article "The Old Man and the Beer" indicates that *The Old Man and the Sea* must have occasioned this attack and the earlier discussions about his nomination for the Nobel Prize may have added fuel to the fire.

When Hemingway was awarded the Nobel Prize in 1954 the *NDL* renewed its attack. Aina Gill called him an "*asocial outsider*" while still acknowledging his artistic mastery.

Apart from the judgements of Soviet criticism and its official organ, the *Literaturnaja Gazeta*, [25] East Germany's opinion on American literature is further determined by the "Literaturbriefe", the literary letters from the pen of Howard Fast in New York. In the fourth of these letters, Howard Fast dealing with *The Old Man and the Sea* delivered a virulent attack on Hemingway, using phrases like "*nonsense*" and "*the intellectual level of a twelve-year-old.*"

From then onwards it was more and more permissible to parody Hemingway, as is indicated by an essay by Paul Hilbert in the *NDL* for May 1955, entitled "The End of Something Called Ernest."

Nevertheless, readers in the Eastern Zone were every now and then offered sections of Hemingway's writings: In 1956 the East German periodical *Aufbau* printed a long extract from *The Old Man and the Sea* without any commentary, and in July of the same year the *NDL* printed Hemingway's *Appeal to the German People* of 1937. [26]

Examining some of the critiques in detail we find that purely aesthetic — and this also includes stylistic — qualities are generally given only a very secondary place. Even in 1948 when Hemingway still received recognition in Eastern Germany, the critics measured him by their conventional yardsticks, social criticism and class warfare. Despite Hemingway's nihilism, there was a willingness to discover the positive qualities of this highly gifted outsider. For example, Adolf Volbracht in a review of *The Sun Also Rises* [27] said : " *First of all the reader will be surprised to find that Ernest Hemingway [...] manages to hold our interest while describing banalities — endless drinking bouts — and with a photographically realistic picture of the animalism of a few good-for-nothings... Even readers with a literary training will find it difficult to explain how such a realism turned objectivism manages to fascinate us.* "

Of course Volbracht is not at all pleased that Hemingway presents a decadent bourgeois society, without at the same time denouncing it. Nevertheless, he feels it impossible to reject *The Sun Also Rises* out of hand because its characters — as far as the motives for their actions are concerned — are not entirely worthless. " *This picture of people and things, which appears at a first glance so very crude, gains depth and meaning upon closer examination. In spite of their alcoholic bouts and nights of love Hemingway's characters in the end do emerge as decent, if badly-behaved boys and girls who may profess to hate sentiments but who, in their 'dark urge' nevertheless do the right thing.* "

Similar opinions were vented in the two leading communist papers of East Berlin on the occasion of Hemingway's 50th birthday. The author of the article in the *Sonntag* mentions the nihilism of *The Sun Also Rises* and the pessimism of *Men Without Women* but continues : " *That is the secret of this style : to move deeply in an indirect manner. In* A Farewell to Arms *he has achieved this superbly.* " He further remarks that with *For Whom the Bell Tolls* Hemingway has overcome his pessimism. He says : " *The last thought of the dynamiter Robert Jordan 'The world is a fine place and worth the fighting for and I hate very much to leave it' gives the lie to Hemingway's nihilism.*" [28]

In her article on Hemingway in the *Berliner Zeitung* of July 21st 1948 Susanne Kerckhoff, representing the more radical criticism, applies Marxist principles much more consistently. " *The subjects Hemingway deals with are clearly subjects of our time. The First World War, the post-war years, and the antifascist resistance in Spain all pose one question : How does man survive in an age of technical power, in fear of death and loss ? How can he break with the conventions of a rotten social order ?* " She sees Hemingway's description of the meaningless as his way of shattering antiquated values. Even if *"his antitheses do not result in a synthesis"* his honesty is more valuable than " *those rash syntheses of mediocre writers who try to turn abysses into pleasure gardens and thus are nihilistic — because dishonesty is nihilistic.* "

The moderately approving attitude towards Hemingway was however supplanted in 1953 by an altogether derogatory one — in accordance with which judgements about his earlier works were now revised. The Russian attitude showed a similar shift as can be demonstrated from the pages of the official *Literaturnaja Gazeta*. On the 3rd of September 1955 a reader asked for more information about Hemingway, Caldwell, and Faulkner. On the 25th of August 1956 the answer came in the form of an article by T. Motyleva. The article is among other things remarkable for the whole-hearted approval of Kaschin's judgement on Hemingway in an article entitled " On Reading Hemingway. " He quotes : " *His attempts to overlook many things, or at least not to think about many things, have limited and impoverished his creative possibilities. Hemingway cannot or will not recognize the source of the flood of stagnation which poisons his whole world.* " These critics however at least do not go so far as to treat Hemingway as a secondary writer with only a small group of readers in the USA. The temptation to do this was refuted in an article by Ilja Ehrenburg in the *Literaturnaja Gazeta* who listed the works of Hemingway together with those of Dreiser, Sinclair Lewis, Steinbeck, Faulkner and Caldwell as essential elements of modern American literature.

The greatest difficulty for Marxist critics was that Hemingway had refused to draw the Marxist consequences from his attitude of social and even class criticism. A writer of his stature ought not to have avoided the necessity of openly and directly attacking bourgeois society after he had fully realized its morbid and sick state. I should like to illustrate this situation by comparing it with the present Marxist appreciation of the realistic novel of the 19th century. Marxist literary critics dealing with Balzac found themselves in a strange dilemma : they could not deny that he was a great writer, nor could they deny his being a very decided reactionary. They extricated themselves by saying that he was a protagonist of his own — if reactionary — class because he had appraised it realistically as a powerful force in the structure of the society of his time.

For most Western critics the question of class was of little importance. For the average bourgeois citizen the characters in Hemingway's work were beyond class — "déclassé" — anyway; their problems were not connected with a political or economic struggle for existence but with the moral survival of the individual. Thus Western critics were little concerned with the fact that on close inspection Hemingway's novels often take place, as it were, in an economic vacuum although they originated at the time of the great economic depression. Of course we do not need to enter here into the particular subject of the political discussion aroused by *For Whom the Bell Tolls* — although in fact this discussion turned out to be quite different from the reaction anticipated by the original popularizers in Germany. It was namely seen as a political novel in the sense that Tolstoi's *War and Peace* could be considered political. [29]

We have now to give a critical survey of the numerous obituaries that were published in July 1961 in the Eastern as well as Western part of Germany. The Western publications are not very interesting as most of them repeat those factors in

Hemingway's life and death that were interesting for the reading public already at the time of the publication of his various novels. There are one or two obituaries in the West not in conformity with the others. The reviewer in the Düsseldorf paper *Der Mittag* stresses the fact that he was not and that he is not an admirer of Hemingway's works because Hemingway is, so to speak, a member of the "school of force" in contemporary American literature. He, of course, makes an exception : *The Old Man and the Sea*. But at the same time he points out the fact that the admirers of Hemingway would refute his opinion with the remark that this work is not typical of Hemingway.

What strikes the reader when he sees the obituaries of the East is first their great number and secondly their much more positive criticism in comparison with the reviews published in former years. The Berlin paper *Der Morgen* thus says : "*We too mourn over the death of Ernest Hemingway. And that does not mean this paper only but the whole Eastern zone of Germany.*" Whereas *The Old Man and the Sea* was at the time of its publication somewhat severely reviewed the book is now praised as the last important work of Hemingway and a great literary achievement, in which Hemingway overcame the nihilism of his early works. The Christian symbolism of this work is not mentioned.

On the other hand the papers of the Eastern zone of Germany use a phrase that was not unknown formerly in the Western world. They call *The Old Man and the Sea* a work of Greek simplicity and greatness. Even the awarding of the Nobel Prize was at the death of Hemingway no longer a bone of contention. And *Der Neue Weg* even mentions a paragraph from Hemingway's Nobel Prize acceptance speech.

If we are looking for the reason of the change of opinion in the East German papers it might be found in the fact that according to those papers Hemingway made a declaration in favour of Cuba at the beginning of the revolution in that country.

In quite a number of the papers of the Eastern zone the political and sociological viewpoints are not forgotten, though they are not stressed in the same degree as before. According to those papers Hemingway's literary success and merit may be explained by his criticism of the society of his time, his antifascism, and anti-militarism.[30] It is not surprising that here we find the only reservations. The Eastern papers still try to lay the blame especially on Hemingway's *For Whom the Bell Tolls*. The *National Zeitung* regrets that this book has no clear political outlook.

In both parts of Germany the interest in the life of Hemingway was thus revived by his death, which was felt to be quite in accordance with his life legend.

NOTES

1. The analysis of the first period must from lack of material be very short as the archives of the publishing house Rowohlt as well as the great German newspaper libraries and the Reichstagbibliothek were destroyed during the war.
2. Friedrich SCHÖNEMANN, book review in *Die Literatur*, 31 (1928-29).
3. W. SPEYER, *Vossische Zeitung*, 1928, Unterhaltungsbeilage 295.
4. M. DIETRICH in *Hochland* 3, 2 (1932-33).
5. *Der Querschnitt*, 13 (1933).
6. Dietrich BEHRENS in *Berliner Tageblatt* 1934.
7. Helmut PAPAJEWSKI, " Die Frage nach der Sinnhaftigkeit bei Hemingway ", *Anglia*, 70 (1951).
8. Gerhard PRAUSE, *Welt und Wort*, 6 (1951).
9. G. PRAUSE, *op. cit.*, p. 50.
10. Wilhelm GRENZMANN, *Weltdichtung der Gegenwart*, Bonn, 1958, p. 406.
11. H. STRESAU, in *Deutsche Universitätszeitung*, Göttingen, 1957, Heft 23/4.
12. Günter BLÖCKER, *Die neuen Wirklichkeiten. Linien und Profile der modernen Literatur*, Berlin, 1957, p. 246.
13. W. GRENZMANN, *op. cit.*, p. 410.
14. G. BLÖCKER, *op. cit.*, p. 244.
15. Joseph BAUR in *Welt und Wort*, 8 (1953).
16. G. BLÖCKER, *op. cit.*, p. 245.
17. Hermann PONGS, *Neue Deutsche Hefte*, 1954/55, p. 708.

18. There are of course primitive imitations of Hemingway. They are for instance, to be found in H. J. Soekring's novel *Cordelia*. Some of the first enthusiastic critics of his work called him the German Hemingway whereas such a careful critic as Friedrich Sieburg wrote an ironical review of this novel and its method.

19. W. GRENZMANN, *op. cit.*, p. 409.
20. Arnold GEHLEN, *Urmensch und Spätkultur*, Bonn, 1956, p. 127 f.
21. W. GRENZMANN, *op. cit.*, p. 408 f.
22. *Berliner Zeitung*, July 21, 1948.
23. When Hemingway was attacked in 1954 because of his nomination for the Nobel Prize, Aina Gill drew the ammunition for her onslaught from a distinction in Johannes R. Becher's book *Erzählen oder Gestalten*. Here Becher says about *For Whom the Bell Tolls* : " *The fascist terror is merely told here and thus is easily eradicated from the reader's memory — if it penetrates there at all — whereas the so-called red terror is given artistic form in all its details and with a wealth of literary finesse — thus determining the character of the work.* " Aina Gill concludes her article by saying : " *What good is it that Hemingway later apologized to the Spanish republicans for this book ? It continues to be read in its original form...* "
24. *NDL*, 5/1953, p. 211.
25. There are of course exceptions. When the translation of an American book is published earlier in East Germany than in the Soviet Union the appreciation can be different. That seems to have been the case chiefly with the translation of *The Old Man and the Sea*. Cf. Carlos BAKER, *Hemingway and His Critics*, New York, 1961, American Century Series, p. 158.
26. Another extract of this *Appeal to the German People* appeared in *Weltbühne*, *NF*, 1,5/135.
27. *Aufbau*, 8 (1948), p. 713.
28. *Sonntag*, July, 18th, 1948.
29. *Die Gegenwart*, April, 15th, 1949.
30. It is noteworthy that in this respect the words and the phrasing of the East German papers are nearly the same. This might be explained by a political coordination of the Ministry of Information.

HEMINGWAY IN ITALY

by Mario Praz

1. The Italian Background.

IF an Italian of the beginning of the present century, after having slept for about fifty years like Irving's Rip Van Winkle, should have awakened in 1960, and, hardly recovered from his astonishment caused by a new and different world, should have turned to the literary scene in the hope of finding there a link with the past and tradition, he would have experienced a no less alarming disappointment. With a taste formed on the works of D'Annunzio, Pascoli, and Fogazzaro, but chiefly of D'Annunzio, then at the zenith of his reputation, he would have had to recall, among his own minor readings, the novels by Giovanni Verga (*I Malavoglia*, *Mastro Don Gesualdo*) and by Grazia Deledda in order to find something not altogether unfamiliar in the three most representative productions of the Italian literary climate in 1960 : Vasco Pratolini's novel, *Lo scialo*, Giovanni Testori's play, *L'Arialda*, and Luchino Visconti's film, *Rocco e i suoi fratelli* : I am mentioning a film among literary works, because Italian neo-realism after the second world-war made its appearance on the screen (with *Roma città aperta*, *Sciuscià*, *Ladri di biciclette*, etc.) earlier than in fiction.

D'Annunzio, at the beginning of the century, was no doubt the arbiter of taste, and although the common people occasionally supplied subjects to his inspiration (as in *Le Novelle della Pescara* and *La Figlia di Iorio*), his style and predilections belonged to that "aureate" Italian tradition, instinct with nobility and decorum, which had all but frustrated the attempts at realism every now and then made in the course of the nineteenth century. What are, instead, the characteristics of those three works which we have just selected as typical of the 1960 climate?

Characters usually taken from the low classes and even from the underworld, usage of the vernacular and slang in the dialogues, an absolute lack of reticence, no hesitation in showing the sordid and even repulsive aspects of everyday life, finally a distinctly leftist social orientation in calling the social structure to account for the horrible happenings, as well as in seeing glimpses of goodness only in humble and simple folk. The scene of Pratolini's novel is the Florence of the hooligans of the left bank of the Arno, the scene of Testori's drama and of Visconti's film is the gloomy industrial Milan which visibly dominates both the stage and the screen with the sinister, oppressive blocks of suburban apartment houses.

Unnatural loves, unbridled or downright bestial passions, are insisted upon. One may notice a somewhat decadent indulgence in Luchino Visconti's film : every now and then he gives the impression of having chosen a low and outrageous subject through that same perversion of taste which caused Huysmans' Des Esseintes (in *A Rebours*) to feel a loathsome appetite for the *immonde tartine* of bread, onion and strong cheese eaten by a disgusting street arab ; but it would be difficult to find decadent implications in Pratolini's or Testori's works. Visconti's film, dealing with the tragical experiences of a Southern family come to Milan in search of fortune, is, I think, too well-known abroad to need an account. Pratolini's novel is long (upwards of 1300 pages), complicated, and, rather than for its meandering plot, which casts a sinister light on the decay of the bourgeois class under Fascism (the profile of a typical Fascist scoundrel, Leandro, is outlined with an overdose of caricature), deserves consideration on account of its rendering of the Florentine milieu which equals the best pages of Aldo Palazzeschi (*Sorelle*

Materassi) and Bruno Cicognani (*La Velia*). Testori's drama lends itself to an easier summing-up.

The play opens with dialogues of couples of lovers who meet in the evening in a suburban district. Conversations of a crude and clumsy character match those anybody might catch at any street corner. This is a kind of realism which finds, its model, rather than in Aretino's dialogues, in Hemingway's fiction, which, as we shall see, has enjoyed a great vogue in Italy. Soon afterwards the plot is disclosed, and its chief theme could have formed the subject of an Italian sixteenth-century comedy. A middle-aged spinster, Arialda, a sewing-woman by profession, and a penniless Neapolitan widow, Gaetana, compete for marriage to a well-to-do widower, the greengrocer Amilacare Candidezza. Gaetana, from fear that her matrimonial project may come to nothing, tries to prevent her daughter Rosangela's love for one of the greengrocer's two sons, Gino. Arialda, having come to know that Gino and Rosangela have made love in his father's house during his absence, and having obtained as a proof of it a rouge-stained handkerchief with the girl's initials (possibly the rouge is only a substitute for a more tale-telling red, owing to the intervention of censorship), shows the handkerchief in a scene she makes to Candidezza when he comes back home in Gaetana's company. But she goes even further : in order to frustrate her rival's plans, she persuades her brother, Eros, a homosexual (and the responsibility for this vice is laid at the door of rich perverts), to push a little prostitute, Mina, who loves him unrequited, into the arms of the lecherous greengrocer, so that he may no longer care for Gaetana. The latter is shown the door in due course, and in her despair she finds nothing better to do than to throw herself at Arialda's feet, imploring her aid ; rebuffed, she kills herself. Lino, the boy " protected " by Eros (in whose turbid imagination are mingled threads of Socratic love, as if he might be able to put him on the way of purity and honesty), dies in a motor-accident provoked by one of Eros's rivals : he falls from the motor-bike Eros has given him as a present. Arialda, tormented by remorse, shaken by the sorrow of her brother (who, in his despair, once again rejects Mina who tries to console him), invokes the dead that they should take away the living with them, since the human condition is so intolerable.

This conclusion harps on a tune common to the chorus of many a Greek tragedy, and actually some critics have spoken of Greek tragedies apropos of *Rocco e i suoi fratelli*. No comparison could be more out of place. There is no metaphysical structure such as one finds at the back of a Greek tragedy behind these works of Italian neo-realism, so that Arialda's final invocation remains a mere *flatus vocis*. Equally out of place are certain remarks prefixed by Guido Aristarco to the edition of the text and the staging of *Rocco* (a volume issued in the series " Dal soggetto al film " by the Milan publisher Cappelli, 1960). Seeing the problem of Visconti's " cinema antropomorfico " in terms of Lukacs's critical theories, Aristarco writes :

What is actually that reality of which artistic creation must be the faithful mirror ? This reality is not the mere surface of the outside world as it is immediately apprehended : the causative, momentary, punctual phenomena. What is more important and decisive is the reflection of what actually is, not of what only appears : the essence of the phenomenon, not its external aspect... Realism aims at the utmost profundity and comprehension ; it probes, as deeply as it can go, the mainsprings hidden beneath the surface, and it does not represent them in the abstract, separating them from the phenomena by way of contrast ; it rather brings to life that dialectical process through which the essence is turned into a phenomenon... Naturalism is confined to the " average ", realism aims at the " typical ". The typical is characterized by the fact that it is the meeting point where all the chief trends of that dynamic unit, in which the genuine realistic literature mirrors life, are linked together in a single living and contradictory whole : all the most important contradictions — social, ethical and psychological — of a given historical period.

Actually the physical images in Visconti's film are so predominant that we hardly succeed in seeing anything else beyond them ; he is satisfied with nothing short of the very fact he intends to represent before our eyes. The ideal of photography is to give of a thing an image which cannot be distinguished from the thing itself, and although photographic objectivity is merely an approximation, because the photographer's eye cannot help intruding, that objectivity may be reached with such a slight divergence from reality that the very impression of reality is conveyed. The ideal of a performance, for Luchino Visconti, is a photographic one : he wants to give us the very thing. One has seen this in his staging of plays, in which, for instance, it was not enough that a certain character of Chekhov should read a Russian paper : that newspaper must actually belong to the period of the play, with a plausible date, as in the newspaper which is seen in the foreground of *Iron and Steel* by the Pre-Raphaelite painter William Bell Scott where one could read a whole article on " Garibaldi in Italy " with its date March 11th 1861. Realistic art is possible in literature and painting, where the medium allows for a modicum of abstraction, but to aim at realism through photography is tantamount to reproducing reality in its barrenness. A research pushed so far may be called art only in the sense that one may call art the delusion of wax figures with real hairs and clothes, who upset and even frighten us more than reality itself owing to the sheer consciousness and complacency of their exemplary simulation.

Art is not a mere cast of reality, but, in Hegel's words, a " conciliation with reality " (*Versöhnung mit der Wirklichkeit*), and this is true also of literature, of drama. Photography allows for less choice than the written word ; the medium employed by a writer is never a close cast of everyday reality. It is not so in Joyce, in whom the wealth of accessory and apparently meaningless details forms by itself a deformation of reality (in the real world such elements vanish in perspective, whereas in Joyce they all command attention in the foreground) ; it is not a close cast even in Hemingway's famous technique of the dialogue, in which common, casual, meaningless sentences acquire a hallucinatory intensity by dint of being repeated and bandied about as if they were endowed with a mysterious spell, so that the transition from the " natural " dialogues of the

American writer to Péguy's extremely artificial style may take place almost unawares. But the dialogues of *L'Arialda* actually aim at being a cast, almost as if those conversations had been recorded on a tape.

Such lack of "conciliation with reality," this absence of choice are responsible for that impression of formlessness, monotony and brutal crudity which is conveyed by so many works of Italian neo-realism. In the long run boredom and nausea would prevail were it not for censorship, which, by displacing the problem on to the ground of artistic freedom, creates for them an interest largely out of proportion with their actual worth. Flaubert in the last century had urged writers to describe the cesspools (*les latrines*), chiefly the cesspools, and his recommendation had its point in that period of definite aversion to face the facts of reality; but in our day, in which literature cannot certainly be accused of reticence or squeamishness, one would rather invite the readers to meditate on the passage in *Robinson Crusoe* about the goats: "*by the position of their opticks, their sight was so directed downward, that they did not readily see objects that were above them.*" What I have just said about Testori may be repeated for another neo-realist writer in the limelight, Pier Paolo Pasolini, into whose novels (*Ragazzi di vita, La Vita violenta*) the often arbitrary and bizarre usage of the Roman dialect succeeds however in introducing a picturesque and fanciful element which draws them closer to art.

A foreigner, familiar with the characteristics of classical Italian literature, may naturally wonder through what agency of events and influences contemporary Italian literature has come to possess, in its main outlines, such traits as are directly opposite to its traditional ones. It will be therefore worth while to trace the various stages of that process.

The position of Italy in the fields of literature and the arts underwent a steady decline after the middle of the seventeenth century, a decline which touched its lowest point in the very period when there were evident signs of Italy's reawakening in the political field, i.e. during the Risorgimento, in the mid-nineteenth century. In the eighteenth century Italy's position had shifted from the centre to the fringe; not only had she ceased to be the source of new currents in the arts, but those few original artists and thinkers she produced failed to obtain recognition abroad. If we compare the enormous vogue Machiavelli enjoyed abroad with the lack of interest aroused there by Vico, a later great Italian thinker, we realize how far the diffusion of a writer is helped not only by his genius, but also (we could almost say : above all) by the fashion his country is enjoying among foreigners at the time. In Machiavelli's time Italy was in the limelight, in Vico's she was little more than a geographical expression, as Metternich called her in the next century. The penalty which a nation pays for existing on the fringe does not limit itself to the lack of response abroad; it inevitably reacts on the character of the national production which, cut off from the main currents of literature and art, becomes provincial. There is no denying that such was, on the whole, the character of Italian art and literature in the nineteenth century. The only redeeming feature of provinciality is, occasionally, a simplification and a lack of sophistication which cause literary or artistic products to become widely popular at home, i.e. easily accessible to the lower strata of society. A narrowed outlook, also, by an exclusive concentration on the immediate surroundings, may extract such a quintessence from them as to outweigh the disadvantages of narrowness.

One fact must be borne in mind when considering Italian art and literature in the nineteenth century : that with Canova and Foscolo that aureate, aristocratic character which had been for centuries a characteristic of Italian art came to an end (a later reappearance of this tradition, with Carducci and D'Annunzio, at the end of the century, was short-lived). Italian art, when it made its voice heard again, was always, in one way or another, linked with the people, either by inspiration or character. Carlo Porta and Gioacchino Belli adopted the dialect, the former of Milan, the latter of Rome, for their picture of the life of the lower classes of their respective towns, which by far exceeds the production of any contemporary poet writing in the literary language in its vividness and wit. Verdi in music, Mancini in painting, were popular artists to the point of occasional vulgarity. Manzoni and Verga made humble people the subjects of their novels. Only in the case of Leopardi did the provinciality of the surrounding culture act as an irritant, and deepen the poet's sense of solitude. But even the greatest poems of the aristocratic Leopardi were not those conceived in the solemn, time-hallowed form of the *canzone* (*All'Italia, Ad Angelo Mai*, etc.), but the idyls suggested by humble life around him, *Il Sabato del villaggio, La Sera del dì di festa, Il Passero solitario, A Silvia*.

While on the whole the romantic vogue in Italy affected only external elements, such as the use of mediaeval instead of Arcadian paraphernalia, or ghosts and apparitions instead of classical allegories and divinities, there was one side of romanticism familiar to the English through the poetry of Wordsworth, which struck firm roots in Italy : that interest in the lives of humble folk, which found its first expression in Gray's *Elegy* became the leading theme of Wordsworth, and culminated in the message of George Eliot :

> When I began to enquire,
> To watch and question those I met, and held
> Familiar talk with them, the lonely roads
> Were schools to me in which I daily read
> With most delight the passions of mankind,
> Souls that appear to have no depth at all
> To vulgar eyes....
> .... There I heard,
> From mouths of lowly men and of obscure
> A tale of honour, sounds in unison
> With loftiest promises of good and fair.
> Of these, said I, shall be my Song : of these,
> If future years mature me for the task,
> Will I record the praises, making Verse
> Deal boldly with substantial things, in truth
> And sanctity of passion, speak of these

> That justice may be done, obeisance paid
> Where it is due : thus haply shall I teach,
> Inspire, through unadulterated ears
> Pour rapture, tenderness, and hope, my theme
> No other than the very heart of man... [1]

This is almost the programme of Manzoni in writing the *Promessi sposi*, which owes only the external form of a historical novel to Walter Scott : in reality it could be called, as *Silas Marner* has been called, a " lyrical ballad " in prose. Manzoni, too, takes the dignity of the humble, the true, and the ordinary for his theme, and his language is calculated to appeal to the heart and enlist the sympathies of everybody through its direct simplicity : like Wordsworth, he aimed at doing away with the time-hallowed distinction between the language used in literature and everyday speech. Manzoni believed that every man should live in the freedom and truth of his own soul in order to fulfil his duties ; his sympathy goes to the victims, the oppressed, and the humble, to the obscure sacrifices of downtrodden communities, which are ignored by the professional historian ; he detests the heroic scoundrels who loom large in politics and diplomacy. He sees the role the humble folk play in history, indeed in his eyes it is they who really make history, and not all of them together as armies or social groups, or indiscriminate crowds, but each one on his own, with his individual face, and his little patrimony of feelings, ideas, and good works. Manzoni's creed in this respect comes very close to Tolstoy's, who in *War and Peace* (Book IV, Part I, 4) insists on the importance of the anonymous crowd, of the acts which history fails to record ; for him only unconscious activity bears fruit ; George Eliot embodied the same democratic creed in *Felix Holt* (Vol. I, ch. XVI) :

> We see human heroism broken into units, and say this unit did little — might as well not have been. But in this way we might break up a great army into units ; in this way we might break the sunlight into fragments, and think that this and the other might be cheaply parted with. Let us rather raise a monument to the soldiers

whose brave hearts only kept the ranks unbroken, and met death — a monument to the faithful who were not famous, and who are precious as the continuity of the sunbeams is precious, though some of them fall unseen and on barrenness.

The *Promessi sposi* is the epos of the humble and oppressed, a tribute to their impulsive goodness, to the treasures of compassion, patience and resignation contained in their souls; indeed the whole of Manzoni's production, including his lyric poetry and tragedies as well as his great novel, is instinct with sympathy for the oppressed, for those no one has ever comforted in the course of centuries, for the toil and the sacrifices which form the web of History, for the weak who tremble in silence, for the dispersed and nameless tribes. In one important point, however, Manzoni's idea of humanity is different from Wordsworth's on one side and from Tolstoy's on the other : humility is for him a disposition of soul rather than a social position ; only the man who does not presume to fashion his own life but accepts it as it is, is truly humble. For some of Manzoni's followers (Cantù, Balbo, Carcano) humility lost this meaning and, through the influence of Saint-Simon's ideas, which they tried to reconcile with Catholicism, became identified with a social position, and often degenerated into rhetoric and sentimental posturing ; later, Manzoni's influence became merged with V. Hugo's, e.g. in Antonio Ranieri's *Ginevra, o l'orfana della Nunziata* (written 1836-7). Finally in Verga the theme of the dignity of the humble folk lost all evangelical references, and took on the definite social connotation of a primitive, barbaric world.

The repeated attempts of minor Italian poets during the nineteenth century to adopt the language of real life were doomed to end in grotesque failures : a typical instance, Tommaseo's poem, *Una serva* (written 1837), whose very title sounded like a challenge, exhibits continuous clashes between humdrum expressions and cadences and stiff poetic diction, an effect which makes one recall Victorian utilitarian implements decorated with classical trimmings (e.g. a " Gothic " sewing machine or a steam engine masquerading behind Doric columns). [2]

Those attempts indicate in any case in which direction the genius of Italy was likely to find expression in the nineteenth century: in the close study of nature and the people, and of the everyday drama of humble folk, and in the steady cult of a sane, clear-sighted observation of human destinies, mixed with humour and pathos. Realism was a widespread tendency in Europe in the second half of the nineteenth century, and no country was better prepared for it than Italy. Thanks to the use of dialect Porta and Belli succeeded better in suiting their technique to their subjects than writers using Italian, on whom the academic tradition weighed heavily. Manzoni attained his simple familiar style only after repeated attempts, but neither his miraculous balance of wisdom and humour, of human emotion and Christian teaching, nor his compromise between literary dignity and everyday language could be repeated. We miss it in Ippolito Nievo, the author of the *Confessioni di un ottuagenario*, who learned much from Manzoni, but was unable to fit his language, which has a strong literary flavour, to the human substance of the story.

In the course of the century there were several attempts to introduce a breath of fresh air into poetry, the ablest of them being that of Vittorio Betteloni who, following the models of Byron's " talk in verse " and of Heine, gave Italy a kind of *genre* painting in verse which may be compared to Coventry Patmore's *Angel in the House*. For instance:

> Dice quel fil di voce piano piano :
> " Vittorio, stavo rincalzando il letto
> A mamma per l'appunto
> Quando venir t'ho udito di lontano. " [3]

Betteloni complained :

> Mai non s'usò in Italia
> Scriver come si parla,
> Mai non s'ebbe il coraggio
> Di scrivere il linguaggio

> Di chi intrattiensi e ciarla
> O si spiega ai suoi simili.
>
> Anzi ci vuole un abito
> Posticcio e d'etichetta,
> Dove il pensier s'impaccia;
> Però fra noi s'ha taccia
> Che la mente più eletta
> Non sappia farsi leggere. [4]

Edmondo De Amicis, that late follower of Manzoni, decidedly knew how to write to be readable; he was the first popular writer of united Italy, a moralist of the schoolteaching kind, and in the end a moderate socialist. He saw his limits and took pride in his benevolent mission. His is a typical Biedermeier creed:

> Great writers stir admiration and enthusiasm; the others, only affection and sympathy. Now, were its effect only to awaken sympathy, I think a book would be justified, because sympathy is a benevolent disposition of the heart, and a benevolent disposition is half of a good action. Besides, should the great exclude the small, the beautiful, the graceful? Should there not be little daisies and violets because there are roses and sunflowers? Does Dante's poem prevent me from crying and being comforted while reading Thouar's [5] short stories?

Human sympathy is the keynote of *Cuore*, De Amicis's popular book which vies in lachrymosity with Dickens's most mawkish passages, a classic for Italian boys no less than Collodi's *Pinocchio* (1883), which, though steeped also in Biedermeier feeling, has a subtler quality of fantasy and psychological observation.

A period like the 'sixties and 'seventies of the last century which considered it a daring felicity, when Betteloni gave in his verse the price of the frock worn by the milliner he loved, when Olindo Guerrini followed him with "*a grey frock costing 4.50 a yard*" for his ideal girl, and when Vincenzo Riccardi di Lantosca began a poem with "*Era il settembre del milleottocento — cinquantaquattro...,*" had certainly travelled a long way from the classical paraphernalia and the romantic sighs which had characterized the first half of the century. The change was the more noticeable in painting, where historical and Biblical subjects, which for long had been the hallmark of a painter's worth, gave place to trivial and " unpoetic " *motifs*, with a parallel choice of human types selected from the most ordinary, and even ugly, specimens of Humanity. Also in painting native talent turned to naturalism : first in the landscape, by preferring details, a tree, a field, an ox, a haystack, or a country-lane, to stagy academic compositions ; then in reproducing insignificant episodes of everyday life, without any intention of " telling a story, " as was usual with ordinary *genre* painting which was very popular in Italy at the time, in keeping with the Biedermeier taste. Not only were fragments preferred to grand compositions, but fragments of humble life, peasants, nameless folk, and landscapes with no special distinction to recommend them : briefly the diminutive idyllic world which at the end of the century formed the subject of Giovanni Pascoli's first and best book of verse, *Myricae* (1891), whose title is explicit enough (from Virgil's " arbusta iuvant humilesque myricae "). It was as if the Italians wanted to start from scratch, deliberately ignoring their great past because this had become identified with the hated academic teaching. For Italian painting even more appropriately than for literature we might repeat certain often quoted lines of the poet Domenico Gnoli (1838-1915) :

> L'antico spirito ? È morto.
> Entro al sudario della storia
> Sta nel mausoleo della gloria :
> E Lazzaro solo è risorto.

> Pace alle cose sepolte !
> E tu pure sei morto : il vento
> Dell'arte non gonfia due volte
> La tua vela, o Rinascimento.
> .....
> O padri, voi foste voi.
> Sia benedetta la vostra
> Memoria ! A noi figli or la nostra
> Vita : noi vogliamo esser noi ! [6]

The realistic tendency which had become more and more prominent in Italy in the course of the nineteenth century culminated in the work of Giovanni Verga. There is a *verismo* which fascinates us by its documentary accuracy, through which objects, by becoming unfamiliar, in the course of time acquire a hallucinatory power : such is the *verismo* of Federico De Roberto (*I Viceré*, 1894) : but when *verismo* coincides with great art it has the power of resisting the years ; it is always contemporary ; such is the *verismo* of Giovanni Verga. Even if the customs of the people described are not contemporary, but belong to a backward race, like Verga's Sicilians, who are still swayed by jealousy, honour and revenge, and repay insults with physical violence like animals at bay. Verga had imbibed the lesson of French realists ; the objectivity of the artist, the scrupulous reproduction of human data, the so-called *tranche de vie*, etc., were canons in which he believed, and these canons formed the programme of Flaubert, the Goncourts and Zola.

Verga was a long time in finding himself : he had a passionate Sicilian nature to express, and the canon of objectivity, for all the jeers of D. H. Lawrence (in his translation of Verga's short stories), acted as a convenient check to what might have been too exuberant. After having written a number of novels on the *beau monde*, which breathe the spirit of French fiction in the Goncourts' time, Verga, when about forty, came back to his native place, and found his inspiration in the passionate primitive race around him. It was for Verga not so much the discovery of a " popular " content for his art which aimed, as fiction did in Italy at the time, at appealing to the people ; nor even an idea of social propaganda, as was common in a period when, national unity once achieved, the new ruling class became aware of the deficiencies of the triumphant revolution and of the precarious character of the newly liberated nation. There was no burning desire for reform and redemption of the masses in Verga, who was in this respect very much unlike the European, particularly English and Russian, novelists of the nineteenth century. There was, in him however, a sense of wonder, which was developed by his sojourn on the Continent, at the discovery of the virgin, almost mythical, world of Sicilian peasants.

Striking away from the aureate tradition of Italian prose, Verga made the Sicilian shepherds talk their own language : it was, at the end of the nineteenth century, in Italy, a repetition of Wordsworth's discovery of the virgin world of peasants and humble people, unadulterated by the sophistications and conventions of society. According to Leo Spitzer :

> The originality of Verga's technique consists in this, that the narrative of an entire novel, from the first to the last chapter, is systematically filtered through a semi-real chorus of popular talkers who integrate the narration by means of gestures and conversations... For instance, Verga does not describe Bastianazzo's death in his fisher-boat "Provvidenza", but (in the third chapter of *I Malavoglia*) the process by which this death becomes real for the village and his mother, through the words, the gestures and the attitudes in general of all the members of that community... The story-teller has chosen to narrate the events as they are reflected in the mind of his characters. [7]

Verga does not believe, with Tolstoy, in the spiritual advantages of poverty and humility. "*Verga's peasants are certainly not Christian-like,*" Lawrence remarks, "*whatever else they are. They are most normally ugly and low, the bulk of them. And individuals are sensitive and simple. Verga turns to the peasants only to seek for a something which, as a healthy artist, he worshipped... He worshipped every manifestation of pure, spontaneous, passionate life, life kindled to vividness. Verga turned to the peasants to find*, in individuals, *the vivid spontaneity of sensitive passionate life, non-moral and non-didactic.*"

One cannot talk of Italian neo-realism, both in fiction and in the cinema, without seeing its antecedents in Verga's art, an art which has a regional and vernacular character, and taps the still fresh sources of the remote disctricts of the South and the islands. Recent Italian best-sellers abroad — like Ignazio Silone and Carlo Levi — are late followers of Verga, and their stature would appear in the proper light if Verga were better known abroad.

Verga's influence is, however, insufficient to account for all the aspects of Italian realism of our present time. There merged into it another influence, an American one, Hemingway's prose.

2. The Influence of Hemingway.

The first article that ever appeared in Italy on Hemingway was published in the Turin daily paper *La Stampa* in June, 1929, with my signature. Hemingway's first important book, *In Our Time*, had been published five years before, in 1924, and it was T. S. Eliot, I think, who first drew my attention to it. [8] In my article on " Un giovane narratore americano " I saw Hemingway's subject-matter and style by contrast with a then widespread type of *intimiste* literature, largely influenced by Proust and Henry James, and to such literature overripe with culture I offered as a curative the example of an art which seemed to spring from virgin soil. Mine was only a partial view : I had before my mind only the Biedermeier side of the Italian nineteenth century tradition, and my reaction to Hemingway was almost as naive as that of eighteenth-century people to Macpherson's *Ossian*. On the one side I failed to foresee a possible link with a kind of realism which had already borne fruit, and what magnificent fruit, with us in Verga's work ; on the other side I was blind to the late romantic and even decadent aspects which have been detected since in Hemingway's world. [9] Here is the substance of what I wrote :

Now Ernest Hemingway has a new accent in this multitude of story-tellers ; it would be next to impossible to find in him an echo of the current recipe. Maybe because he is an American, and America may be considered relatively virgin soil, so far as literary traditions are concerned. If you have to think of somebody else, you may think of Defoe, who in *Moll Flanders* causes his heroine to talk in a sublimated version of the style of a maidservant's letter. Nothing, at first, seems simpler than Hemingway's technique : he confines himself to repeating speeches almost drily, to describing the scene with the barest particulars. His style adheres to the outline of things with an almost impersonal firmness. If one can talk of an objective style, it is his. There is nothing in him of that cerebral tendency which cannot do away with certain standards and categories, and no sooner contemplates an object than it deforms and judges it, so as to give an artificial, rhetorical, vision of the world... It would be difficult to imagine a more elementary style than Hemingway's : the greatest possible economy of means, as in a natural process. He wraps things round by a repeated verbal contact; he seems to possess the spontaneous wisdom of the dowser, who divines the presence of underground water. Hemingway relates half a sentence, sketches the expression of a face, a twitching of the lips, a nothing; but this nothing throws light on a whole situation : a maximum of evocation with a minimum display of means. One may object that this can be said of the art of every great story-teller ; but the novelty consists in this, that the austere firmness which in a European is, as a rule, the result of a laborious process of simplification seems to exist naturally in this American. He cannot help adhering to the things he describes, so much so that a sophisticated reader may find his way of approach monotonous in the long run. Any subject is good for Hemingway : a fishing party, a conversation overheard in a military hospital or in a sleeping-car or in a bar, a boxing-match, a bullfight. He has a definite propensity for subjects of this latter description, since he seems sometimes to identify " life " with the display of violence and brutality, so that blows and blood appear occasionally to be regarded as high human values... One is indeed at a loss to imagine what his readings may have been. Hemingway's point of view has so little in common with the aesthete's that occasionally it may even appear strictly utilitarian. He singles out details of a practical character with the humdrum precision of the man in the street.

I was trying in my article to convey what D. S. Savage has said much more forcibly in the London literary miscellany *Focus* (1946) :

Hemingway is, within very narrow limits, a stylist who has brought to something like perfection a curt, unemotional, factual style which is an attempt at the objective presentation of experience. A bare, dispassionate reporting of external actions is all that Hemingway as a rule attempts in presenting his characters and incidents. His typical central character, his 'I', may be described generally as a bare consciousness stripped to the human minimum, impassively recording the objective data of experience. He has no contact with ideas, no visible emotions, no hopes for the future, and no memory. He is, as far as it is possible to be so, a *de-personalized* being.

These words express admirably what I wanted to convey to a public of Italian writers and readers, steeped in the delicious sea of Proust. I did not try to see behind the façade, to reveal what view of life was behind that de-personalized style. This has been done, however, in Mr. Savage's essay, where he shows how the entire extrusion of personality into the outward sensational world makes Hemingway's characters the inwardly-passive victims of a meaningless determinism; how the profound spiritual inertia, the inner vacuity and impotence which is a mark of all Hemingway's projected characters, ends in a deadening sense of boredom and negation which can only be relieved by violent, though still meaningless, activity; how the final upshot of it all is the total absence of a sense of life, so that life is brought into a sensational vividness only by contrast with the nullity of death.

I did not try to see through Hemingway's world; what interested me was the aspect hinted at in these words of Savage: "*A novelist, of admitted literary merit, who lacks all the equipment generally expected of a practitioner of his art except a certain artistic scrupulousness and poetic sense, is something of a phenomenon.*" For Savage, Hemingway represents "*a special form of that which might be termed the* proletarianization *of literature : the adaptation of the technical artistic conscience of the sub-average human consciousness.*" As an instance of Hemingway's style I quoted in my article a long passage from " Cat in the Rain, " and advised a study of " Big Two-Hearted River. "

My article in *La Stampa* was resented in certain quarters : it was said, among other things, that long ago Italian literature had gone through the phase represented by Hemingway's stories; one must not forget that these were the years of the Fascist rule, and nationalism was rampant, so much so that when, in 1936, I wrote about Hemingway's *Green Hills of Africa*, the Fascist censorship must have been caught napping when it allowed the article to appear at all : Hemingway's name was taboo among us because of his attitude during the Abyssinian campaign.

In the meantime, however, other critics had been speaking of Hemingway with praise, chiefly on account of his novel about the Italian front, *A Farewell to Arms* ; and what information the Italians could not get from their own literary reviews they gathered from French magazines, always widespread in our country. By 1941, Hemingway's work was not only so well known but so widely imitated that one of our leading critics, Emilio Cecchi (who had helped to acquaint the Italian public with Hemingway) wrote in the *Corriere della sera* : " *We keep stumbling everywhere against this type of dialogue, whether we read a short story or a reporter's correspondence : its usual form consists in repeating, taking up again and chewing, a common, careless, meaningless sentence, in altering it imperceptibly, in giving it a certain mysterious intonation, and then in calling it back again, bandying it about and swallowing it up, in making it issue forth again out of a sleeve or a nostril, endlessly.* "

Among the first to learn from Hemingway, as well as from American novelists, Elio Vittorini became known in the thirties through his translations of D. H. Lawrence as well as original short stories and impressions of places (*Piccola borghesia, I Morlacchi*) : he was then a Fascist and had himself photographed with the front page of the *Corriere della sera* under his eyes, with the " Discorso del Duce " well in evidence : he was then very young. In 1941 he wrote his best book, *Conversazione in Sicilia*, whose final scene with the ghost of the brother killed in action derives from a well-known chapter in Thomas Wolfe's *Look Homeward, Angel* ; [10] in the previous year he had published a selection of short stories by William Saroyan (*Che ve ne sembra dell'America ?*). Hemingway and Saroyan are the evident literary sponsors of the book which he published in 1945, *Uomini e no* : from the very title, which sounds very quaint in Italian until one realizes that the model has been supplied for it by Hemingway's *To Have and Have Not*, combined with Steinbeck's *Of Mice and Men* (*Uomini e topi* in the Italian translation). *Uomini e no* claims to be the novel of the Italian resistance and partisan war : the Italian counterpart of *For Whom the Bell Tolls*. Vittorini had come out of the war a blossoming Communist, the editor of the Communist review *Il Politecnico* which tried to imitate Russian weeklies even in external appearance. Vittorini and another Sicilian, the painter Guttuso, both proletarian artists, were, together with Silone and Carlo Levi, the only names international literary correspondents had got hold of for a time in post-war Italian art and letters. In an English miscellany *New Road* (no. 4, 1946) one could read with no little amusement the title of an essay by Paul Potts, " Not since Dante : Ignazio Silone, A Footnote, " explained in the course of the article by the curious statement that no one had done so much as Silone to lead Italian literature back towards the glory it had not known since the days of Dante and Guido Cavalcanti. And when Stephen Spender came to Rome, the only name of a young Italian writer he seemed to have heard was that of Vittorini : he and Guttuso were the prominent figures in a gossipy piece on Italian art and letters which appeared in *Vogue*.

The reader has not long to search in *Uomini e no* to discover its secret. The lyrical tone obviously goes back to Saroyan, but the continuous dialogues, the tough manner, the delineation of characters, the crudity of certain episodes, could not have existed without the example of Hemingway, particularly of *For Whom the Bell Tolls*.

The minute narration of the torture of the peddler Giulaj, on whom a German officer sets his dogs, finds a counterpart in the description in Hemingway's novel of the massacre of all the fascists of a small town, done to death between two lines of peasants armed with flails. Enne 2, the protagonist of Vittorini's book, is in love with a girl, Berta ; they go to the house of an old woman, Selva, who belongs to the movement. Now Selva's behaviour to the lovers reminds one immediately of the behaviour of elderly Pilar, the partisan woman, to Robert Jordan and Maria. Both elderly women push the young ones into the arms of the young men, and at the same time are jealous of their youth and beauty. A passage from Vittorini's novel will also illustrate the peculiar mannerism of his dialogue, a subject to which I shall have to return in a moment :

" Do you think it is odd ? " Selva said. " It isn't odd. We've never seen you with a companion, and we want you to have a companion. Can't we want you to have a companion ? "
She fixed glowing eyes on the man and the woman.
" Can't we want this for a man who is dear to us ? A man is happy when he has a companion. Shouldn't a man be happy ? "
" Thank you, " Enne 2 said. " Thank you, Selva. But... "
" To hell with 'but', " old Selva said. " Can't we want a man to be happy ? We work in order that men may be happy. What good would it do to work if it didn't serve to make men happy ? That's why we work. Isn't that why we work ? "
" That's why, " Enne 2 said.
" Then it is why ! " Selva said.
And she kept on fixing her eyes on the man and the woman.
" God ! " she said. " Men must be happy. What sense would our work make if men couldn't be happy ? You tell me, young woman. Would our work make any sense ? "
" I don't know, " Berta replied.
And it was as if she hadn't replied, she was very serious ; and she lifted her face a moment, but it was as if she hadn't lifted it.
" Would any of our work make sense ? "
" No, Selva, I don't think it would. "
" Would it make sense ? No, it wouldn't make any sense at all. "
" It wouldn't make sense. Nothing on earth would make sense. "
" Nothing on earth would make sense. Isn't it so, young woman ? "
" I don't know, " Berta replied again.
" Or would something make sense then ? "
" No, " Enne 2 replied, " I do not think so. "
" Would our clandestine newspapers make sense ? Would our schemes make sense ? "
" I don't think so. "
" And our men who get shot ? Would they make sense ? No, they would not make any sense. "
" No, they wouldn't make sense ".
" Would anything in the world make sense ? Would our bombs make sense ? "

"I don't think anything would make sense."
"Nothing would make sense. Or would the enemies we kill make sense?"
"Not even they. I don't think they would."
"No, no. Men must be happy. Everything makes sense only if men can be happy..."

Later on, Selva is alone with Berta:

Selva got up and went behind the table. She looked to see if the water was boiling.
"I hoped you were his companion," she said.
She broke off, but still she did not let Berta speak. She went on: "A man has to have his companion. Even more so if he's one of ours. He must be happy. What can he know of what men need if he isn't happy? We are fighting for this. For men to be happy."
She turned round leaning on the table with both hands. "Do you follow what I'm saying?"
"It's simple," Berta replied.
"Very simple," Selva said. "A man who is fighting in order that men may be happy should know what men need in order to be happy. And he must have a companion. He must be happy with his companion."
"Hasn't he a companion?" Berta asked.
Selva looked again to see if the water was boiling. "You ask me? I hoped you were... I never knew that he had one." She came around the table with the teapot and two cups. "The first time I saw you," she said, "I thought immediately that you ought to be his companion. You are just what he would want a woman to be. But you," she added, "do you believe what I am saying?"
"Why not?" Berta said.
"If I were young," Selva continued, "I would like to have been his companion. But I might be his mother. But when I saw you I thought that you must be the one."

If we read after this the various passages in *For Whom the Bell Tolls* where old Pilar eggs the two lovers on, we shall find a similarity of situations, of atmosphere, of treatment, although no single passage of Vittorini can be said to imitate Hemingway closely. In both authors the scenes consist almost exclusively of dialogues. I shall quote one passage only (p. 154). Pilar, Robert and Maria are sitting under a pine tree, and Pilar asks Maria to lay her head on her arms, then she strokes her.

— You can have her in a little while, *Inglés*, she said. Robert Jordan was sitting behind her.
— Do not talk like that, Maria said.
— Yes, he can have thee, Pilar said and looked at neither of them. I have never wanted thee. But I am jealous.
— Pilar, Maria said. Do not talk thus.
— He can have thee, Pilar said and ran her finger around the lobe of the girl's ear. — But I am very jealous.
— But Pilar, Maria said. It was thee explained to me there was nothing like that between us.
— There is always something like that, the woman said. There is always something like something there should not be. But with me there is not. Truly there is not. I want thy happiness and nothing more... You are for the *Inglés*. That is seen and as it should be. That I would have. Anything else I would not have. I only tell you something true. Few people will ever talk to thee truly and no women. I am jealous and say it and it is there. And I say it.
— Do not say it, Maria said. Do not say it, Pilar.
— *Por qué*, do not say it, the woman said, still not looking at either of them. I will say it until it no longer pleases me to say it. And, — she looked down at the girl now, — that time has come already. I do not say it more, you understand ?
— Pilar, Maria said. Do not talk thus.
— Thou art a very pleasant little rabbit, Pilar said. And lift thy head now because this silliness is over.
— It was not silly, said Maria. And my head is well where it is...
Pilar said : .... So simple I am very complicated. Are you very complicated, *Inglés* ?
— No, nor not so simple.
— You please me, *Inglés*, Pilar said. Then she smiled and leaned forward and smiled and shook her head. Now if I could take the rabbit from thee and take thee from the rabbit.
— You could not.
— I know it, Pilar said and smiled again. Nor would I wish to. But when I was young I could have.
— I believe it.
— You believe it ?
— Surely, Robert Jordan said. But such talk is nonsense.
— It is not like thee, Maria said.
— I am not much like myself today, Pilar said. Very little like myself... I will leave the two of you. And the talk of jealousness is nonsense. I am only jealous that you are nineteen. It is not a jealousy which lasts. You will not be nineteen always.

The passage from Vittorini's novel illustrates a peculiarity of his dialogues as compared with Hemingway's. True, there are repetitions in Hemingway's dialogues, as there are in ordinary life, [11] but we very seldom get from them the impression of exercises in conversation (such as we might find, with all the cases and tenses and moods, in a foreign-language grammar). There are pages and pages of Vittorini which read like such exercises. The nucleus of his dialogues is a triplet. First a statement, then the same repeated with a query, then repeated again as a stronger asseveration :

— Lui ora non ha da fare con molte compagne.
— Lui ha da fare con molte compagne ?
— Non ha più da fare con molte compagne.

Very frequently the echo extends beyond the triplet :

— Sembra che si vedano le montagne.
— Sembra ? Si vedono. Sono le montagne.
— Sono le montagne ?
— Sono le montagne.
— Si vedono le montagne da Milano ?
— Non le vedi ? Si vedono.
— Non sapevo che si vedessero.

Thus Hemingway's technique, devised to carry the impression of actual life by reproducing word by word a dialogue of short sentences, becomes in Vittorini a mannerism, because he is not such an impassive onlooker and listener as Hemingway, but invests everything with a lyrical mood, or merely with a rhetorical emphasis. The effect is very curious. Starting from Hemingway, Vittorini comes near certain effects of Charles Péguy, whose exasperating repetitions give the impression of a person seized with the symptoms of general paralysis. Péguy had caught the rhythm of peasants' talk, and tried to couch it in an artistic pattern ; Vittorini does the same with the talk of the man in the street. But Hemingway never tries to impose a pattern on his dialogues : hence their impression of freshness, even in monotony. Thus the lesson of simplicity and directness of Hemingway has been lost on a writer hopelessly predisposed to mannerism. This does not mean, however, that the lesson is not there. A fake postulates the genuine thing. Vittorini's tone rings false, affected, childishly rhetorical, but his model is still recognizable. The whole thing looks as absurd as an eighteenth-century European imitation of Chinese art, or as a Japanese picture of Napoleon as a prisoner in St. Helena, with the English soldiers in the garb of samurai. Vittorini's partisans talk more like the shepherds in Theocritus's *Idyls* than like the men who fought in Milan against the Germans: *Uomini e no* stands to *For Whom the Bell Tolls* in the same relation as Callimachus to Homer, if for a moment we could call Hemingway a Homer and Vittorini a Callimachus. If to us the result of Vittorini's effort seems therefore to be a new preciosity, we may consider with amusement how far he has travelled from his original intention, which must obviously have been a *proletarianization* of literature, the adaptation of the technical artistic conscience to the sub-average human consciousness, according to D. S. Savage's definition which I have already quoted.

The influence of American fiction, particularly of Hemingway, is also apparent in another Italian war book which caused a certain stir at the time — Giuseppe Berto's *Il Cielo è rosso* (1947). Berto was in the United States as a war prisoner, and although he denies having read Hemingway before he wrote his novel, he must have been affected by the vogue of the American author. Berto's novel is the story of a group of Italian adolescents whom the bombardment of a Northern Italian town has deprived of their parents and homes. Tullio, Carla, Giulia, and a half-witted little girl live in the ruins of a devastated area; they are joined by Daniele, who has come out of a priests' college to find his home destroyed and himself alone in the world. Tullio is the chief of a gang of boys who live by stealing and blackmail; part of their profit is destined to the relief of the poor and to the funds of their party (they are Communists): in a word, he reincarnates the type of the generous outlaw which is a well-known figure of early romanticism. Carla is also a type one comes across in romantic literature, the kind-hearted prostitute : though only fifteen, with the connivance of her lover Tullio, she earns her living as a whore. To this depraved, though not repulsive, couple, is contrasted the pair, Daniele and Giulia, who are essentially honest and good, and find it very hard to adapt themselves to the new circumstances : they pathetically succumb, Giulia by dying of consumption, Daniele by committing suicide. And then Tullio is killed in the course of an unlucky gangsters' expedition. The whole novel is steeped in a profoundly melancholy atmosphere, from the description of the lazy, marshy riverland and the provincial Venetian town at the beginning to the shooting-party in the marshes, which forms the only idyllic episode of the whole book, and on to Daniele's suicide under a train in the end. *Il cielo è rosso* is certainly one of the saddest novels ever written, and, for all its American influence, is tinged with a typical Latin sentimentalism. Italian readers have been reminded of De Amicis' *Cuore* ; if one wants to sum up one's impressions, one could say that *Il cielo è rosso* is Murger's *Vie de bohème* translated into terms of a modern American novel. Yet whatever strictures one may make, the novel remains one of the most remarkable books written in Europe in the immediate post-war period.

One of the most obvious signs of American influence on Berto is again the abundance and character of the dialogues. It would naturally be preposterous to ascribe every occurrence of dialogue to Hemingway's example. But whenever you come across what purports to be a faithul reproduction of conversation, with all its repetitions and apparently meaningless expletives, with its short sentences falling like drops in a vacuum, creating an atmosphere almost by the significance of the pauses, by barely hinted gestures and actions — whenever you come across this, you may depend on it that an American influence is at hand. Take for instance this passage from *Il Cielo è rosso* :

" They're obstinate, " Tullio said. " The most obstinate people I ever saw. Sometimes they stand in front of the town hall or in front of the military command and wait. They wait from morning to night. They don't ask them what they want any more; they'll go on waiting all the same. Maybe some day something will turn up, because they are so obstinate."

Or this:

"Then there is the girl's father," Tullio said. "He's a druggist, the owner of a big pharmacy. The girl will be a druggist too, like her father. I do not know how many years she still has to study, but she's sure to become a druggist, because she's a clever girl. She helps out now once in a while in the store."

A single word is the keynote of both these passages: it is repeated over and over again, so as to give the listener the maximum impact. The bare word is occasionally used in incantation, as if, by sheer repetition, it could take on all the life of the thing itself. Passages like those I have been quoting may not be typical in themselves: but the repetitions, the short sentences, give in the long run the impression of simplicity, of elementariness, of closeness to nature, which we associate with American novels, in particular Hemingway's. An episode of the American soldiers who are distributing food to a crowd of beggars is too long to quote, but a small portion of it will indicate some characteristics of Berto's prose:

"Whom have you got at home?" the sergeant asked.
"Two sisters," replied the boy. "They're smaller than me. They'll be very happy if I bring home some white bread."
"You've no father?" the sergeant asked.
"He died in the bombardment," the boy said. "My mother died in the bombardment, also."
The sergeant came over to the boy and put his hand on his head, then sat down on the box on which the old man had been sitting. "Sit down," he said. The boy sat down again. The sergeant did not speak, and he felt a little embarrassed. "They're singing," he said.
"Yes," said the sergeant.
The melancholy song of the soldiers, with a few notes of a guitar, reached their ears.
"They want to go back home," the sergeant said. "That's why they're singing."
"What do the words mean?" the boy asked.

"That there's a happy country somewhere, far away," the sergeant said.

"It's nice," said the boy.

They listened in silence until the song was over. Then the boy asked again: "Tell me what I have to do."

"Nothing," the sergeant said. "Nothing this evening. Tomorrow, come here at seven."

"O. K.," said the boy. He was still holding the dirty mess tin in his hand and asked: "Should I wash the mess tin?"

"Yes, wash it up," the sergeant said.

The boy went to where the water casks were, and washed the mess tin by rubbing it with earth. A soldier who saw him gave him a piece of soap, and he washed the mess tin again with soap. Then he went back to the sergeant. "I would like to dry it," he said, "but I haven't anything to dry it with."

"You don't have to dry it", the sergeant said. He seemed absent-minded, as if he was thinking of something else. The soldiers at the end of the courtyard were still singing.

This spareness of contours, this bare presentation of things, this reproduction of details which seem unessential, are certainly uncommon in Italian literature. Berto is very fond of describing practical occupations in their minute details. For instance:

Giulia smiled, but finding nothing else to say, got up and did not sit down again. She gave a few more pulls to the pump of the stove and busied herself with the preparations for the meal. She took some canned meat and some eggs out of the box, she lifted a pan off its hook on the wall, and put everything on a table placed against the wall. She opened the can, broke the eggs, and poured everything in the pan. Then she began to mix. Her gestures were slow, unstudied. Daniele looked at her, and looked also at the door to see whether Carla would come back. She had been gone a long time. Then Giulia took the pot off the fire and began to pour out the vegetables. Daniele went to help her, and took in his hand a tin plate with many holes, which was used to drain the vegetables.

Giulia smiled at him with gratitude. "Don't scald yourself," he said. She cautiously poured out the contents of the pot. The vegetables rested on the perforated tin plate, and the water dropped into a basin underneath. A thick white vapor rose, full of the smell of the boiled vegetables.

"Shall I go and throw the water away?" Daniele asked.

"No," Giulia said, "we can use it to wash the dishes."

Now, I won't try to prove that such minute cooking operations (a similar one occurs near the end of the novel, on p. 382) have never before been described in Italian literature, though I would be at a loss to quote anything like them. But open any book of Hemingway, and you will find the model. Take for instance this passage from " Big Two-Hearted River " :

Nick was hungry. He did not believe he had ever been hungrier. He opened and emptied a can of pork and beans and a can of spaghetti into the frying pan.
" I've got a right to eat this kind of stuff, if I'm willing to carry it, " Nick said. His voice sounded strange in the darkening wood. He did not speak again.
He started a fire with some chunks of pine he got with the axe from a stump. Over the fire he stuck a wire grill, pushing the four legs down into the ground with his boot. Nick put the frying pan on the grill over the flames. He was hungrier. The beans and spaghetti warmed. Nick stirred them and mixed them together. They began to bubble, making little bubbles that rose with difficulty to the surface. There was a good smell. Nick got out a bottle of tomato catchup and cut four slices of bread. The little bubbles were coming faster now. Nick sat down beside the fire and lifted the frying pan off. He poured about half the contents out into the tin plate. It spread slowly on the plate. Nick knew it was too hot. He poured on some tomato catchup. He knew the beans and spaghetti were still too hot. He looked at the fire, then at the tent, he was not going to spoil it all by burning his tongue. For years he had never enjoyed fried bananas because he had never been able to wait for them to cool. His tongue was very sensitive.

I said before that I cannot remember anything like this kind of description in Italian literature, and I may as well say, in any other literature I know. If such minute operations have ever been described before, there was no emphasis on them ; they were not meant to stand out like something particularly significant. With Hemingway they have ceased to be part of the background ; they are presented as important episodes. And the same has happened with the seemingly insignificant details of ordinary conversation. Before Hemingway, dialogues in fiction or on the stage were the result of a selection : all immaterial portions were left out ; questions and answers followed a more or less rigid pattern dictated by art. The utmost artificiality prevailed in the *stichomythy* of the Greek tragedies, as well as in Alexandrian couplets of the French plays, or the witty repartees of Restoration comedy ; but even the dialogues in the novels of the naturalist school of the nineteenth century, for all that they pretended to be copied from real life, are arranged so that, so far as the author can help it, there is nothing superfluous. Hemingway has shown the value of the apparently superfluous, the strange beauty of the commonest things when seen from a certain angle, so as to deserve almost the praise Baudelaire gave to the great seventeenth-century French sculptor Puget : " *Toi qui sus ramasser la beauté des goujats.* " Thus he represents the extreme limit of proletarianization so far reached by literature.

At first only kings were considered fit characters for tragedies ; at first only great events were to be a theme for narration : then Montaigne appeared and the apparently insignificant shades of humour and sensibility were brought into literary expression ; then landscapes, bourgeois interiors, still-lifes formed subjects for independent pictures ; and so little by little the humble sides of society and of life have been given attention, until they have come nowadays to the limelight. *Un cœur simple* is only an episode, though one of the greatest, in Flaubert's career : Hemingway's, on the other hand, is a world of simple hearts and simple minds, simple-looking even if they are complex : in him we see the return to primitivism in an age of great technical development, the standard being set by the man in the street as it once used to be by the court.

The man in the street looms large in Italian neo-realism, both in fiction and the cinema, and if we keep in mind the names of Verga and Hemingway, we possess the key to understand the spirit of the works of even the most apparently original authors. Take for instance Moravia's last novel, *La Noia* (1960) : the character who comes most alive in it, the girl Cecilia, does not look to the past or the future, but lives *hic et nunc*, and expresses herself in a rudimentary fashion which reminds one both of Hemingway's characters and of Zazie in Queneau's *Zazie dans le métro* ; on the other hand the protagonist seems to offer a fit illustration of what D. S. Savage said : " *The inner vacuity and impotence which are a mark of all Hemingway's projected characters end in a deadening sense of boredom and negation which can only be relieved by violent, though still meaningless activity, etc.* " Many dialogues, consisting of short, repetitive sentences could be quoted from Moravia's novel (pp. 175-6, 188-9, 270-1), in which Hemingway's influence is ultimately recognizable. [12]

On the other hand the tragic story of humble folk which has been adapted to the screen from Moravia's *La ciociara*, with one of Sofia Loren's best roles, decidedly belongs to that popular, vernacular world which Verga was the first to reveal to the Italians. If we bear in mind those lines Betteloni wrote a century ago :

Mai non s'usò in Italia
Scriver come si parla —

we may think that contemporary Italian literature has reached the very opposite of its tradition, fulfilling and even outvying the attempts at realism and the anti-academic aspirations of the nineteenth century. Indeed the revolution has come full circle : for realism in literature and the abstract in art have become crystallized nowadays into a kind of academy. Official art at the 1960 Venetian Biennale was abstract art, and though Visconti's film *Rocco e i suoi fratelli* was not awarded the Golden Lion at the Film Festival, the reaction against the decision of the jury has been so widespread that one can infer that Visconti's film was " *what was looked upon as right,* " i.e. it embodied the type of taste prevailing (to the point of being conventional) among Italian intellectuals.

NOTES

1. *Prelude*, text of 1805-6, XII, 161-68, 181-184, 231-40.
2. See Nikolaus PEVSNER, *High Victorian Design*, London, 1951,p. 22.
3. " *Says that thin voice very slowly* : '*Vittorio, I was just tucking in mummy's bed, when I heard you coming from afar*'. "
4. " *It never was the custom in Italy to write as one talks, nobody ever had the courage to write the language of people who chatter leisurely or express themselves to each other, rather one needs a borrowed, formal garb, in which thought gets entangled; therefore it is often said of us that even the most distinguished spirit among us cannot write readably.* "
5. Pietro THOUAR (1809-1861), the author of popular edifying *Racconti* for adolescents.
6. " The old spirit ? It is dead. It lies in Glory's mausoleum, wrapt in History's shroud : and only Lazarus was resurrected. Let the dead bury the dead. Thou art dead too : the wind of art does not fill twice thy sail, O Renaissance. Fathers, you were yourselves. Blessed be your memory ! We sons now must live our own life : we want to be ourselves ".
7. " L'originalità della narrazione nei *Malavoglia*," in *Belfagor*, XI, 1 (January 1958).
8. See for further details my essay on " Hemingway in Italy " in *Partisan Review*, October 1948.
9. See : Nemi D'AGOSTINO, " Ernest Hemingway ", *Belfagor*, XI, 1, January 1956 (the same issue which contains L. Spitzer's article quoted above). " *To many American writers and critics about 1930,* " D'Agostino writes, " *the language of young Hemingway appeared as a new miracle of poetic freshness and intensity, an exemplary lesson for everybody, a new road opened to experiment in expression. It was a language for which many literary origins may be found, from Defoe to Twain and Stephen Crane : a language which had been moulded and refined through a skilful assimilation of many modern lessons, from Flaubert to the Russian novelists, from Joyce to Gertrude Stein ; and nevertheless it appeared so spontaneous and racy, anti-literary though very attentive to sound-values, so immediately born out of the very core of Hemingway's feeling, out of his denial of mental elaboration and of the idola of bourgeois culture, the symbol and learned ambiguity. It was a structure of words as fresh as pebbles picked up from a torrent's bed, through which reality seemed for the first time to yield a bare poetry of its own. But ultimately his prodigious transparency, his disenchanted adherence to a narrative imagism, his sheer rational refusal of culture marked his limits. Young Hemingway's most perspicuous style expressed to perfection his fear and incapacity of thinking and getting mature, the pent feeling of his own solitude, the anguished desire of escape.* " " *Hemingway is no easy writer. There are hidden Stendhalian, irrational, Puritan elements in the folds*

of his personality. He has felt the crisis of romantic individualism in a complex way, and his characters unconsciously experience that deep and harassing problem of freedom of which Thomas Mann speaks in My Time. " " The vast influence of his elementary type of narrative on Western fiction has its positive side in the stimulus it has provided for young story-tellers to evade certain closed literary traditions, and renew themselves through a courageous observation of reality, the adoption of a livelier language, and the reconsideration of certain forgotten lessons of the past. "

10. See Glauco CAMBON, " The Italian Response to American Literature, " *Cesare Barbieri Courier*, June 1960, p. 6.

11. Repetitions are found also in Sherwood Anderson, who had imitated certain mannerisms of Gertrude Stein. Hemingway himself gave a parody of this kind of style in *Torrents of Spring*.

12. Among other instances of Hemingway's influence on dialogue, see Vittorio G. ROSSI, *Preludio alla notte*, Milan, 1948, p. 17 :

" Why are there sea-urchins in the sea ? Why do they live ? " Monica asked.
" To live ".
" And the limpets, why do they live ? "
" To live ".
" And we, why do we live ? " Monica asked.
" To live ".

See also pp. 20, 28, 51, 55, 59, 80, of this novel.

HEMINGWAY IN NORWAY

by Sigmund Skard

Norway is a nation of 3.5 million inhabitants, located on the outskirts of Europe. Its economic and literary resources are by necessity limited and its points of international contact few, as compared to those of most other countries. The Norwegian reception of Hemingway could hardly be expected to present much that is radically new. Notwithstanding, even this sketchy survey of his influence will show that neither in timing, strength or development is it a simple replica of that in other nations, even in Scandinavia. Indirectly the material may thus emphasize the complexity of the game of literary interrelations. [1]

Hemingway's strong Norwegian impact is somehow unexpected. A number of those general factors that explain the importance of the young American writers of the 1920's to other countries do not seem to apply to Norway at the time of his emergence. The little nation had seen no war since 1814 and had been allowed to develop its political and social democracy peacefully. In the war of 1914-18 Norway, like neighbouring Sweden, maintained a profitable neutrality, at the safe edge of world catastrophe. In the 1930's, depression was met with an optimistic and successful policy of social reform that was felt to be in the national tradition. There was no general breakdown of moral values, no " lost " generation of embittered and cynical returning soldiers, like the one that took Hemingway to its bosom in other parts of Europe.

This situation was to some extent paralleled in the domain of literature. In many European countries the American authors of the inter-war period appeared against the flattering background of a national wiiting that was intellectualized, academic and thin. Norwegian literature at the time was not similarly obsolete. The period saw a marked flowering of realistic fiction and lyrical poetry, based on a literary tradition of religious, humanitarian and social responsibility. Norwegian literature was felt by most of its readers to be relevant and close to life. Even in style there was little of the " Biedermeier " note. Writing was neither bloodless nor precious. The young Americans were bound to appear as less of a novelty in Norway than they did in many other nations.

But these factors were counterbalanced by others, no less important. While Norway did not participate in the First World War, the conflict soon was followed by social convulsions, brought on by sudden industrialization and sharpened by international recession. In some of the Norwegian youth of the 1930's unemployment created a mood of despair. These tensions became the background of a vanguard of young radicals, most of them communists of the Trotzkyite type and tightly organized in a " Clarté " group. Like radical Norwegian writers in the previous century they were internationally minded, sharing the anguished idealism of their contemporaries abroad ; and this feeling of fellowship was intensified during the 1930's by the general growth of the totalitarian political systems. They felt traditional Norwegian 'reformism' to be old-fashioned and tied to a dying past. In intellectual life as well they were bent on debunking puritan and provincial conventions. Norwegian literature they felt to be bourgeois, lacking in sophistication, and unconscious of post-war modernism. They saw it as their task to break that isolation.

While the radicalism of these critics was sometimes dogmatic and shallow, they captured attention by their brilliance and acumen. But they never completely dominated the scene. There were moderate and conservative groups, which also had their national traditions and international bearings, and defended their positions with increasing vigour. Contemporary literature became one of the battlegrounds in a keen and many-sided debate.

In this conflict the United States came to play an unusual part. Norway traditionally feels closer to America than almost any other European nation does. This fact is partly due to Norway's worldwide shipping and its general westward orientation, but above all to an immense emigration across the Atlantic, exceeded only by that from Ireland in percentage of the population, and a deep-rooted sense of democratic fellowship with the United States. All through the 19th century the American example was a direct stimulant in Norwegian politics; two American presidents are the only foreign statesmen to have their monuments erected in Oslo. Even censure of American civilization was always tempered by sympathy. Knut Hamsun's famous diatribe of 1889 was largely a footnote, and never moulded public opinion in the country itself as it did, for instance, in Sweden. From the 1890's to the 1930's there was a continuous discussion of American civilization by friendly critics and scholars, conservatives and political radicals alike (H. Tambs Lyche, Halvdan Koht, S. C. Hammer, Arne Kildal, C. J. Hambro, Charles Kent).

Translation of American literature before the 1930's was miserably slight as compared, for instance, to similar translation in contemporary Sweden. Norway was just breaking away from its dependence on Denmark, both in publishing and language. But the Norwegian translations were growing in number, and in 1926 for the first time needed their own section in the National Cumulative List of Books. In 1928, on the eve of the discovery of the young school of American writers, Knut Hamsun himself retracted his opinion of forty years before by declaring that "*the young novel in the States is the freshest and most original in the world, a source of renewal and an example for imitation to Europe.*" [2]

The break-through itself was largely due to Sigurd Hoel

(1890-1960), novelist, critic, and herald of new ideas, including psychoanalysis. At the suggestion of the publisher Harald Grieg, director of Gyldendal Publishing House where Hoel was the leading reader, Hoel in 1929 accepted the editorship of a *Series of Modern Novels* called the " Yellow Series " from the color of its covers. In all, it ran to more than 100 titles. Around fifty of the books in the series appeared before 1940, and more than one third of these were American.[3]

Exaggerated claims have been made about the pioneering character of this undertaking. But the facts suffice to secure for the " Yellow Series " an honorable place in the history of contemporary translation, and not only with regard to its American volumes. Sigurd Hoel and Gyldendal were among the first in Europe to translate authors like Julian Green, Richard Hughes, Rosamond Lehmann, Elizabeth Madox Roberts, and Thornton Wilder. They shared with Sweden the European priority in presenting Louis Bromfield (1929) and James M. Cain; with Denmark and Sweden in translating John Steinbeck (1938); with France and Italy in translating Kafka (1933). And they were the first in all Europe to introduce William Faulkner (1932) and Erskine Caldwell (1935), both of whom were published in French only in 1933 and 1936, in other languages only from 1935 and 1939 onward.

While most of the books appeared in small printings (2,000 in the 1930's) they became immensely popular in literary circles, and soon entrenched modern American literature solidly in the Norwegian reading public. As early as 1938 statistics of the lending activity of Oslo's leading public library showed, that among authors in English the Americans were in the majority. Their general influence can be gauged by the lively translation in the 1930's even of older American literature. The recognition was established as a fact when, in 1940, Francis Bull in his *History of World Literature* written in Norwegian declared the Americans to be the leaders of European writing in the interwar period, together with the French.

But at the same time, judgment was sobered, and balanced

by realistic knowledge of everyday America. There is little in Norway of that twisted romanticism and primitivism that in other nations created the worship of an American « littérature noire » and the establishment of a fabulous « style américain ». Hemingway was at the very center of this new interest. [4] Sigurd Hoel happened to read *In Our Time* in Paris in the spring of 1926 ; the book had appeared in the previous fall. He has vividly described the impression, " *one of those experiences which come only very few times in life... The book made me calm and troubled at the same time. It responded to a vague longing ; I had not realized that it existed before, and even now I had no words for it.* " When *The Sun Also Rises* appeared in the same year, Hoel persuaded Harald Grieg to buy it for the planned library of novels, and it was published in 1929 in Gunnar Larsen's translation as the first volume of the " Yellow Series, " simultaneous with Thornton Wilder's *The Bridge of San Luis Rey*. Along with the German and Finno-Swedish editions of the book (1928, 1929) the Norwegian version was the first European translation of a Hemingway novel, a fact which Hemingway himself, in his later years of fame, remembered gratefully. Gyldendal followed up by translating, in and outside the " Yellow Series, " Hemingway's entire production except *The Torrents of Spring* and *The Fifth Column (Death in the Afternoon* appeared in 1963.) The translators were of high quality, most of them authors of renown in their own right. In 1951-53 the *Collected Novels and Short Stories* appeared in nine volumes, the first collected edition in Norwegian of a living foreign author. Beside a Danish pocket edition, where the unnumbered volumes are sold separately, this Norwegian edition is presumably still the only Collected Works of Hemingway in any language.

The sale, distribution and reading of these books in Norway have been impressive. They have appeared in 24 different printings (four of them pocket books), which, up to 1962, had sold around 270,000 copies. In 1954 the total sale of Hemingway's books in Swedish translation up to that date was stated to be well above 250,000 copies. Even if some Swedish sale has to be added for the succeeding eight years, the Norwegian sale is noteworthy, in a nation with a population only half the size of that of Sweden. The most successful Hemingway novel in Norway, *A Farewell to Arms*, has sold more than 70,000 copies to date; in Sweden before 1954 it also had sold 70,000.[5] To these figures has to be added the sale of editions in English, for which no statistics are available. Remembering the proficiency in English among the Norwegians one may assume that the distribution of Hemingway's books in the original has been considerable.

This popularity is confirmed by a spot test of present circulation of his works in Norwegian libraries.[6] The Public Library of Bergen, Norway's second city (115,000 inhabitants), in 1961 owned 81 copies of Hemingway's books in Norwegian translation, and 10 copies in English. (The relatively small number of original editions was temporary, since many of these books were worn out at the time and were being replaced.) During the year 1961 the average circulation of each copy of the translations was 18, of the originals 12, "*an amazing frequency.*" In comparison, individual popular novels by Norwegian authors (Hamsun, Sigrid Undset) may have an average circulation figure as high as 24. But if one counts the entire work of the writer, the figures are much lower, for a popular contemporary novelist like Sigurd Hoel only around 15. On this basis "*Hemingway is beyond doubt our most popular author.*"

This lasting position in the broad layers of the Norwegian population is, of course, primarily due to the strong popular appeal of Hemingway the writer. But if he has become so well known, it is the result of a number of contributing factors. Quite important, in Norway as elsewhere, is doubtless the continuous and effective propagation of the Hemingway legend in the magazines and illustrated press. Since the 1950's American literature has been an obligatory part of the study of English throughout the Norwegian educational system, and Hemingway texts have been included in anthologies and curricula for schools and universities. But even more important has been his critical reception. A surprising number of signed reviews and serious discussions of the author and his books, and of books about him, have appeared in the Norwegian periodical press ever since 1929, even in small newspapers of stiictly local circulation.

The figures of publication, sale and loan make it clear that Hemingway and his American contemporaries encountered little in Norway of that condescending attitude that, in Sweden, postponed real recognition of the lost generation writers until the 1940's and 1950's. Some of the first Norwegian reviewers of the " Yellow Series " still expressed their surprise at the emergence of such literature in " *dull and vulgar* " America. But these ideas obviously did not prevent understanding and appreciation. A similar objective curiosity was manifest in the reception of Faulkner, who had to wait for his first Danish and Swedish translations respectively for seven and twelve years. But apart from this general openness of mind, the critical appraisal in Norway is extremely chequered. It reflects the contrasts in Norwegian society and in Hemingway himself, contrasts that are ultimately irreconcilable in both.

He was launched by the " *radical* " school, as their discovery. Sigurd Hoel was already the recognized intellectual leader of the group, although their ways soon parted politically; and it was his introduction to each volume in the " Yellow Series " which, above all, " *placed* " Hemingway as an author in the minds of Norwegian readers. Long before the building up of a Hemingway legend he was accepted as a symbol of the " *new times.* " In 1933 a Norwegian writer, born in 1911, could talk of the youth that " *did not grow up with movies, radio, air travel, automobiles, Freud, Watson, Huxley, and Hemingway.* " [7] His early writing thrilled many young Norwegians, who had never seen war, but who sensed the " *modernism* " of the new author, were delighted to get " *good and lost* " with him, and regarded his Parisian heroes with the gaping admiration of Middletown.

But this passive and slightly affected attitude was not typical of the group which launched Hemingway. On the contrary, its members were a band of fighters, and used him and his American colleagues as provocative examples of a militant radicalism, which was in no doubt about its aims, and certainly not about sexual matters. The more conservative groups fought back violently on behalf of established standards, giving the critical discussion an ideological harshness that is well known in Norway.

Extremes were not dominant, however. From the very beginning there were notable attempts at unbiassed understanding. The radicals were not alone in praising Hemingway the writer, the conservatives not alone in acknowledging the limitations of his art. Important was the undogmatic independence of Sigurd Hoel himself. For all his foreign orientation he felt loyal to a national tradition which insisted on viewing literature rationally, in its moral and social context. The running discussion of Hemingway which gradually got under way, may not have offered much that had not been thought or said before. But some striking evaluations appeared. And the debate shows a certain dialectic equilibrium : the image of Hemingway that emerged, was many-sided and, as a whole, balanced. [8]

Among the serious reviews of his first translated book, *The Sun Also Rises* (there were around twenty of them), only few raised any protest on behalf of morals. But there was a good deal of irritation, among critics and readers alike ; there were those who "*found the book to be somehow directly insulting*" (Hoel). Some regarded it as insignificant and fatuous. More critics thought it to be unbearably tedious with its repetitious descriptions of surface detail. Some reviewers ascribed these features to a belated photographic naturalism, " *as boring as the original one,* " others to a " *careless and haphazard* " journalism, labels that were singularly unfortunate. Other negative observations were more adequate : the touch of empty virtuosity and mannered jargon, the wordiness and looseness of structure in parts of the book, the narrowness and lack of deeper interest in the characters, and the shallow psychology of questionable relevance, points of criticism that have recurred ever since.

But even Norwegian critics who did not like *The Sun Also Rises*, were struck by the amazing novelty of its form. And they also realized other aspects of its value. The leading reviewer from a Christian point of view, Ronald Fangen, began by finding the novel " *rather flaccid and lacking in contour,* " but ended by praising its honesty and courage and emphasizing in Brett that quality that the translator of the book once called " *the moral beauty of being immoral.* " In the most friendly reviews, moreover, above all in those written by Hoel himself and by his immediate followers, one may find, even at this early date, the keywords to Hemingway's artistic strength, put down at a time when discussion of him was limited everywhere : the concrete, no-comment factuality of words and acts ; the " *sulky reticence* " with its economy of words and its fear of the abstract and superfluous ; the undercurrent of unsentimental sensitivity and intensive stoic despair ; the sure and unconventional psychology, limited though it was ; the fine sense of shades in thought, emotion and experience ; and the discreet irony, all of it expressed with a " *dewy simplicity* " of style, which reveals reality through its details " *without diluting it,* " and with an unbelievable power of captivating and holding the reader's attention.

Above all, these critics felt the timeliness of the new author. In Hoel's words : " *Perhaps the novelty of his form corresponds to something new in the reality of our time.* " [9]

This promising overture was succeeded in the following year by Hemingway's critical break-through in Norway with *A Farewell to Arms*. As before, some of the more cautious reviewers maintained their censure of the " *sophomoric touch* " and " *chattering note* " of the author, his " *sissy affectation* " and " *superficial elegance,* " the endless dialogues " *natural, tiring and irrelevant,* " and the " *Zolaesque naturalism* " — " *truthfulness is not enough!* " But in general the book made an overwhelming impression of *"serious honesty,"* a beauty *"chaste"* and *"sacred,"* a *"simple purity"*, a wise understanding of men at war, a style *"perfect and of one mould,"* and a completely new *"eminently modern technique."*

Some of the previously severe critics now headed the chorus of praise. The reserved Kristian Elster admitted the power and internal grandeur of the chapters in the book following Caporetto. Ronald Fangen still regretted the complete lack of a pronounced hope and a *"more far-reaching perspective"* in Hemingway, but bowed to the *"rich and candid"* love story he had told, his mixture of virility and shyness, his fine and warm humour, *"the sober and undaunted grasp of reality"* which made the book *"uniquely representative,"* and the *"fruitful lack of milieu"* which allowed for *"an almost primitive, but conscious, total stylization."* [10] In his introduction Sigurd Hoel happily underlined that by now he was not presenting a controversial beginner any more, but a world celebrity. And he added a number of penetrating observations on Hemingway's psychology and the sensuous character of his style.

With *A Farewell to Arms* Hemingway was accepted as a first-rate author in Norway. Respectful articles about him appeared in the two large Norwegian encyclopedias (both in 1932) as well as in the Swedish one (1935), at a time when he was not even mentioned in similar English, French, German and Italian works of reference. But the remaining years of the 1930's represented something of a let-down in Hemingway's career in Norway, as it did in France. The social tension among American writers of the time was largely unknown. Hemingway's strongest work during these years, the short stories, which sometimes reflected this struggle, was not translated yet — short stories were regarded as unsaleable. The original collections were sometimes competently commented upon, with emphasis on their *"earnestness toward life and their human understanding,"* but their influence was, of course, limited. [11] Hemingway's books on African hunting and Spanish bullfighting also remained outside the Norwegian horizon in the 1930's.

When *To Have and Have Not* appeared in the "Yellow Series" in 1938, the book, therefore, lacked background, and the impression was confused. In his preface Sigurd Hoel took the middle road. While he had to admit to Hemingway's political childishness, he found it balanced by a widened human sympathy which broke a dead circle and "*a cult of virility turning stale.*" But when read carefully, Hoel's general conclusions were quite skeptical. Some reviewers accepted Hemingway's supposed change of attitude more hopefully. Others were openly revolted and called the book a failure. They denounced the "*depressing banality*" of the author's social analysis, his shallow and ineradicable anarchism, and his lack of eternal values. Behind this attitude there was now an outspoken impatience with the radical school that had carried Hemingway to his fame, and its "*inevitable*" praise of everything he did : "*he has become the obsession of our younger readers.*" [12]

Hemingway's participation in the Spanish Civil War was followed with sympathy by many Norwegians ; the international import of the conflict was urged upon the nation by the radical group. *The Fifth Column* was played over the Norwegian Broadcasting System in 1938, although Hoel characterized it as a poor literary work. For political reasons Hemingway, therefore, became a forbidden name during the German occupation of Norway 1940-1945. In occupied Denmark, reprints of his earlier books were allowed to appear, only advertising was suppressed. In Norway the "Yellow Series" stood for everything the Nazis abhorred, and it was strongly attacked in public, a fact which immensely stimulated sales ; the editor eventually had to escape to Sweden, the publisher was removed and imprisoned. In 1942 the remaining copies of *A Farewell to Arms* and *To Have and Have Not* were confiscated by the Germans and withdrawn from all library shelves together with a number of other volumes in the series ; *The Sun Also Rises* was already out of print. [13]

Some news items about *For Whom the Bell Tolls* were published in the Norwegian press, however, and were surprisingly overlooked by German censorship. Even a few copies in English (probably in a Swedish reprint) reached the country, where they were fast read to pieces. When after the liberation the book appeared in Norwegian translation in 1946, it was received with overwhelming enthusiasm. There were striking parallels between Robert Jordan's struggle against fascism and what had occurred in Norway itself. Even from a more general point of view recognition was without a shadow; the book seemed to give exactly what many readers had missed in Hemingway's earlier work. His change of style was regarded as a renewal, parallel to his hard-won faith in basic human values.

Soon, however, there was a growing note of dissatisfaction, due to the changing mood of the post-war years. The " young " critics of the 1920's now gradually appeared as sedate gentlemen of mature age, together with their idols; and their various brands of radicalism were no longer accepted as meekly as before. There was a rising wave of conservatism, politically and otherwise, a growth of philosophical and religious interest that challenged dogmatic radical concepts, and a concern with literary modernism even more modern than that of Hemingway. And such ideas were now expressed with less hesitation than they were in the 1930's. When Hemingway's *Short Stories* appeared in 1947, the first complete edition in Scandinavia (a selection followed in 1953), reception was still enthusiastic. But strong qualifications were also expressed about the superficiality and spiritual poverty of the stories, and their " *powerful, but depressing and monotonous description of man.* " In the first comprehensive Norwegian evaluation of Hemingway's work Odd-Stein Andersen in 1947 related and subordinated all the surface attitudes of the author, including his social *engagements*, to his basic personal problem : his futile effort in " *breaking his prison without leaving it* " and solving the metaphysical riddle of death by means of the palpable facts of terrestrial life. [14]

These dissensions were brought to the fore with extraordinary violence by the publication of *Across the River and Into the Trees* (1950). Some of Hemingway's veteran champions still read their old love into the book. They spoke of it as a "*moving human document*" revealing "*new emotional depths,*" praised its autumnal beauty under "*the fine frost fog of resignation,*" and found "*a tender, silvery note of hope*" in the colonel's "*faithfulness to true passion.*" But the negative attitude was overwhelming. The communist paper presented its review under the headline "Farewell to Hemingway" — "*this surely must be the bottom.*" At the other end of the line conservative critics regretted the "*sour tedium*" of the book, and the author's "*closed perspectives*" and failing power, which proved him to be *passé*.

Most striking was the denunciation coming from old Hemingway fans, who were disappointed by his sentimentality and coquettishness, his "*intellectual bankruptcy*" and "*pasted-on idealism,*" "*only too manifest to the young generation.*" The most wholesale condemnation of the "*nauseating*" volume appeared in the leading business journal of Norway, a paper famous for its coarse language. The review showed a curious mixture of political and literary hatred and love. Hemingway still remained the magician of old. At the same time, in his fake romanticism and "*bottomless spiritual poverty*" he had for thirty years been the moving power behind the radical intellectuals with their "*flanking attack on all moral values.*" [15]

A more articulate evaluation along the same lines came from the pen of a young poet and critic Erling Christie, born in 1928, in a review of the republished translation of *The Sun Also Rises* (1953). To Christie the book was the outstanding expression of the idea of man as a product of biology. Nobody has, like Hemingway, passively registered the details in this "*reduced image of man,*" even with regard to his intellectual possibilities, leaving observation and blind action his sole obligation. But "*much has happened since the 1930's*": Hemingway's cynicism and self-pity now seem trifling beside *our* atomic agony, our ethical and spiritual quest. For that reason, the "*tyranny of taste*" which Hemingway still exerts, remains dangerous because of its narrowness. He is alien to the thought of centuries, and even to the real American tradition with its ideas of responsibility to society and mankind. Because of him and his followers Norway is still largely ignorant of authors like Willa Cather, Thomas Wolfe and Maxwell Anderson, who are closer to true Americanism. [16]

But this divergence of opinion was only a sign that Hemingway was now moving into a distance where it would gradually be possible to see him in full figure, both as an author and as an influence in Norwegian life. The pendulum of readjustment swung back — but not all the way — with the publication in 1952 of the Norwegian translation of *The Old Man and the Sea*. The book was praised unanimously by conservatives and radicals alike, including the communists. It was called perfect in its kind, "*pure and noble and sincere,*" borne by humble and wondering tenderness, freed from the endless circumlocution and narrow individualism of Hemingway's youth, and therefore humanly relevant. But recommendation was not blind. Some of Hemingway's old admirers were careful to qualify their praise by calling the book an interesting document and a beautiful prose poem of nature mysticism, but "*no masterpiece,*" monotonous, and "*extremely limited as a work of literary art.*" [17]

The same doubleness of judgment reappeared when *The Green Hills of Africa* was translated in 1955. The book was received as an interesting collection of material for the better understanding of the artist. But eulogy was mixed with familiar reservations, and not too flattering comparisons with the human depth and warmth of the African books of Karen Blixen. [18]

The contrasts were confronted for the last time, so far, in the attitudes expressed toward Hemingway's Nobel Prize in 1954, and in the necrologies at his death in 1961. The communists now wrote him off as "*an author dead for many years.*" Religious and conservative critics of many brands again denounced his "*self-abandoning fatalism,*" his hollow image of man, his "*complacent and self-deceiving irresponsibility,*" a philosophy of *nada* surrounded by the waiting vultures. But many more, regardless of their own views of life, expressed their affection and gratitude toward the writer, now in a larger perspective. They recalled not only his artistic fastidiousness, now recognized by friend and foe alike, but his comprehensive human experience and stubborn courage, creating "*a purity of stylistic truthfulness*" that is rarely equalled in his imitators and explains the timelessness of his tragic dimension. Above all, he now appeared to his Norwegian readers in his real stature as the expression "*beyond anybody else*" of their own time. In writing about his personal anguish he has "*vicariously liberated millions of fellow human beings from theirs.*" [19]

A more connected and detailed analysis could not be expected from this day-to-day criticism, which largely appeared in newspapers. No full-length book has been written on Hemingway in Norway as yet. But some good-sized evaluations have appeared in periodicals and collections of essays, particularly since the Second World War; and several critics have followed Hemingway through the years, basing their statements on coherent ideas. [20] Typical of the best among them is an effort to show the extremely complicated nature of Hemingway's character and his art, as different from the simplified and vulgar legend, and thus penetrate to the roots, both of his limitations and his strength. In consonance with Norwegian literary tradition few of the critics have still done full justice to the *poetic* side of Hemingway, the magic and mystical depths, the ritual and symbolic dimension, all that goes beyond his surface realism, — those features that made the author himself compare the modulation in the opening chapter of *A Farewell to Arms* to Bach. But something has to be left to future analysts.

Two important critics made their most pertinent remarks in connection with Hemingway's "*imperfect masterpiece,*" *To Have and Have Not*. [21] To Johan Borgen the "*real*" Hemingway exists on the artistic level alone. The miscarried tragedy about Harry Morgan is the twisted symbol of Hemingway's own desperate and inevitable defeat, that incurable wound of eternal loneliness which awaits all "*poetic natural-*

ists. " His quest was for " *the expression behind the expression,* " the moment of ecstatic congruity when " *the real thing is its own symbol;* " and it is forever unattainable.

Sigurd Hoel starts from the same point, but moves in a different direction. Hemingway's perhaps most lasting contribution is a literary method, forcing him to a precision in observation and description that was hardly ever attained before him. This precision curiously combines with his art of indirection : telling something by saying nothing about it, revealing it by saying something else. And this device is one of the secrets of his appeal to his own time : " *some have a sensitivity they try to conceal, others have nothing, but very many love the mask.* "

But here two questions arise. About Hemingway himself : where does shyness end and coquettishness begin ? And what about his future ? In world literature, the strongest power of survival has always been in the simple, direct expression of genuine emotion ; " *the song of a bird is never dated.* " Compared to the masters of indirection it is the innocents who last, the naïve, the unconscious and instinctive. Hemingway never was unconscious in that sense of the word. On the contrary, he made a system of his hide-and-seek, whether he was aware of the deepest reasons in himself or not. But do we have to believe that it will be necessary to mankind even in the future to hide its sensitivity behind a mask ? Or will times come that are more simple and natural than ours, when man is allowed to acknowledge his real nature ? In this little article of Hoel's, the Norwegian discoverer and literary champion of Hemingway is being corrected by the psychoanalyst and social critic, in the strongest qualification of his work that has appeared on Norwegian soil.

As this cursory survey will show, Hemingway has played an important part in Norwegian critical debate ever since his first appearance in 1929. He has exerted an even more important influence on Norwegian writing. At Hemingway's death the President of the Norwegian Authors' Association, Hans Heiberg, stated that " *in this generation Hemingway is the foreign writer*

who has been of greatest importance to Norwegian literature."
But upon closer inspection the problem raises many difficulties. As yet, it has not been investigated in detail, and one may question whether it will ever be. [22]

Criticism abundantly demonstrates that Norwegian readers were immediately struck by the novelty of Hemingway's literary material and his handling of it, even apart from his famous style : his description of war and the underworld with its recurrent note of violence and death, his absorption in sports and love, hunting and bullfighting, his typical heroes with their cynical disillusion and tragic stoicism, and the shocking bluntness of his approach. Many of these traits ran counter to Norwegian literary traditions and accepted procedures. For that reason imitation was doubly tempting, and apparently easy. During the years immediately following his appearance there was a feeling that such imitation was almost general.

Today, one is inclined to speak more cautiously. What "*smacks of Hemingway*" in Norwegian literature since 1929 often is part of a wave of "*modernism*" which was connected with general changes in the way of life both in and outside Norway. Of literary sources many may come into the picture, even of contemporaries, from the great literature of war in the line of Barbusse — Remarque — Malraux to the other American novelists who where made available to Norwegian readers at the time. Within this general impact it is not always possible to distinguish Hemingway's special note. In addition, the nature of his material and the originality of his method served as a warning. Few Norwegians could write on Hemingway's subjects from personal experience ; and authors with self-respect would be cautious about *pastiches* that could be so easily traced back to their model.

This does not rule out an extensive and deep penetration of Hemingway in Norwegian writing of the time ; and occasionally the influence can be established beyond reasonable doubt. Directly, he inspired his own first translator, a relationship that is known even in other countries. Gunnar Larsen began his own interesting work by writing two novels (published in 1932 and 1933). The former is a love story that is clearly related to *A Farewell to Arms*, the latter a study in violence (the hunt for two murderers), where the typical observation simultaneously of nature and of simple human beings facing death is even more intensive and severe than in his model. Another instance of direct apprenticeship seems to be Arthur Omre, "*the master of the Norwegian short story,*" who, in his early career, was probably encouraged by Hemingway to use as literary material a personal experience similar to that of Hemingway himself.[23] Further research may reveal more examples of such connection.

But even in these few instances Hemingway has rather served as an inspiration than as a model to be copied. This, doubtless, is the really important part of his influence. Together with his contemporaries he has called forth, or strengthened, in Norwegian writers many trends that appeared in the 1930's and 1940's : a new concern with international material ; a new interest in " tough " or brutal subjects within the Norwegian framework ; a new interest in complicated, marginal, or morbid characters ; a new awareness of the close interplay of body and soul. In a general way he may similarly have influenced literary technique in the more strict sense : the concentration on barren, but revealing facts ; the intensity of dialogue ; the bluntness of sexual description ; the terseness of psychological suggestion ; the faster pace of the tale ; and — most of all — that general " atmosphere " of sensuous delight, of observation mixed with bitter irony, that is no less real because it is hard to define.

In particular, his influence was bound to be active in the brief literary form. In the words of Johan Borgen at Hemingway's death : " *the short story writer who has been able to avoid infection from him, must either be immune by conscious resistance, or by lacking musicality.* " Borgen himself, one of the finest short story writers in the language, is a case in point, but only one among many. Sometimes, for instance in his early love scenes, when Hemingway still rang in the writer's ears, the connection is too close. But to him, and to other authors of talent, Hemingway largely has been of assistance in their quest for personal identity. One may hardly talk of a Hemingway "school" in Norway.

This problem is closely tied to the impact of the Hemingway style. Here again, there is no doubt about the strength of the first impression. Sigurd Hoel wrote that even Hemingway's literary language was "*something one had long been waiting for without knowing it.*" [24] To contemporaries, the influence of his style appeared as all-pervasive, only to be compared to the influence of Hamsun on the prose of some European countries some decades before. And in this field, at least, one should expect Hemingway's voice to be clearly discernible both among Americans and Europeans. It is important to note in this connection, that his excellent Norwegian translators, almost without exception, were able to reproduce the essentials of his style even to readers who did not themselves know English. But here matters are again complicated, this time by the Norwegian background.

What made Hemingway's literary language burst upon European writing like an explosion, was its deceptive simplicity, which so strangely fused with his indirection. He seemed untouched by traditional expression, its abstraction and involution, its decorative and bookish vocabulary and long-winded Latin syntax. He built his effects on brief paratactic sentences, on dialogue phonetically transcribed, and on terse and concrete, pithy and precise verbs and nouns of popular origin. In Norway, for special reasons, literary prose had for several generations been moving in exactly the same direction. And it was not only a question of parallels, but of common roots. The transforming power within Norway's Danish-born written idiom was the spoken Norwegian dialects with their traditions back to saga and folk tales. Whether Hemingway himself has known the sagas, is an open question. But it has often been pointed out, not least by Sigurd Hoel, how close the two styles come to each other in their tight-lipped expressiveness. The same holds good for important features in common speech, not too different in the two countries.

On a more literary level, the strongest revolutionary power in Norwegian prose before Hemingway was Knut Hamsun. He broke away from tradition for his own capricious purposes, but often with similar effects. One of his disciples was Sigurd Hoel, who once characterized Hamsun's style almost in the words he has used about Hemingway, *" the ability to say great things by small words, and suggest even much more almost or completely without words. "* [25] Now, Hamsun is among the writers to whom Hemingway himself explicitly acknowledged that he " *owed most,* " [26] — as they both admired Mark Twain, probably for similar reasons. Here the lines are again running parallel. Even Hemingway's most immediate literary background, the style of American journalism, occasionally may have left its mark in Norway independently of Hemingway himself.

This development, which was well under way in the 1920's, in many cases makes it difficult in Norway to trace details of style back to Hemingway : they may have different or mutual origins. The situation was unwittingly brought out by an American scholar writing about Sigurd Hoel : " *his style, like modern Norwegian in general, translates most naturally into the American idiom, rather than into French, or German, or British English.* " [27] It is typical that some of the Norwegian authors who in a general way resemble Hemingway in their writing, had moulded their own style long before their acquaintance with him.

These qualifications of course do not apply to that Hemingway style that is unmistakeably his own and can easily be pointed out. In Norway this style made itself felt in journalism right away ; many of Hemingway's warmest admirers were themselves journalists. An observer found in the Norwegian press " *experiments in the simple universality of Hemingway's style* " one year after the appearance of his first book in translation. Equally strong was the impact among fiction writers. A Norwegian critic could state in 1938 that Hemingway now "*appears in cheap reprint in almost everyone among our younger writers.*" [28]

In Norway as elsewhere, however, this immediate influence often proved to be superficial and cheap, the mannerisms of the master without his art. Sigurd Hoel has wittily characterized such imitators, "*speaking out of one corner of the mouth to the very edge of being unintelligible.*" [29] As was the case in regard to subject matter and literary technique, his lasting impact is the subtle one by which he helped Norwegian writers find their *own* style. Here Hemingway could be of particular importance because he strengthened tendencies that were already there. His own personal way of writing could work as a general liberating force, demonstrating how a national style could become "modern" without slavish imitation, loosening the structure, whittling down the wordiness, sweeping away traditional decorations, and tightening expression, giving it a rhythm more close to our time.

By definition this influence cannot always be traced back to Hemingway with certainty. But doubtless it has been important, and doubly so the more thoroughly it has become assimilated. A critic described this kind of osmosis when he wrote in 1954 that Norwegian youth after the Second World War has no longer need to imitate Hemingway's style: "*it has entered into their blood and become nature.*" [30] This assimilation, combined with the continued general interest in his writing, makes it probable that his work will remain a motive power even within that movement *beyond* realism that is now on the rise, and which is increasingly recognizing similar elements in Hemingway's own style.

Shortly before his death Sigurd Hoel was questioned about the allegation that modern Norwegian literature is inferior to British writing because of a slavish submission to the Americans from which the British have now liberated themselves. Hoel retorted that British authors, to their own detriment, had never learnt "*that writer's discipline that is represented by the Hemingway school,*" and that they could still need to learn from

"*Norwegian writers who have.*"[31] To what extent this statement is really true, we may never know exactly. But beside the impression of Hemingway the man, and the struggle to understand his art, this anonymous, but real penetration may, nevertheless, in the long run, prove to be the most indelible mark he has left on literature. Whether he changed the general trend of Norwegian writing remains doubtful. But he certainly has been an important force in modifying it, and adding to it a new dimension.

NOTES

1. For works on the American impact on other Scandinavian nations, see the introduction to L. Åhnebrink's article in this volume. For Norway in particular, see my books *American Studies in Europe* (Philadelphia, 1958), 2, 428-439, with bibliographies, and *The Study of American Literature* (Philadelphia, 1949). A brief, but excellent survey of Hemingway's impact on Norwegian literature is found in Philip HOUM, *Norges litteratur fra 1914 til 1950-årene* (Oslo, 1955), — see the Index of names. Both in ideas and substance this article owes much to Philip Houm. He has also been kind enough to read this article in manuscript; so has Harald Grieg, Director of Gyldendal Publishing House.
2. H. GRIEG, *En forleggers erindringer*, Oslo, 1958, 2, 498 f.
3. For the "Yellow Series", see GRIEG, *l. c.*, 1, 272-282, and Th. JONSSON in *Festskrift til Sigurd Hoel på 60 årsdagen*, Oslo, 1950, 223-225.
4. See HOEL in *Vinduet*, 5, 1951, 761 ff. and *Arbeiderbladet*, 1954, Oct. 29.
5. For Swedish sales figures, see L. Åhnebrink's article in this volume. The Norwegian figures are given by Gyldendal Publishing House.
6. Information was kindly imparted by the library itself.
7. Waldemar BRØGGER in *Samtiden*, 44, 1933, 51.
8. The critical material from newspapers quoted in this article is available in the extensive clipping file of Gyldendal Publishing House, and can easily be identified there. Reference is therefore made only to authors of important articles. Some reviews may still be hidden in the files of periodicals.
9. For mostly negative reviews, see in particular Johs. A. Dale, Kr. Elster, Ronald Fangen, A. Poulsson, Rolv Thesen, and W. Brøgger (*Janus*, 2, 1934, 334), on the positive side Paul Gjesdahl, B. S. Tranøy, and a few local papers. Hoel's introductions to the "Yellow Series" are reprinted in his volumes *50 gule* and *De siste 51 gule* (Oslo, 1939 and 1959). Hemingway's translator is quoted from HOUM, *l. c.*, 484. The book was also admired by Knut Hamsun; see GRIEG, *l. c.*, 2, 499.
10. Most important reviewers : Johs. A. Dale, Inge Debes, Kr. Elster, R. Fangen, Jean Føyen, A. Poulsson, Ø. Ree.
11. Arne KILDAL in *Amerikas stemme*, Oslo, 1935.

12. Positive reviewers : Johan Borgen, P. Gjesdahl, F. Halvorsen, A. Kildal, G. Reiss-Andersen, H. L. Tveterås ; negative : C. J. Hambro, Barbra Ring, and many minor figures. In the anthroposophical review *Janus* Alf Larsen called Hemingway and his contemporaries " *half-idiots who can write* " (7, 1939, II, 783).
13. Hoel's introduction to *For Whom the Bell Tolls*.
14. Compare, for instance, J. Borgen and R. Myhre. Odd-Stein ANDERSEN'S article in *Vinduet*, 1, 1947, 253-267.
15. P. Bang, Edv. Beyer, J. Borgen, A. Chr. Meyer, Egil Rasmussen, S. Riisøen and Per Vogt (" Audax " in *Farmand*).
16. *Morgenbladet* 1952, Nov. 12. Compare similarly A. HOELL in *Vinduet*, 2, 1948, 545 (complaining about the neglect even of Dos Passos, Farrell, Faulkner, and E. Glasgow), and ten years later Ø. BOLSTAD, *ibid.*, 12, 1958, 106.
17. Typical are reviews by Edv. Beyer, N. Chr. Brøgger, Kjell Krogvig, Arve Moen, and S. Riisøen. Qualified praise was expressed by J. Borgen and Arne Skouen.
18. In particular P. Bang, J. Borgen, Alf Harbitz, Eugenia Kielland, Arve Moen, E. Rasmussen, and A. Skouen.
19. Comments regarding the Nobel Prize, see in particular N. Chr. Brøgger, Kåre Holt, A. Moen, Ø. Parmann, S. Riisøen, and A. Skouen. Necrologies, see particularly J. Borgen, Hans Heiberg, Kåre Holt, and A. Myhre. A poem in Hemingway's memory was published by W. Nordahl.
20. HOEL in his introductions, *l. c.*, and in *Vinduet*, 5, 1951, 761-767 ; Trygve BRAATØY, " Fragmenter om døden " (in his : *Kjærlighet og åndsliv*, Oslo, 1934, 119-147) ; Odd-Stein ANDERSEN, 1947 see note 14 above ; Per AAMOT in his : *Streiftog* (Oslo, 1948), 67-85 ; Tor MYKLEBOST, *Drømmen om Amerika. Den amerikanske roman gjennom 50 år* (Oslo, 1953), 92-99 ; Sigmund SKARD, " Hemingway i dag og i morgon " *(Syn og Segn*, 67, 1961, 289-295 and *Dåd og dikt* (Oslo, 1963), 368-385).
21. Hoel in his introduction to *To Have and Have Not ;* Borgen in an unpublished lecture (July 7, 1958) in the archives of the Norwegian Broadcasting System.
22. See for the following discussion a number of pertinent remarks in HOUM, *l. c.*
23. HOUM, *l. c.*, 439 ff. and 482 ff.
24. *Vinduet*, 5, 1951, 762.
25. HOEL, *Tanker om norsk diktning*, Oslo, 1955, 96.
26. GRIEG, *l. c.*, 1, 279.
27. M. Joos in *Festskrift til Sigurd Hoel, l. c.*, 92.
For an interesting discussion of the similarities and parallel backgrounds of the Icelandic saga style and that of the American hardboiled novel, see S. BERGSVEINSSON, " Sagaen og den haardkogte Roman " (*Edda*, 42, 1942, 56-62).
28. Review in *Tidens Tegn* of *A Farewell to Arms ;* H. L. TVETERÅS in *Stavanger Aftenblad*, 1938, May 21.
29. HOEL, *Tanker om norsk diktning, l. c.* 268.
30. Ø. Parmann in his comment on the Nobel Prize.
31. *Vinduet*, 16, 1962, 182.

HEMINGWAY IN SWEDEN

by Lars ÅHNEBRINK

1. Two Radical Critics.

IN any discussion of Hemingway in Sweden emphasis must be laid on two critics who early recognized the American writer's particular genius : Artur Lundkvist (b. 1906) and Thorsten Jonsson (1910-1950), both of them creative writers of considerable merit. In newspapers, in magazines and in books the young enthusiasts played a significant part in introducing Hemingway to Swedish readers.

In 1932 Lundkvist, a poet, novelist and left-wing critic, brought out his first volume of criticism entitled *Atlantvind*. Although he was more interested in such writers as Carl Sandburg, Sherwood Anderson and Eugene O'Neill, he also gave a brilliant sketch of Hemingway and his art. Lundkvist was struck by Hemingway's style, which seemed to him " *concise, exact, effective : short sentences with muscular verbs and concrete nouns, utterly lacking vague adjectives and irrelevant emotionalism. A style akin to athletic bodies and modern steel furniture : strong, elastic, without patina. An antimetaphysical style, completely directed toward exterior reality...* " [1] Hemingway was a master at reproducing the polished lustre of cars and conveying the sensation of a woman's perfume. He had also given adequate expression to a new type of man, a man who expected nothing and everything, who confronted utter confusion or the deepest tragedy or the greatest happiness as the most natural or the most banal thing in the world. He was a "*man with a mask : the mask of pessimism, of disillusion, of cold unaffectedness.*"[1] What did it hide? Anguish, pain, weakness? Or modern man's complicated web of rationalism and instincts, civilization and primitivism? Hemingway worshipped movement, action, activity. He worshipped them for their own sake, as a value *per se*. He seemed to despise thought, reflection, passive perception. To Lundkvist Hemingway was a pessimist who worshipped the fleeting moment, the vital sensations of the present registered with the quick and effective factuality of a modern precision instrument.[2]

Despite Hemingway's insistence on sober facts there was also a warm, vitalistic streak in him. The love scenes in *A Farewell to Arms* were described with sensuous warmth and opulence. Hemingway's pessimism did not "*prevent him from a positive attitude toward the more lustful aspects of life.*"[3] It was in fact his pessimism that made him a lover of life, a worshipper of the moment. Consequently the present dominated his world, which had no future and no purpose. Living was everything.[3]

Lundkvist deepened his analysis of Hemingway's art in *Amerikas nya författare* (1940). Hemingway, the restrained artist, the careful observer of reality, was contrasted with Faulkner, the romantically subjective visionary. As an artist Hemingway seemed like an *instrument*, a perfect precision instrument. He represented also the hero of the modern age, an immense photographic enlargement of the man in the street,[4] completely absorbed by what was going on without asking why or how. The actual events, which seemed inevitable, were his only reality, and surrounded him hermetically. His only desire was to live and if possible to enjoy life. His heroism consisted in stoically enduring everything without thinking, "*if possible also without feeling.*"[5] Hemingway was haunted by fear, fear of his own fear. His world was without mercy, tenderness and pity.

Hemingway was reproached for having somewhat romanticized his hero because of his supposed invulnerability and emotionless self-sacrifice. Similarly, Hemingway seemed to have regarded the Spanish Civil War as simply a seasonal event : "*the lofty sport of war instead of bull-fighting and big game hunting, the superior adventure of death for the professional hero of our time.*"[6] Despite these objections the American writer had created "*a style and an attitude toward life which, for better or for worse, had put its imprint on contemporary literature.*"[6]

In 1942 Lundkvist brought out *Diktare och avslöjare i Amerikas moderna litteratur*, in which he devoted one chapter out of twenty-one to Hemingway, emphasizing his earlier opinions. The same year saw the publication of Thorsten Jonsson's *Sex amerikaner* (Hemingway, Faulkner, Steinbeck, Caldwell, Farrell, Saroyan). The chapter on Hemingway was entitled " Dödens närhet " (Nearness to Death), a new and significant approach. A novelist, short story writer and liberal critic, Jonsson began his long and perceptive essay with a discussion of Hemingway's style. Although this style did not have the dignity of movement of an iceberg, it possessed a living force and a greater mass than was first realized. Hemingway's descriptive passages were written with a carefully pruned economy and his dialogues, resonant with hidden implications, had "*an evasive laconism (quite unlike that of the Icelandic Sagas) often more explicit about peripheral matters and reticent about what was essential.*"[7]

Concerning Hemingway's brutality and his attitude toward violence, Jonsson maintained that the problem was a complicated one. Hemingway had won his public by exploiting the Robert Wilson aspect of his personality. He had appeared as the Clark Gable of literature and he had had the ambition of being the hero of our time.[8] This aspect of the American writer was not always attractive. Hemingway was not only a Robert Wilson, a brutal he-man, but also a Francis Macomber.

In 1934 the Norwegian critic Trygve Braatøy[9] made an attempt to refer Hemingway's eccentricities to a castration complex. Jonsson rightly rejected this interpretation and explained the dualism in Hemingway on the basis of his childhood and war experiences. The fear and terror of death which he had felt so keenly both as a young boy and as a soldier and which he had described so well in the Nick Adams stories and in his novels, was the root of all his anguish. The essence of Hemingway's psychosis was his fear of death.[10] He could never get rid of his terrible war experiences. Even in his book about bull-fighting in Spain, *Death in the Afternoon*, he had to make a digression in order to write a Natural History of the Dead, which was nothing but an attempt to liberate himself from his anguish and terror of death. That he admired the technique and the courage of the matador is well known, but what he was fascinated by was hardly the gory spectacle in the arena. He saw "*in the killing of the bull a symbol of man's victory over the domain of death.*"[11]

Death, as described by Hemingway, was a death which he sought to defeat with violence. He had to be brutal, because he had his anguish to conquer and he used his brutality "*to conquer his experiences.*"[12] Nothing would be more wrong than to make Hemingway a spokesman of violence, Jonsson maintained. The genuine spokesmen of violence were those to whom violence seemed morally valuable and esthetically appealing. They wrote "*no natural histories about the dead.*"[13]

2. Hemingway's Popularity.

The honour of having introduced Hemingway to Swedish readers goes to Holger Schildt, who published the first Swedish translation of *The Sun Also Rises* in 1929. Since 1932 Bonniers have been Hemingway's publisher in Sweden. With the inauguration of *Bonniers Litterära Magasin (BLM)*, ably edited by Georg Svensson,[14] this firm helped to familiarize Swedish readers with new literary tendencies abroad. Even in the first year of its existence *BLM* printed short stories by Louis Bromfield, William Faulkner and Ernest Hemingway ("The Killers").

The introduction of these writers was symbolic of the re-orientation of literary and critical opinion in Sweden. Special letters from New York written by outstanding critics (Alfred Kazin was one of them) supplied fresh information about the changing literary situation in America. No alert reader could any longer be unaware of the dynamic forces at work in American literature.

Bonniers brought out eleven books by Hemingway between 1932 and 1962, the last one being *The Torrents of Spring*, originally published in 1926. Most of Hemingway's novels were translated shortly after publication, but it was nineteen years before *Green Hills of Africa* was translated and twenty-six before *Death in the Afternoon* appeared in Swedish.

The most congenial translator was perhaps Thorsten Jonsson, who rendered into beautifully crisp Swedish the often difficult Hemingway idiom of *To Have and Have Not*, *For Whom the Bell Tolls*, and a number of short stories.[15] Other translators were Bertel Gripenberg,[16] Louis Renner, Olov Jonason, Mårten Edlund and Arne Häggqvist.

Hemingway has been a popular writer in Sweden ever since he gained general critical acceptance in the forties. In 1954 Sweden (population ca. 7 million) could boast that the total sale of Hemingway exceeded 250,000 copies and that among non-Swedish Nobel Prize winners Hemingway was unsurpassed as far as sales were concerned. In 1962 the total sale exceeded 525,000 copies. His most popular books have been *The Old Man and the Sea* with a total sale of 181,440 copies, *To Have and Have Not* (87,120), *Farewell to Arms* (87,000) and *The Sun Also Rises* (46,590). The least popular books in Sweden have been the short stories. The large sales of some of Hemingway's novels have been made possible by inexpensive reprints, such as Bonniers Folkbibliotek, Svalan and Aldus/Delfin.

3. The Critical Battle.

Even though Sweden had shared the common European idealistic attitude toward colonial and revolutionary America, there began to emerge among Swedish critics toward the end of the 19th century a strong distaste for America and American culture. The new animus against America was reflected in essays and reviews on America by three significant critics, Per Hallström, Henning Berger and Gustaf Hellström. Both Hallström [17] and Hellström were members of the Swedish Academy, which is responsible for awarding the Nobel Prize for literature. In the main they continued the Norwegian novelist Hamsun's attacks on what they regarded as the typically American sins of materialism, vulgarity, hypocrisy and smugness. Like Hamsun, these writers had arrived full of hope in America in the eighties and nineties, only to return a few years later in bitterness and despair.

This hostile attitude seems to have prevailed among Swedish critics well into the twenties. Gradually America became the most interesting country in the world and Sinclair Lewis was soon hailed as "*the best known author of modern American literature.*" With the award of the Nobel Prize to Lewis in 1930 a barrier of resistance was broken down and American literature was eventually recognized and accepted in Sweden. [18] Although the air was cleared, much resistance still continued. In 1932 in a review of Blankenship's *American Literature as an Expression of the National Mind* Anders Österling, a member of the Swedish Academy since 1919, emphasized the new interest in American literature. "*It has taken a comparatively long time,*" he wrote, "*for American literature to become an extremely important factor here in Europe. Individual American authors have, of course, already won recognition all over the world and given a foretaste of a transatlantic uniqueness. But the great change has in fact taken place only since the War. During the last fifteen years America has actually taken the lead as a land of literature. Literary curiosity is for the first time directed toward the books which are written in America, in contrast to those written in England, France and Germany.*" [19]

In his review of *Och solen har sin gång* (*The Sun Also Rises*) Österling was hardly enthusiastic about the American writer. He felt that, despite its nonchalant tone, the novel possessed a deeper purpose. But he seemed to have missed the essential point of the novel. After having mentioned the motto and the epigraph from Ecclesiastes, he went on : " *Yet, one does not at all get the impression of a deep despair in these characters. These Americans are no decadent types — they are not pained by the poison of the disease of reflection nor are they brooding over the purpose of existence. Their main problem is thirst. They drink like barbarians...* " [20] Since Hemingway literally drowned his narrative in liquor, his aim must have been to vex his countrymen during the era of Prohibition. This comical effect was exploited beyond all limits. Compared with Sinclair Lewis' *Dodsworth*, Hemingway's narrative shrank into a special study of limited scope. Österling was nevertheless impressed by the truth of the portraits of Cohn and Brett and by the fiesta scenes, which were first-rate reporting. And then the American tempo — " *smooth running in highest gear, lightning acceleration and other qualities borrowed from the technique of the automobile, which Hemingway's style seeks to emulate. This is not enough to make a good book, but it is typical.* " [20]

An earlier anonymous reviewer was clearly irritated by Hemingway's alcohol-smelling description of American life in Paris à la Murger. " *Murger's heroes,*" he concluded, " *can still amuse, but Mr. Hemingway's moderately sober and extremely unintelligent company makes no European reader happy.* " [21]

The critic in the liberal *Dagens Nyheter*, Carl-August Bolander, was not particularly pleased with the novel, which seemed " *a somewhat monotonous and unimportant story about young Americans drinking in Paris and in the Pyrenees, no doubt characteristic of American Bohemians in Europe, but somewhat tiring because of their eternal drinking.*" [22] Artur Lundkvist was able to see a deeper meaning in the excesses of these bohemians. "*Their way of life is appallingly dreary and sterile,*" he wrote, "*but they accept the meaninglessness with brave matter-of-factness. They have no ambition, no purpose, no future. They believe in nothing and possess no enthusiasm. They live in an age of steel.*" [23] Their pleasures seemed sterile. The symbol of the book was the impotent American desperately in love with a frustrated English lady. This tragic motif grew almost imperceptibly out of the somewhat nonchalant narrative. "*The inner story which gives the book its meaning,*" Lundkvist added, "*must be read between the lines, it is hidden beneath all the sensations of the style and the senses. Such is Hemingway's method.*" [24] To Thorsten Jonsson the hero's impotence was symbolic of the entire postwar generation. The novel was "*compact, hard, and aggressive,*" but it had an undertone of warmth, particularly in the description of the Spanish farmers. [25]

In his lukewarm introduction to *Farväl till vapnen* Sten Selander, a poet, essayist and humanist critic, emphasized the notion that Hemingway was perhaps the most "European" of the younger generation of writers in America. His sober and effective style with its somewhat calculated simplicity had a French ring. In no respect was it typically American. [26] Like most of the younger generation, Bromfield, Wilder, Dorothy Parker, Hemingway was not interested in attacking Mr. Babbitt and other American vices. In order to do so a certain amount of social pathos and belief in humanity were needed. Hemingway was too disillusioned to indulge in such naive and utopian efforts. His Europeanized, cynical and extremely liberated characters [27] had no interest whatsoever in Mr. Babbitt, Zenith or the spiritual freedom of the United States. They were hardly interested in anything but their private eroticism and equally private consumption of alcohol. Their connection with God's own country was limited to the fact that they had happened to be born there. They belonged to the international intelligentsia who felt at home wherever there were "*bars and loafers on the sterile asphalt chaussée of modern thought.*" [28] Proust, Gide, Huxley and other European writers were the spiritual fathers of Hemingway's moral nihilism and his contemptuously entertaining human interest rather than the typically American Dreiser, Lewis and Sandburg.

Selander felt that "*the smell of alcohol, the intellectual snobbery and defeatism in Hemingway's early books*" [29] were too marked for his taste. But *A Farewell to Arms* was a remarkable novel, which surpassed everything the American writer had written before. It was no wonder that this book had made Hemingway popular among the general public. But there were many reservations. It was characteristic of Hemingway to choose a deserter as his hero and even more characteristic of the author was the reason given for the hero's desertion : he had grown tired of the war and had realized how stupid and meaningless it was. [30] The book's sensualism was also revolting to the Swedish critic. The pleasures of the body and the senses were to Hemingway the only essential factor in the relationship between man and woman. His particular "*belief in life*" avoided responsibility and thoughts of the future. Consequently Catherine's child was an unwelcome stranger who killed its mother. [30] The critic could not accept either the tendency or the philosophy of life inherent in the novel, yet he was impressed by the artistic quality of the book and the intensity of its scenes. Few books had given a better picture of the prevailing mood of the twenties, the decade of hopeless despair. No reader therefore needed "*to regret an acquaintance with a book, which the future, as far as one could judge, would recognize as one of the classic documents of the mentality of the post-war years.*" [31]

A virulent attack was launched on Selander for having called the novel a classic document of the post-war years by a critic in the *Reformatorn*, the weekly organ of the Stockholm Good Templars, founded in 1888. The reviewer found it incomprehensible that such a good critic as Selander should be duped by *A Farewell to Arms*. The book was a complete failure. To read it was a waste of time. The hero was more interested in women and alcohol than in the destiny of the people and consequently the reader was completely indifferent to the events of the novel. Hemingway's experience of life, the critic went on, was too limited, his egocentricity too great to lift the book to the level where literature proper began. [32]

Another conservative critic, Anna Lenah Elgström, praised Hemingway's simple and charming style but missed a deeper purpose in his writings. The American's indifference to life, his dryness of emotion, his brutal negativism — a vice comparable to that of Huxley and Aldington — seemed disgusting to her. The novel had none of America's good qualities : "*freshness, the mind of youth, the naive belief in progress and in the power of good will.*" [33] Other critics, to whom Hemingway's world was a chaos of cynicism and empty bottles, reacted also against the novel's frank eroticism [34] and empty dialogue. [35]

There were, however, a few reviewers who admired the perfect art with which Hemingway had intertwined the tragedy of humanity with the tragedy of two persons. The charm of the novel was its lack of pathos and gestures of accusation, its simplicity and naturalness. In its individualism and sensualism Hemingway reminded the reviewer of George Moore and he was very curious to see what this anti-Comstockian would say about his own country, when he chose to do so. [36] The liberal and perceptive critic, Henning Söderhjelm, was impressed by the novel despite its undisguised sensualism and an unsavoury spirit of hopeless disillusion. The book radiated a frank modernism akin to that of Aldous Huxley; it was an original piece of art and Hemingway's narrative technique was impressive : he never explained or analyzed anything ; an exterior calm hid the violent inner anxiety. [37]

Before *A Farewell to Arms* was reviewed in *BLM*, the magazine had published a translation of " The Killers " [38] and introduced the American writer to their readers. The writer stressed the American quality in Hemingway, an author "*who had liberated American literature from European dependence. He is the leading and perhaps the most articulate representative of a whole group of American writers, who have emerged since the war and who, with their disillusioned, almost brutally honest philosophy of life, revolt sharply against what is generally understood as Americanism.*" [39] And he added : "*In his fear of false emotionalism and his subjective transformation of reality he hides every emotion behind a curt, metallic form, which is nevertheless exceedingly expressive and deceptively artless.*" [39]

In his laudatory review Svensson compared the novel with the great love stories of all time : *Romeo and Juliet*, *Anna Karenina* and Hamsun's *Victoria*. Opposing Selander, Svensson maintained that Hemingway's style was not French but American. The tension between the hard, metallic surface and the hidden, emotional sensibility was responsible for Hemingway's effective style. [40] To Artur Lundkvist *A Farewell to Arms* was undoubtedly America's strongest contribution to war literature, [41] a much better novel than *The Sun Also Rises*. Thorsten Jonsson, on the other hand, affirmed that the war novel was not as good as the Paris novel, because the prose was more impersonal and the narrative contained too many melodramatic effects. [42]

A Communist critic admitted that Hemingway was a master of narrative art, but he was annoyed because the author suggested no road out of despair. Since he realized the meaninglessness and absurdity of the bourgeois system, Hemingway's solution could only be one : hopelessness. [43] Another Communist reviewer was irritated because the novel was not revolutionary enough : it afforded only bourgeois anarchism and pessimism. Its valuable aspect was "*its free and open relationship between man and woman.*" [44] It had a great deal to offer the working classes and could therefore be recommended.

Death in the Afternoon was a real shocker to Sten Selander ; it was an exceptionally "*disgusting*" book. This was due to two factors : the subject-matter and above all the spirit in which the subject was treated. Both were peculiarly alien to the Swedish tradition and temperament. "*Bullfighting,*" he went on, "*is to him* [Hemingway] *nothing strange or alien, it is rather a picture of his own, normal world, where brutality, cruelty and raw egotism reign supreme and the only values are a hard skin, sure instincts and freedom from the inhibitions created by civilization. The forces which strive to check the best within us are in his view openly hostile.*" [45] Hemingway's concept of justice was hardly distinguished from the worst kind of hooliganism. Selander had to admit the beauty and restraint of the style, but Hemingway's reflections about sexual perversity and venereal diseases were extremely vulgar. The American author suffered from "*tasteless exhibitionism and a sadistic desire to torture the nerves of the reader.*" [46] Selander refused to read another line by Hemingway.

In a review of *Winner Take Nothing* Artur Lundkvist praised Hemingway's technical virtuosity, but he expressed certain reservations. The author had created a new type of man, had offered the youth of the 1930's an attitude to adopt and a model to follow. Hemingway "*has posed as the Byron of our age,*" Lundkvist wrote, "*a representative of the hardboiled generation and the sad young man.*" [47] But Hemingway's attitude toward life, like that of Maupassant, was not quite genuine. He was a bit snobbish about his indifference to life. "*He wanted to conquer his secret inner sentimentality and the result was brutality; he denied the sexual instinct by regarding it as a sensation, an athletic feat and the result was sadism. He was locked in his attitude, enclosed in his style as in armour.*" [47]

Two years later, in his review of *Green Hills of Africa*, Lundkvist again expressed his concern about Hemingway. The new book, meager and monotonous as it seemed, was a feat rather than a creation. Was not Hemingway on the point of "*falling into his own trap, of becoming a victim of his own attitude as the hero of our time? He seems to be more and more locked up in his role and his style as in a hard shell. He is too occupied with what Peter Fleming called 'the importance of being Ernest.' This must lead to sterility; we may soon have reason to talk about 'the impotence of being Ernest.'*" [48]

Hemingway's third novel and the third book to be translated

into Swedish, *To Have and Have Not*, was not favourably received in Sweden. It was definitely a book for men, both fascinating and repulsive.[49] The novel showed "*no advance in the author's monotonously brutal narrative art.*"[50] To Gustaf Hellström it was a disappointing book. Hemingway ought to know how futile his admiration for violence was. "*Violence — and admiration for violence — not only brutalize the emotional life, but also blunt the intellect.*"[51] Other conservative critics affirmed that Hemingway had written a "*blood-dripping monster of a novel,*" which was coarse and morally degrading and without any artistic merits whatsoever.[52] The kind of primitivism illustrated in the novel was a clear indication of a degenerating civilization. Its will to live was nothing but convulsive twitches and spasms and its fresh complexion was the result of octagonal bottles. The book was like a "*morsel of coagulated blood*" to Elmer Diktonius.[53] Hemingway simplified life and people too much.[54] The novel, whose *tempo furioso* called for admiration, revealed a primitive, almost barbaric poverty of feeling. Esthetically it was a failure and ethically it was disgusting, an apotheosis of brute force and openly destructive in its tendency.[55] Henning Söderhjelm called his review "A Hymn to Brutality," in which he stressed the fact that Hemingway was more important for literary history than for the reading public. Social pity was not the driving force behind the novel but Hemingway's admiration for the man and the adventurer Harry Morgan.[56] The weakness of the book, according to Thorsten Jonsson, was Hemingway's attitude toward his hero,[57] but it showed clearly that the author had broken his isolation.

The Swedish left-wing critics were the only ones who praised the novel more or less unreservedly. To them the book was fundamentally a social document of great importance. What the author wanted above all to call attention to was the shocking social conditions and injustices in America, where the gulf between wealth and poverty was more alarming than in any other civilized country.[58] After having abused Sven Stolpe for his false and bourgeois articles about America, Stig Ahlgren

praised *The New Masses* and *The New Republic* and concluded :
" *Hemingway's book is one of the most perfect I ever read...* " [59]

Such was the reaction in the thirties. The change which came in the next decade was largely due to the effects of the analyses of Hemingway's art, his cult of violence and brutality written by Lundkvist, [60] Jonsson and other intelligent critics. Hemingway's manly façade hid a horror of death which was never subdued. Under the hard surface there worked human and tender impulses. The fact that Hemingway liked to be photographed in front of enormous fish and wild game, was nothing but a pose which proved the critic's case. This kind of revaluation, together with the popularity of *For Whom the Bell Tolls*, helped to gain critical recognition for Hemingway in the forties.

In his favourable introduction to *Klockan klämtar för dig* (1941) Anders Österling noticed with satisfaction that Hemingway's theme was the spiritual solidarity of mankind. He stressed also the author's human interest, which was eventually liberated from the attitude of contemptuous cynicism. The hero was perhaps somewhat reminiscent of Gary Cooper, but he was natural, courteous, and a good model for the young, and he deserved his brief moment of bliss with Maria. [61] To Artur Lundkvist the novel was Hemingway's greatest book, perhaps *the* book of his life. He emphasized the author's maturity, his trust in life and his feeling for human beings. No snobbery or banal heroic pose ; instead a human heroism of rare quality. [62] These two comments from a conservative and a radical critic are symptomatic of the chorus of agreement among Swedish critics. It was noted with satisfaction that Hemingway had developed from nihilism and pessimism to revolutionary humanism. He retained his belief in sexual romanticism as a kind of substitute for religion.

Över floden in bland träden (1951) was considered an interim book, below the level of Hemingway's earlier achievement. One critic prophesied this was the end of Hemingway, who, anyhow, had not risen above the level of comics. [63] Typical headlines were : " Hemingway's Bankruptcy, " " Tired Old Hemingway, " " The Bell Tolls for Hemingway, " " Bitter Repose. " Lundkvist called the book "*infantile*" and a "*catastrophe,*" since the author had worked so hard on it, [64] and Anders Österling found that the new book did not increase Hemingway's glory, nor did it show any signs of development. [65]

A year later (1952) the same papers printed headlines such as " Doomed Author Takes Revenge. " *Den gamle och havet*, which appeared five days after the American and English editions, was a brilliantly conceived symbol of man's eternal battle. In this book we feel, the critics agreed, that the battle, even though it leaves us without any reward, and perhaps leaves us more empty-handed than when we began, is still worth fighting.

A number of obituary notices were printed on January 25, 1954. [66] Most of the writers agreed that Hemingway had been an important force in the history of literature and that his impact had been remarkable all over the world. He had been an incarnation and a mirror of our time. [67] Many critics deplored the fact that Hemingway had not received the Nobel Prize, which he had deserved more than many others.

4. The Nobel Prize.

When Hemingway was awarded the Nobel Prize in 1954 it was generally agreed that the Prize came too late. Hemingway's candidature had been eagerly discussed ever since the thirties. In 1937 Georg Svensson maintained that the center of gravity of the literature in the English language was moving toward America. Yet none of the emerging writers, Dos Passos, Hemingway and Faulkner were ready for the greatest literary distinction. [68] When in the following year Pearl Buck was awarded the Nobel Prize the same critic stated that Hemingway and T. S. Eliot were both worthy of the Prize, but, he added, they were "*perhaps not quite presentable.*" [69] Although no prizes were awarded during World War II, several candidates were eagerly discussed during those turbulent years. A newly started Danish periodical, *Bogrevyen*, mentioned Hemingway as a worthy candidate for 1943. His rivals included, among American writers, Willa Cather and Theodore Dreiser. [70] In 1945, after the death of Paul Valéry, one critic maintained that from the point of view of literary history the names of T. S. Eliot and Ernest Hemingway surpassed all others. They, more than anyone else, had put their imprint on the poetry and prose, respectively, of the last fifteen or twenty years. A prize to either of them would remunerate a daring type of literature that fought for new modes of expression instead of following conventional and popular patterns. [71] Hemingway was also among the dozen writers mentioned for the 1947 award. His rivals included : Gide, Mauriac, Malraux, Eliot, Faulkner, Dos Passos, Neruda, Øverland, Nexø and Lagerkvist. The closest rivals were, however, Gide and Eliot. Gide won, and was awarded the Prize for 1947, whereas Eliot was the supreme candidate for 1948. His influence on poetry had been almost as great as that of Walt Whitman.

An article in *BLM* entitled " Vem bör få nobelpris 1950 ? " may have substantially influenced the Academy in their choice. Leading newspapermen and critics in the United States, on the Continent and in Scandinavia were asked to answer this question. The result of the survey was that Faulkner's name topped the list, whereas Hemingway was the runner-up. Again Hemingway was the loser. The resistance of the Academy was eventually conquered by the brilliance of *The Old Man and the Sea*, which won Hemingway the Nobel Prize for 1954.

The choice was not altogether popular. When the winner was announced, Swedish newspapers printed few evaluations of Hemingway's literary activity. Most critics were either concerned with his picturesque personality or his position in contemporary literature. The attitude of the reading public may be described as one of reluctant respect and not undivided sympathy. Malicious critics pointed to the fact that Hemingway had not long before been declared dead both literarily and physically. One of the obituary articles was signed by Anders Österling, secretary of the Swedish Academy. To give the Prize to Hemingway now was nothing but ostrich politics and *esprit d'escalier*. Moreover, Hemingway was too old (56) and none of the writers of the fifties read him. Consequently he was felt to be worthless. One ironic critic affirmed that it seemed a bit generous to give the award to one more American, because he had made a few changes in the usual syntax. Such syntactical changes were nothing but linguistic coquetry, original in the same way as the scroll of a signature, but hardly worth a Nobel Prize. [72]

Ivar Harrie, a notorious enemy of Hemingway, maintained that Laxness, the Icelander, was at the real center of interest, whereas Hemingway's influence and way of writing belonged to the past. Laxness should have had the Prize, for he had renewed epic art after Hemingway and independently of Hemingway. To give the award to such writers as Churchill and Hemingway was nothing but a concession to public opinion. Others, however, felt that Hemingway had been worthy of a Nobel Prize for a very long time and it was better to give it to him now : he might not be able to cheat death once more.

In his justification of the award Österling praised Hemingway's "*powerful and influential stylistic mastery of the art of modern narration.*" [73] Åke Runnquist was among the Swedish critics who defended Hemingway and the Academy. He stated that since Gœthe's young Werther there had not been a literary character more influential than Hemingway's tough and sentimental hero. Runnquist also felt that the original quality and the special attraction of his work were not altogether evident twenty years before. *The Old Man and the Sea* displayed not only great artistry but a new and positive attitude toward life which had direct bearing upon present-day problems. [74]

Since the Nobel Prize, interest in Hemingway has been kept alive by more translations [75] and by fresh evaluations of Hemingway's art and mind. *Afrikas gröna berg* was brought out in 1954, immaculately translated by Mårten Edlund and magnificently illustrated by Erik Palmquist. The volume was considered one of Hemingway's best books because of its revelation of the author's psychology : a man among men squeezing as much life as possible out of the fleeting moment. In an evaluation in the *Dagens Nyheter* [76] Olof Lagercrantz saw Hemingway and his hero as a soldier who never returned, a new type of man, born of the war, icily alone, full of anxiety and without any hope for the future, a type most influential both in literature and in real life.

5. IMPACT ON SWEDISH WRITERS.

There were only slight repercussions of post-war pessimism in Sweden after World War I, during which the country was neutral. The mood of despair was somewhat incongruous in view of the official welfare state ideology. The new generation of Swedish writers, the proletarians, who did their best work in the thirties, were basically optimists. Their source of salvation was the new primitivism.

The first Swedish writer to employ the typical Hemingway idiom was Walter Ljungquist in his short novel *Ombyte av tåg* (1933). At the time of his literary debut he was photographed in his study, with a large picture of Hemingway, one of his literary ancestors, on the wall. [77] The popularizer of the hard-boiled style in Sweden was not Ljungquist but Thorsten Jonsson, one of Hemingway's translators. Jonsson's own collections of stories, *Som det brukar vara* (1939), *Fly till vatten och morgon* (1941), *Dimman från havet* (1950) and the novel *Konvoj* (1947) bear the Hemingway stamp. One critic even referred to Jonsson's style as " hemingwayska. " [78] In particular the stories from 1941 marked a new departure, a kind of behaviorist narrative art, in Swedish prose writing. [79] They exerted an immediate influence on the younger generation, who felt that this style was an adequate expression of the pulse of modern times. The new subject-matter, modern man's struggle against the world, appealed particularly to existentialist groups. The years 1943-46 which Jonsson spent in New York as a special correspondent for the liberal Stockholm paper *Dagens Nyheter*, were of great importance for his own development as a writer and critic.

It is more difficult to pinpoint Hemingway's impact on Artur Lundkvist, whose role as introducer and sponsor of new American writers was and still is significant. His particular brand of brutality and vitalism is reminiscent of Whitman, Hemingway and D. H. Lawrence. Such writers of the older generation as Ivar Lo-Johansson, [80] Eyvind Johnson, Sven Stolpe and Jan Fridegård may also have been stimulated by Hemingway's literary technique.

It was not, however, until the forties that the impact of Hemingway and the hard-boiled school of writing was generally felt. It is safe to speak of a Hemingway school in Sweden. The American writer was considered the leader of the American hard-boiled school, which also included writers like Faulkner, Caldwell and Farrell as well as James M. Cain, W. R. Burnett, John O'Hara, Horace McCoy and Jerome Weidman. [81] Most of Sweden's Hemingway epigones made their literary debut in the forties. They learnt only a certain formula or mannerism from the master (in some cases perhaps through Thorsten Jonsson) and they mistook Hemingway's deceptive lack of emotionalism for cynicism and filled their pessimistic books with tedious descriptions of mortuaries, battlefields and brothels. In Norway the war had blown away this Nazi type of contempt for human beings, but in neutral Sweden it was still fashionable to be hard-boiled and disillusioned. "*The American influence on the most recent Swedish literature is undeniable,*" wrote Georg Svensson, "*and occasionally it finds childish expression. It implies an acceptance of a manner of writing and an attitude toward life which in America is already vieux jeu.*" [82] It was not to be wondered at that a reaction set in before the end of the decade, [83] and an anthology entitled

Hårdkokt (1950), seemed to have given the deathblow to the school in Sweden.

There are at least a dozen mostly minor writers that should be mentioned in this connection. Interest in somewhat simple and primitive people and a more restrained form of writing are typical features. One young Swedish writer told an interviewer: " *To write in the American way in Sweden is to use a straightforward word order and to describe sexual intercourse.* " [84] In Bertil Lagerström's *Trasdockor* (1943) the theme is the rootlessness of modern man; in Sven Bergström's *Fjärran är havets rand* (1944) and in Harry Ahlberg's *Söndag med hög hatt på* (1944) the war is partly responsible for the authors' Waste Land reality. The hard-boiled style is particularly obvious in Mårten Edlund's *Tag vad du vill ha* [85] (1944), Gustaf Rune Eriks' *Hänryckningens tid* (1944) Sven Forssell's *Syrsorna i St. Florentine* (1948), Peter Nisser's *Blod och snö* (1941), *Irrande liv* (1948) and *Sällskapsdamens dilemma* (1950), Sven Rydberg's *Konversation under en lampa* (1941) and in certain writings by Lars Ahlin, Sivar Arnér, Tuve Ambjörn Nyström, Gösta Petterson and Arne Trankell. Something of Faulkner's fury may be felt in Dagerman and Lindegren.

In the thirties Hemingway's hard-boiled style and philosophy of life stimulated a few Swedish writers. But it was not until the forties and the influence of another war that we could speak of a Hemingway school in Sweden. It is safe to say that certain aspects of the literature of the forties — a decade characterized by its particularly neurotic psychology, its possessed study of the loneliness of the human heart, its disillusion and pessimism, its nihilism, its Kafkaesque symbolism and its existentialist discussion — can only be fully understood if one takes into account the impact of Hemingway and the hard-boiled school on Swedish creative writing.

NOTES

1. Artur LUNDKVIST, *Atlantvind,* Stockholm, 1932, p. 71.
2. *Ibid.,* p. 72.
3. *Ibid.,* p. 75.
4. Artur LUNDKVIST, *Amerikas nya författare,* Stockholm, 1940, p. 4.
5. *Ibid.,* p. 5.
6. *Ibid.,* p. 18.
7. Thorsten JONSSON, *Sex amerikaner,* Stockholm, 1942, p. 10.
8. *Ibid.,* pp. 13-14.
9. His collection of essays was entitled *Kjærlighet og åndsliv.*
10. *Sex amerikaner,* p. 22.
11. *Ibid.,* p. 25.
12. *Ibid.,* p. 26.
13. *Ibid.,* p. 27. See also : JONSSON, *Sidor av Amerika,* Stockholm, 1946.
14. I am particularly indebted to Dr. Georg Svensson for his valuable aid in connection with this article. The Bonnier archives contain innumerable Hemingway items. The firm's *Amerikansk litteratur i GULA SERIEN* (The Yellow Series) included such writers as Sherwood Anderson, Louis Bromfield, Edna Ferber, Joseph Hergesheimer, Eugene O'Neill, John Steinbeck, Edith Wharton and Thomas Wolfe.
15. Jonsson also translated into Swedish Steinbeck's *The Grapes of Wrath* and some stories by Caldwell.
16. Translator of *The Sun Also Rises* (1929). In 1927 Gripenberg translated *Spoon River Anthology,* which had an immediate impact on Swedish writers.
17. Hallström was elected in 1908 and Hellström in 1942.
18. See : Carl L. ANDERSON, *Swedish Acceptance of American Literature* (Stockholm, 1957).
19. " Amerikansk litteratur, " *Svenska Dagbladet,* September 17, 1932.
20. " Amerikansk bohem ", *Svenska Dagbladet,* June 15, 1929.
21. " Sommarlektyr, " *Sydsvenska Dagbladet,* June 6, 1929.
22. " Amerikansk krigsroman, " *Dagens Nyheter,* July 9, 1931.
23. *Atlantvind,* p. 72.
24. *Ibid.,* p. 73.
25. *Sex amerikaner,* p. 28. When a new translation of the novel appeared in 1948, Viveka Heyman wrote : " *There are not very many who were injured in the war the way Jake was, but there are numerous individuals whom the war has wounded in their souls so that they cannot love or be loved. Hemingway speaks for these people.* " *Arbetaren,* March 6, 1948. To Gunnar Ekelöf, on the other hand, this book with its tragedy seemed peculiarly remote. We had now become used to living close to the edge of the abyss without

dancing on it. The feeling of impotence so frequent during World War I was due to a desire to make up for things lost, a desire too deep even to be completely satisfied. " Tjugu år efteråt, " *BLM*, XVII (July-August 1948), 449.

26. It has been suggested that Selander consciously aimed at de-Americanizing Hemingway in order to make him more attractive to Swedish readers. See Stig AHLBERG, " Farväl till vapnen, " *Sydsvenska Dagbladet*, October 19, 1932. Ahlberg praised the novel, whose hero reminded him of Huxley's John Bidlake and the heroine of Martin Arrowsmith's *Leora*.

27. Selander evidently had *The Sun Also Rises* in mind.
28. *Farväl till vapnen*, Stockholm, 1932, p. v.
29. *Ibid.*, p. vi.
30. *Ibid.*, p. vii.
31. *Ibid.*, p. viii.
32. E. V., " Från bokhyllan, " *Reformatorn*, October 29, 1932.
33. " Två amerikanska författare om krig, cocktails och kvinnor, " *Social-Demokraten*, November 6, 1932. See also *Göteborgs Posten*, November 24, 1932.
34. C. B-n, *Nya Dagligt Allehanda*, October 23, 1932. Other critics praised this erotic quality in lyrical and almost prophetic terms. See particularly *Aftonbladet*, September 27, 1932.
35. P. G. P., " En bekväm, " *Stockholms Tidningen Dagbladet*, October 16, 1932.
36. Carl-August BOLANDER, " Amerikansk krigsroman, " *Dagens Nyheter*, July 9, 1931. Cf. also N. M., " En desertör, " *Uppsala Nya Tidning*, September 19, 1932.
37. " Desillusion, " *Göteborgs Handels-och Sjöfarts-Tidning*, September 26, 1932.
38. " Mord på beställning, " *BLM*, I (April 1932), 52-58. Russell Blankenship had praised " The Killers " and Sherwood Anderson's " I'm a Fool " in his literary history and he evidently influenced Georg Svensson's choice of stories for the magazine.
39. *BLM*, I (April 1932), 58.
40. *BLM*, I (September 1932), 74. It should also be added that the film version stimulated the general interest in Hemingway. See *Fönstret*, IV, No. 9 (1933), 22.
41. *Atlantvind*, p. 73.
42. *Sex amerikaner*, p. 28.
43. *Ny Dag*, December 3, 1932.
44. *Folkets Dagblad Politiken*, September 28, 1932.
45. " Tjurfäktningen som världsbild, " *Dagens Nyheter*, May 1, 1933.
46. *Ibid*. For another disappointed critic, see *Svenska Dagbladet*, November 13, 1932. When the Swedish translation appeared in 1958, critics felt that the esthetics of killing was not so important as what the book revealed about the author himself.
47. *BLM*, III (April 1934), 43.
48. " Böcker från England och Amerika, " *BLM*, V (October 1936), 623.
49. Anders ÖSTERLING, " Att ha och inte ha, " *Stockholms-Tidningen*, June 16, 1939.

50. *BLM*, VI (November 1937), 771. Clifton Fadiman gave a report of the American reaction to the novel in *ibid.*, VII (January 1938), 40-43.
51. " Våld och utveckling, " *Dagens Nyheter*, May 5, 1939.
52. *Sundsvalls Posten*, May 30, 1939. Cf. *Skånska Dagbladet*, May 30, 1939.
53. *Arbetar Bladet*, July 5, 1939.
54. E. N. TIGERSTEDT in *Svenska Pressen*, May 27, 1939.
55. *Svenska Dagbladet*, June 19,1939. Negative were also *Lunds Dagblad*, June 16, 1939 and *Aftonbladet*, May 8, 1939.
56. *Göteborgs Handels-och Sjöfarts-Tidning*, June 20, 1939.
57. *Sex amerikaner*, p. 31.
58. *Ny Dag*, October 23, 1939 ; *Arbetaren*, October 2, 1939. The book's power and masculine force were praised by *Jämtlands Tidning*, May 23, 1939 and by *Gotlänningen*, June 12, 1939.
59. " Hårdkokta författare, " *Arbetet*, May 22, 1939.
60. Lundkvist wrote a long and penetrating analysis of Hemingway's *The Fifth Column and The First Forty-Nine Stories* for *BLM*, VIII (March 1939), 198-204. He criticized Hemingway's style for its mechanical automatism ; it was his Achilles' heel. Lundkvist referred the reader to Wyndham Lewis' article about Hemingway, " Men Without Art. " Another long and seminal article by Robert Penn Warren emphasized the code, the discipline, the style in Hemingway's writing. See *BLM*, XVI (September 1947), 563-574.
61. *Klockan klämtar för dig* (Stockholm 1941), p. 6.
62. *BLM*, X (February 1941), 127-129. See also *ibid.*, XI (November 1942), 733-734.
63. *BLM*, XIX (December 1950), 806.
64. *Morgon Tidningen*, March 4, 1951.
65. *Stockholms-Tidningen*, June 22, 1950. See also Thorsten Jonsson in *Dagens Nyheter*, March 18, 1950 and Sten Selander in *Svenska Dagbladet*, February 12, 1951.
66. Nils BEYER, " Ernest Hemingway död, " *Morgon Tidningen*, January 25, 1954. See also Anders Österling's fine appraisal in *Stockholms-Tidningen*, January 25, 1954. A good summary of Hemingway's achievement appeared in *BLM*, XXX (September 1961), 500-501.
67. Sten SELANDER, *Svenska Dagbladet*, January 25, 1954. Cf. also " Morgontidningarna har mördat Hemingway, " *Aftonbladet*, January 25, 1954.
68. *BLM*, VI (November 1937), 696.
69. *Ibid.*, VII (December 1938), 739. Dreiser was also considered a worthy candidate.
70. *Ibid.*, XII (November 1943), 692.
71. *Ibid.*, XIV (September 1945), 548-549.
72. Paraphrased in *BLM*, XXIV (October 1955), 643.
73. See also Österling's Nobel speech, in which he praised Hemingway's heroic pathos and manly predilection for danger. *Stockholms-Tidningen*, December 11, 1954.
74. *BLM*, XXIII (November 1954), 684.
75. A translation of Leicester Hemingway's biography, *Min bror Ernest Hemingway* appeared in 1962 published by Bonniers.
76. October 29, 1954.

77. *BLM*, XIX (December 1950), 751. Gunnar Larsen was an equally early Norwegian imitator. Ivar Harrie maintained that Ljungquist's second novel, *Släkten står på trappan*, exhibited a virtuosity similar to that of Hemingway. *Ord och Bild*, XLV (1936), 102. But Hemingway's fanatical matter-of-factness and sadistic pleasure in revelation were of course alien to Walter Ljungquist. See *ibid.*, XLVI (1937), 570. In 1939 Sven Stolpe stated that there were many admirers and disciples of Hemingway in Scandinavia. " Litterärt New Yorkbrev, " *BLM*, VII (May 1939), 378-381.

78 *BLM*, XIV (January 1945), 5.

79. See Artur LUNDKVIST, " Novellens förnyelse, " *BLM*, X (November 1941), 743-744.

80. See also his laudatory review of Hemingway's short stories in *Lantarbetaren*, XLIV (1942), 5.

81. Åke RUNNQUIST, " Den ensamme spårhunden. Några drag hos den hårdkokta romanen och dess hjältar, " *BLM*, XVIII (April 1949), 291.

82. " Om s. k. hårdkokthet, " *BLM*, XIV (January 1945), 6. In the same article Aksel Sandemose poked fun at the Swedish imitators of Hemingway.

83. Georg Svensson, " Den siste Hemingway, " *BLM*, XV (February 1946), 101-102.

84. Örjan LINDBERGER, " Svenska romaner och noveller, " *Ord och Bild*, LIV (1945), 568.

85. The hero is a nihilistic he-man who despises sentimentality. A scene of sexual bliss cut short by chance is also included. *Ord och Bild*, LI (1942), 423.

SWEDISH TRANSLATIONS

BOOKS.

1929 *Och solen går sin gång (The Sun Also Rises)*. Transl. Bertel Gripenberg. Stockholm : Schildt, 1929.

1932 *Farväl till vapnen (A Farewell to Arms)*. With an Introduction by Sten Selander. Transl. Louis Renner. Stockholm : Bonnier, 1932 (1941, 1943, 1947, 1953, 1954, 1956).

1939 *Att ha och inte ha (To Have and Have Not)*. Transl. Thorsten Jonsson. Stockholm : Bonnier, 1939 (1952, 1954, 1958).

1941 *Klockan klämtar för dig (For Whom the Bell Tolls)*. With an Introduction by Anders Österling. Transl. Thorsten Jonsson. Stockholm : Bonnier, 1941 (1942, 1944, 1954, 1955, 1957).

1942 *Snön på Kilimandjaro och andra noveller (The Snows of Kilimanjaro, etc.)*. Transl. Thorsten Jonsson. Stockholm : Bonnier, 1942.

1947 *Och solen har sin gång (The Sun Also Rises)*. Transl. Olov Jonason. Stockholm : Bonnier, 1947 (1954, 1960, 1961).

1951 *Över floden in bland träden (Across the River and Into the Trees)*. Transl. Mårten Edlund. Stockholm : Bonnier, 1951 (1954).

1952 *Den gamle och havet (The Old Man and the Sea)*. Transl. Mårten Edlund. Stockholm : Bonnier, 1952 (1954, 1959).

1954 *Afrikas gröna berg (Green Hills of Africa)*. Transl. Mårten Edlund. Illustr. Erik Palmquist. Stockholm : Bonnier, 1954 (1955).

1955 *Noveller (Short Stories)*. Transl. Mårten Edlund & Thorsten Jonsson. Stockholm : Bonnier, 1955.

1958 *Döden på eftermiddagen (Death in the Afternoon)*. Transl. Arne Häggqvist. Stockholm : Bonnier, 1958.

1962 *Vårflod (The Torrents of Spring)*. Transl. Olov Jonason. Stockholm : Bonnier, 1962.

SWEDISH REPRINTS.

1942 *A Farewell to Arms*. Stockholm : Continental Book Co., 1942 (1945, 1947). *Zephyr Books*, Vol. 1.

1943 *For Whom the Bell Tolls*. Stockholm, 1943 (1945). *Zephyr Books*, Vol. 26.

1947 *The Sun Also Rises*. Stockholm, 1947. *Zephyr Books*, Vol. 146.

HEMINGWAY'S REVIVAL IN THE SOVIET UNION
1955-1962

by Stephen Jan PARKER

THE WORKS OF ERNEST HEMINGWAY were first published in the Soviet Union in 1934. In the following five years, through 1939, his short stories, the novels *The Sun Also Rises, A Farewell to Arms, To Have and Have Not*, and the play *The Fifth Column*, were published. His popularity was immediate and impressive. In the mid-thirties, *International Literature*, a monthly journal, asked Soviet writers in a questionnaire which contemporary authors they "*considered to be the most significant.*" Hemingway ranked first in almost all of the replies.[1]

I

The Soviet critiques of Hemingway's early works (*The Sun Also Rises, A Farewell to Arms*, and his short stories) were filled with the words defeat, pessimism, pain, despair, tragedy, and fear. In general, the Soviet critics viewed these works as the honest portrayal of bourgeois life after World War I. The war was a source of upheaval for the Hemingway hero; it caused him to reconsider his life among the "*imperialists.*" He found need for escape, whether in athletics, as the critic Olga Nemerovskaia[2] asserted, in nature as Ia. Frid[3] claimed, or in liquor as A. Mingulina[4] maintained. Both Jake Barnes and Frederick Henry longed for a worthy life. Incapable of finding it in their

Reprinted by permission of *American Literature*, © 1964 by Duke University Press.

society, they were forced to stand by themselves as individuals. They thus faced a common fate of despair and death.

The Soviets were chiefly concerned with the works published during the years of the Spanish Civil War. In *To Have and Have Not*, they felt that Hemingway was at last struggling with a social theme. Though they realized that he had not yet recognized the dialectics of social existence, they widely heralded the dying words of the pirate-smuggler Harry Morgan, " *A man alone ain't got no bloody f...ing chance,* " [5] as Hemingway's first awareness of the social conflict. They widely publicized his journalistic writings, such as " Who Killed the War Veterans in Florida ? " and " The Americans Fallen in Spain, " and his scenario for the anti-fascist film, *The Spanish Earth*. The play, *The Fifth Column*, was held as further evidence of Hemingway's emergence as a social writer. [6] The Soviets felt that the author at last was submerging the "*formalistic,*" style-conscious Hemingway and asserting the vitally concerned man-Hemingway who was outraged at the horror of fascism.

Knowing that Hemingway had promised to write a lengthy novel on the Spanish Civil War, the Soviets anxiously waited for its publication. *For Whom the Bell Tolls* was received unfavorably in the Soviet Union and was considered unsuitable for publication. The disparaging remarks Hemingway made about the Comintern figures, André Marty and Passionara ; his humane treatment of the Fascist officer Lieutenant Berrendo ; his lengthy description of the brutal slaughter of fascists by the loyalists ; and his persistent reiteration of the theme that no cause is ever worth the taking of a man's life were sufficient reasons to have prevented the book's publication. Thus, in 1940, publication of Hemingway ended in the Soviet Union, and he was seldom referred to in the press for the next fifteen years. [7]

With the appearance of *The Old Man and the Sea*, in 1955, the fifteen-year moratorium was broken. The story first appeared in the monthly *Inostrannaia literatura* and in a separate volume in 1956. It drew considerable comment.

In 1955, prior to Soviet publication, the critic Viktor Gorokhov reviewed the English version. As an introduction to this commentary, Gorokhov reviewed Hemingway's past heroes. The characters in the post-World War I works were " *sterile, useless,* " Those like Frederick Henry made a " *separate peace* " with " *painful reality, and in the end ran from it.* " Others stood alone, " *daily throwing challenges, people precise in their own affairs; adroit, bold, strong —people of heroic deed.* " [8] Gorokhov saw a dualistic Hemingway, the Hemingway romanticist and the Hemingway realist.

The Hemingway romanticist sings of the beauty of the solitary challenge. The Hemingway realist pitilessly reveals the senselessness of a fight alone. [As for the Civil War works], Hemingway overcame the barren, tragic individuality of his heroes; the writer and his heroes sought the road to the people, to intelligent struggle, to real optimism. But, in his works, in the cracked voice of the people, everything still sounded of courage turned to the courage of individual despair. The final pages of his last novel were filled with impenetrable pessimism. (p. 27)

The Old Man and the Sea was a story which " *outwardly* " seemed to illustrate the recurrent cycle of " *the desire for a heroic deed—the deed—and at first glance, the defeat of the victor.* " However, said Gorokhov, " *this is no longer the former allegorical conclusion of the vanity of deed and struggle.* " He turned to a statement which would later be quoted by other Soviet critics. After having killed the first shark, Santiago said : " *But man is not made for defeat. A man can be destroyed but not defeated.* " [9] Gorokhov saw Hemingway, the author, speaking for himself through the words of old Santiago.

Pride in the simple man, the toiling man, enlivens the whole story. The writer admires the skill of his hero's craftsmanship in carrying on his own affairs. With deep humanity he describes the burdens of the fisherman's work.... The old man does not die in Byronic solitude like the former heroes of Hemingway. Let him be old, tired, sick, but he does not yield... he goes again to the sea. And goes not alone.... (p. 28)

" *And goes not alone* " was the important point. Santiago had the boy who loved him, learned from him, and would be the future Santiago.

Gorokhov concluded by claiming that the book was the most optimistic work Hemingway had written.

> The old man is not defeated and the old man is not alone. These two life-affirming themes flow together in the finale and determine the optimistic ring of the story.... The hero of Hemingway's story is not an aristocrat of heart or body, selecting by his whims a field of battle. He is a toiler. The image of the old man affirms the elements in the nature of man, his pride and his dignity. (p. 28)

The years 1955-1956 witnessed a literary dispute between the critics Sergei Lvov and Vladislav Drobishevskii. In 1955, Lvov published a critique of *The Old Man and the Sea* in a literary newspaper, *Literaturnaia gazeta*. In this review he stated that the story had " *two layers* " of understanding : " *On the surface—the precise, limited, detailed, captivating craftsmanship story.... But under this layer—a deep, inner philosophical undercurrent.* " [10] Lvov found this undercurrent depressing, best expressed in the saying : " *If only youth was able, if only old age could.*" The critic considered Santiago lonely and defeated.

> The old man knows everything about the sea and the fish.... But he is old and alone. And to him is not given to taste of the fruits of his ability. This is all of his life—the picked bare skeleton of a fish, the useless victory transformed into defeat.

Drobishevskii replied in the May, 1956, issue of *Zvezda*. He did not find the work to be a wholly optimistic one. It was tinged with the motif of solitude, a tragic undercurrent. He found Hemingway's " *usual* " tragic elements present —" *the tragedy of loneliness, the longing of man for man.* " This was the same sentiment expressed in Harry Morgan's dying words. Because of the " *capitalistic conditions of life* " Santiago was alone, and his loneliness was heightened by his old age. But, said Drobishevskii, this was not the prime characteristic of the story. There was a great charge of optimism present, and the work could well be called " *An Optimistic Tragedy.* "

The optimism of the story stems from its hero, a simple man, standing before us in all the beauty of his healthy heart and healthy body.... The story, *The Old Man and The Sea*, is a singular song of the great heart of the simple man, who, in spite of his forced solitude, need, and old age, is able to remain a man and continue to love and fight. [11]

Drobishevskii compared Santiago with Manuel in Hemingway's short story, "The Undefeated." Both characters were old, both suffered bad luck, both struggled, and both earned victory. They differed, however, in the fact that Manuel remained alone in the end, while the old man had the boy.

The return of the boy to Santiago imparts to this story a greater "optimistic ring"... the old man is now not alone.... The figure of the boy in this role... is a new figure in the works of Hemingway. Thanks to his story, *The Old Man and The Sea*, the author approaches a new theme: what a man can do when he is not alone. (p. 170)

Lvov replied to Drobishevskii in the July issue of *Zvezda*. He did not believe that Santiago's statement that a man cannot be defeated was the central point of the story and pointed out that Drobishevskii neglected to state that these words occurred in the context of Santiago's reasoning that birds and beasts are superior to man in having greater courage, and that in the end it is all the same, whether he conquers the fish or the fish conquers him. Lvov felt that the courage of Manuel, the matador, of Santiago, the fisherman, was not as great as that of certain characters in *The Fifth Column*, "The Madrid Chauffeurs," and in the better chapters of *For Whom the Bell Tolls*.

Lvov further contended that the reader must look for "*the conflict of motives which converted the life of Santiago into a mortal dual, one against one, with the elements and creatures of the sea.*" This conflict must be found in the social sphere, and since the battle has never been truly resolved, the conflict remains. In Lvov's opinion, the sum of Santiago's life was "*the uncovering of the primitive struggle for existence.*" The conflict was beetwen "*the magnificent human qualities of Santiago and the inhuman life which he [knew].*" Hemingway, Lvov concluded, sensed the existence of this conflict but did not know how to present it. In no way could one consider *The Old Man and The Sea* an " *Optimistic Tragedy.* " [12]

In 1956, three students from the University of Moscow wrote an open letter to Hemingway on the subject of *The Old Man and the Sea*. They were impressed by the book and found in it similarities to the Burguete fishing episode in *The Sun Also Rises* and to the struggle for life on the sea by the " *hero-toiler* " Harry Morgan. Other aspects which they enjoyed were the precision of Santiago's labor, the warm relationship between the man and the boy, and Santiago's statement that man cannot be defeated. In summarizing the book they wrote :

Everywhere people fight for happiness, for a life worthy of man. They do not always win ; they must endure both adversity and defeat. But he who *knows how* to gain victory does not despair after his heavy failure—does not despair and continues the fight. [13]

In 1960 the Soviet Union published *Across the River and Into the Trees*. The novel appeared in serial form in the monthly journal *Moskva*, and the only discoverable review of it is a three-page introduction to the initial instalment. [14] The reviewer was partial to the book, finding it a story of a man who lived as he wished, though threatened by impending death, a story of love, and a story of anti-war sentiment. Colonel Cantwell was a humanist who abhorred war as much as did Frederick Henry and Hemingway.

The book had been badly received in the United States, in the reviewer's opinion, because it was published during the Korean War and the " *McCarthyite press* " took exception to the following exchange between the Colonel and a waiter :

" How do you feel about the Russians, if it is not indiscreet to ask, my Colonel ? "

" They are our potential enemy. So, as a soldier, I am prepared to fight them. But I like them very much and I have never known finer people nor people more as we are. " [15]

In conclusion, the reviewer apologized for not writing a more complete analysis : " *The book* Across the River and Into the Trees *is an important stage in the artistic work of Hemingway, yet another evidence of his strength as master of the word and as a man, the fierce enemy of war and fascist obscurantism* " (p. 100).

II

Since Hemingway's first publication in the Soviet Union in 1934, Ivan Kashkin has been Hemingway's most prolific and perhaps most perceptive critic. He appears to be the only Soviet critic concerned with Hemingway's private life—his literary associates, his mythical stature in the West. He also has been one of Hemingway's best translators, translating the first published stories, *A Farewell to Arms*, and numerous articles. He has edited and annotated a two-volume edition of Hemingway's collected works [16] and is generally regarded as the Soviet Union's " expert " on Hemingway.

From 1934 through 1961 Kashkin published thirteen articles on the American novelist. [17] A portion of these appeared prior to 1955, but those that have since appeared offer us Kashkin's most comprehensive views on Hemingway's works. In 1956, two lengthy articles appeared, " Alive in the Midst of Death " and " Rereading Hemingway. "

In " Alive in the Midst of Death " Kashkin first questioned whether Hemingway had sought death all his life, as the recurring themes of death and violence in his works suggest : " *He cannot but feel death in the life that surrounds him, and death for him, at least as an onlooker, is one of the main themes of modern decadent art. It is but natural that this should cast a shadow on his work* " (p. 163).

The reason for Hemingway's preoccupation with death, in Kashkin's estimate, was his observation of it in two large and two small wars : " *War made Hemingway see death without disguise or heroic illusion... and he began to treat organized death as a social phenomenon inherent in the world that surrounded him* "

(p. 163). After Hemingway's experiences in World War I, his characters became "*the lost generation,*" victims of "*the social disease of the age.*" They were haunted by "*the end of something*" which dulled all their perceptions of life. This was evidenced in Hemingway's works through *A Farewell to Arms*. Then Hemingway made "*a separate peace with the same rich loafers whom he had so ruthlessly exposed.*" Hemingway became a bullfight connoisseur, fisherman, hunter. With "The Snows of Kilimanjaro" (1936) he realized, along with his character Harry, that "*he had been a hostage in the camp of those with whom he hunts and drinks and talks of art.*"

The realization of the price he has paid comes too late because that price is death—physical, moral, and artistic. The death of the writer Harry is a kind of symbolic purification : He sheds a skin that is dead, but still there is no way into life either for the hero or for the author. (pp. 163-164)

Kashkin pursued this line of argument with the statement : "*Life in a world based on the sordid laws of moneygrubbing, violence, and death is a cruel affair, particularly for the underdog*" (p. 164).

Nick Adams's memories had been of a suicide ("Indian Camp"), the lynching of a Negro (epigraph in *In Our Time*), and an encounter with murderers ("The Killers"). In Hemingway's early stories and in his novels there were many "*gangsters, executions, murders.*" Hemingway continually returned to these types to present them in greater clarity. Kashkin did not believe that Hemingway was obsessed with death for the presence of death was a natural phenomenon in Hemingway's society.

For Hemingway life is inseparable from death and is a fight at close quarters in which his heroes overcome not only the fear of death but the fear of life's intricacies and the disintegration threatening the individual. (p. 165)

The novelist came to partial terms with life through work and struggle. Work had allowed Jake to "*escape*" from his friends at Pamplona, and "*a struggle for a decent life*" had been waged by Harry Morgan, Robert Jordan, and the Spanish guerrillas. This approach to life led Hemingway to the idea "*that life itself should not be spared for a great cause.*" Kashkin said : "*The struggle of common people for a decent existence, their simple and straightforward attitude towards life and death serve as a model for Hemingway's more complex and contradictory characters*" (p. 165). All are faced with death, violence, and fear ; the best of them resolve their problems by looking to "*life, strength, and courage.*" Thus, the "*irresponsibility*" of the lost generation was replaced by the commitment of the El Sordos and Santiagos. When Hemingway asked "*how a simple man could hold his own, and how he could reach and join other simple folks*" in *To Have and Have Not*, the Spanish Civil War and its people gave him the answer :

And even in a book so contradictory and controversial as *For Whom the Bell Tolls*, for all its deficiencies of judgment and artistic drawbacks, victory over death is convincing precisely for the reason that the author gives a picture, be it ever so subjective and even distorted, of a certain part of the struggle against the scourge of humanity, fascism. (p. 167)

Kashkin did not enumerate the "*deficiencies of judgment*" nor the distortions, but only commented on the positive elements : El Sordo's death, the blowing up of the bridge, Andres's trip through the lines, and the character of Old Anselmo. Jordan, in Kashkin's estimation, was still part old-Hemingway, in that the burden of fighting for a cause was too much for him. Commenting on the differences between the deaths of Jordan and El Sordo, he noted that El Sordo died with a full comprehension of his life and the reason for his death, while Jordan, having little to look back upon, died with only the "*joyless stoicism of an unavailing sacrifice.*"

The critic did not find great optimism in Hemingway, but rather an author's pity for his characters and sympathy for their plight—a humanistic note. The most "*humanistic*" of his works, was *The Old Man and The Sea*. In contrast with his former works, this story was "*subdued, gentle, and resigned.*" There had been a change in Hemingway. Instead of writing about strong men's weakness, he now wrote about "*the moral strength of a decrepit old fisherman.*" "*Here there is more faith in, and respect for, man, but life itself has shrunk to the narrow confines of a lonely old man's vision*" (p. 172).

Kashkin commented briefly that Hemingway loved his country in a strange way. He loved the America that was, and thus scorned "*the ideal of hypocritical conventional prosperity, and offers an ethical code of his own.*" This moral code, in Kashkin's estimation, was too simple, it was based merely on fair play and limited responses, inadequate for, and at variance with "*the great truths of life.*" Here he returned to Hemingway's distortion of the events in *For Whom the Bell Tolls*, his inability to see the roots of fascism. Kashkin noted that Hemingway deliberately tried to avoid political questions and "*taking sides*" and offered his own rebuttal on this score.

No work of art, however high its professional merits, will last, if created without regard to time and politics; the latter, naturally, to mean not petty intrigues but the major issues governing the life of millions of people. To ignore these issues cannot but restrict a man's horizon. It is for this reason that the very humanism of Hemingway's heroes is so joyless and stoical, the defective humanism of those doomed by history. (pp. 175-176)

In regard to Hemingway's style, Kashkin complimented him for his frugality, his choice of realistic detail, and, at times, his language. On the whole, however, he disliked the author's dialogue, which was too clipped and easily parodied, his short, unfinished sentences, and his inner monologues. Kashkin considered them devices which, in the hands of his imitators, became "*trite*" and "*empty clichés.*" In concluding, he remarked that Hemingway understood "*the great truths in life*" —death, love, pain; "*while in large works (such as his social novel) he [was] the slave of minor truths and untruths*" (p. 177).

In "Rereading Hemingway" Kashkin employed the term "*blind alley*" to designate Hemingway's failure to see the Truth.

He went further in blending the lives of Hemingway's heroes with the life of the author, establishing the similarity between Nick Adams's life in Michigan and the novelist's in Oak Park, Illinois; the similarity between Tenente Henry's wound in Fossalta with that of Hemingway's; and, in general, the hunting, fishing, and bullfighting experiences of both hero and author. In his discussion of *The Sun Also Rises*, he added a further interpretation not present in his previous articles. The book was not a story of snobbish tourism; but rather dealt with the courage and difficulties of Jake Barnes and the matador Romero. He also considered *To Have and Have Not* at greater length and summarized:

Here is the world of the haves, the rich masters of yachts and their friends, Johnson, Harrison, and others, with their pittance, spiritually destroying the writer Gordon, forcing him to lie in order to live. Directly or indirectly, they doom to destruction the have-nots: the veterans, driven into the workers' camp, the fisherman Harry Morgan.... Hemingway, it seems, understood that the rich were not only bored but were also cruel and frightening people, who with their teeth and claws will defend their right to oppress those whom they do not consider to be people. (pp. 197-198)

Aside from these few additions, and Kashkin's greater emphasis on the writer's need to discover the " roots " of social problems, the two articles of 1956 were identical.

In March, 1960, Kashkin continued with the article, " Of Greatest Importance : The Prose of Ernest Hemingway. " This was the most positive statement the critic had made on behalf of Hemingway. "*For us, of greatest importance in Hemingway is that he, with traumatic power, expressed one of the basic tragedies of man in a world which is broken into solitary cells, in the world of competition, profit, and war*" (p. 215).

Kashkin drew the portrait of the man-Hemingway, forced by his society to live in solitude. Having fled from his motherland, he became the spokesman of the lost generation. " *His misfortune and also his fault was that he tore himself away from native roots. Yes, the limitation of his outlook, at times even his blindness, this is his misfortune, but this is how his life formed beginning with his youth* " (p. 216). Where Hemingway eventually found his niche was in empathy with the " *simple people* " of countries other than his own.

Having thus attempted to vindicate the Hemingway of the lost generation as a natural product of his environment, Kashkin proceeded to develop an argument for the acceptability of the writer. The critic first asserted that since Hemingway's self-avowed literary masters have been Tolstoy, Stendhal, and Mark Twain, and since they were all worthy masters, he deserved a measure of study by all writers. One could view Hemingway's early stories, such as " Hills Like White Elephants, " " Cat in the Rain, " and " Homage to Switzerland ", as experimental work. And although they were concerned with the lost generation they deserved appreciation, for without them Hemingway perhaps might never have developped into the great writer which he became. Most important, it was necessary to understand Hemingway's statement on the aim of a writer : " *To write straight, honest prose on human beings. There is nothing more difficult than this in the world.* " This, Kashkin said, Hemingway had accomplished. At the same time, there was no contradiction between writing " *honest prose* " and complexity of thought. Hemingway had tried to write simply about what he knew best, using a classical yet distinctive style. In his early works he had been excessively terse and concrete, creating effect by selection and placement rather than by comparison and metaphor. But when Hemingway the man became aroused he spoke forth strongly, as in his article, " The Americans Fallen in Spain, " in 1939. In the critic's view, Hemingway was at his best when he dealt with " *the simple people,* " like El Sordo and Santiago— for he was able to make heroes of them, heroes committed to " *a big deed, a big aim, a big fish* " (pp. 216-219).

Kashkin contended that to derive the maximum from his books a " *biographical key* " was necessary, since there was a very close correlation between the lives of the characters and that of the author. In addition, Hemingway wrote in a very personal style. His half-statements and rapid conversational technique required the reader to be attentive to the events which were taking place. He likened this technique to a correspondence between " *dear ones* ", where each understands all references immediately.

The second important aspect of Hemingway, said Kashkin, was his desire to create a good product :

Hemingway does not aspire to create a cheap thing, but a well-created one, one that should last for a while, even forever. This aspiration lies in the basis of the professionally honest and high-grade craftsmanship of Hemingway, especially when he succeeds not in describing, but in depicting. (p. 220)

It was in Hemingway's later years that this artistry became manifest, when he abandoned the " *small* " and concentrated on " *the big fish, the big book.* "

The third significant aspect occurred in his later works, when he stressed " *positive qualities for good, or at least aspiring for good.* " Though Hemingway tried to make the truth of his writing inseparable from the truth of life, " *the scale of his response [was] limited by that which he saw with his own eyes, and this sometimes forced him to inadequate and faulty conclusions* " (p. 220). Hemingway did not develop like Anatole France, Bernard Shaw, Theodore Dreiser, or Lincoln Steffens, other men of his age. These, too, were men of great experience. Yet they not only protested as individuals ; they were also capable of reaching definite conclusions beneficial to mankind.

Kashkin then turned upon Western critics in a defense of the novelist. In referring to the often-published picture of Hemingway with a bottle, he wrote :

One must take into consideration that photographs often reflect not only the face of the subject, but also the face of the photographer, in the way that he views his object. It is the same in criticism, where the face of the critic is reflected. And thus the Western critic of the epoch of comicbooks is only able to perceive " the brutality " of Hemingway. Western criticism eagerly stamps Hemingway as " the singer of death and violence, " intentionally closing its eyes upon the *nature* of the death and *whose* violence. (pp. 221-222)

Kashkin preferred to view Hemingway as the man who " *affirmed life in the midst of death.* " Hemingway was a humanist. " *The humanism of Hemingway is not given in abstract declarations. It is given in his blood and in his art and he shows it in both the greatest and less great of his creations* " (p. 222). Kashkin concluded by saying that Hemingway was neither a fighter-politician nor a philosopher. " *He is simply an honest and talented person.* " " *Even though Hemingway is a solitary and lonely writer, he is nonetheless a writer, surrounded by his numerous characters and books, who influences millions of readers* " (p. 223).

III

Hemingway thus once again has become celebrated by the official Soviet press, and is ranked among the most favored foreign authors. Unpublished Soviet figures on the publication histories of American authors in the U.S.S.R. from 1918 through July 1, 1959, [18] place Hemingway eighteenth on the " *All-Time Best Seller List,* " with seventeen titles published, a total of 487,000 copies, in seven languages. Another register of best sellers, as of July 1, 1960, [19] places Hemingway tenth on the list, with 1,362,000 copies sold. If both of these lists are correct, then in the year between July, 1959 and July, 1960, more than 800,000 copies of Hemingway were sold. Added to this total would be the 100,000 copies of the 1961 edition of *A Farewell to Arms.* [20] There is, unfortunately, no way in which these figures can be checked, yet even an average of these figures over the short period of fourteen years that Hemingway has been published in the Soviet Union would still be more than adequate proof of his great popularity. Ilya Ehrenburg writes about the difficulty in purchasing a book by Hemingway :

Some five years ago it was announced that a new two-volume edition of his works would be sold by advanced subscription. The subscribers were to register personally in a bookshop situated in the apartment house where I was living. It was a cold winter evening. As I drove up to the house, I saw a long queue, the tail of which was made up predominantly of young people. It turned out that they had come there the night before the subscription opened so as not to miss their chance to subscribe. Not all of our books get sold out; there are books that lie on the shelves of bookshops and in the warehouses, but Hemingway's works are unobtainable unless one makes a strenuous effort. [21]

In commenting on Hemingway, the Soviet press has attempted to project a specific image for public consumption. This picture is somewhat at variance with the conception of Hemingway in the West. The Western public associates Hemingway with bullfighting, drinking, trout fishing, soldiering, a devil-may-care attitude — and Hemingway the great writer. In the Soviet Union, the emphasis has been placed on projecting the image of a toiling, diligent worker. In numerous critiques, interviews, and reminiscences of his Spanish Civil War associates, the accepted view of Hemingway is that of a humble, brotherly, devoted, suffering writer. For example, Alexei Eisner, in an article of reminiscence, described Hemingway as a plain person, with great humility, "*a child's smile,*" who never acted like a celebrity or boasted of his abilities. [22] In the published interviews of George Plimpton [23] and Genrikh Borovik [24] the image of Hemingway the writer was developped. Great stress was placed on the fact that Hemingway stood while he wrote, that he wrote six or seven hours a day, and that he kept a list of his word output per day. It was reported that Hemingway said that a writer could not be "*a tourist in life*". A writer did not "*collect materials*" for a book. Books were formed from experiencing life twenty-four hours a day. The emphasis on the toiling writer recalls Mikhail Sholokhov's perennial complaint that the young Soviet writers of today sit in Moscow and fail to journey out to meet and learn from the people.

Another image of Hemingway has been set forth by Evgenii Evtushenko. In his poem, "Meeting," in which he writes about his impressions on seeing Hemingway in the Copenhagen Airport, he presents the image of Hemingway as the rugged, powerful individual.

>   He went, to the crowd of tourists furrowing,
>   As if barely from the helm.
>   And like the sea's foam, the beard,
>   White, bordered his face
>   . . . .
>   The ground under him seemed to cave in—
>   Thus heavily he walked on it.
>   And someone amongst us said to me, smiling:
>   " Look; just like Hemingway! "
>   He walked, in each short gesture expressing
>   The burdened step of a fisherman.
>   Entirely from granite scales hewn out,
>   Walked, as through bullets, through the ages.
>   He walked, bending down as if in a trench;
>   Walked, moving apart chairs and people...
>   He so resembled Hemingway!
>   ...And later I found out,
>   that it was Hemingway. [25]

This romanticized picture of Hemingway the hoary giant is not particularly in keeping with the official image and might best be accepted as a youthful poetic view which perhaps mirrors the young Soviet's concept of the man.

When Hemingway died, the Soviets mourned his passing in words illustrative of great respect and admiration. Leonid Leonov, one of the Soviet Union's most distinguished authors wrote a July 4, 1961, commemoration in *Pravda*, entitled, " Ernest Hemingway : A Writer With a Universal Voice, " in which he said, "*I very attentively watched the stages of his creative genius and I think that his many innovating methods will be examined, interpreted, and in truth, imitated. He was a writer with a universal voice.*" In the " Hemingway Commemorative Issue " of the *Saturday Review* the following letter, written by Alexander Korneichuck, the Secretary of the Union of Soviet Writers, appeared :

> The radio brought us the sad news—Ernest Hemingway has left us forever. One of the brightest stars of our times, who lighted the humane road for peoples of all nations, is extinguished. Together with you, we grieve the untimely loss of a great American writer and a

great friend of our country, the memory of whom will live forever in our hearts.[26]

In the same issue of the *Saturday Review*, Ehrenburg wrote : "*It hurts... that a man should have died who, through the love felt for him, has brought together people and nations otherwise remote from each other.*"[27]

A third testimonial was given by Kornei Chukovsky, Soviet author of children's stories and the Soviet Union's translator of Walt Whitman :

Hemingway, as you know, became the most beloved Soviet writer. It is difficult to find a student who has not read Hemingway. His restless soul, his preoccupation with moral problems, his aspiration, no matter what the cost, to find the genuine truth of life—all of this brings him close to Russian literature which had created Dostoevskii, Chekhov, Gleb Uspenskii.[28]

Hemingway thus once again has been officially reinstated, and his position as one of the most beloved American authors in the Soviet Union now appears secure.

NOTES

1. Ilya EHRENBURG, " The World Weighs a Writer's Influence, " *Saturday Review*, July 29, 1961, p. 20.
2. Olga NEMEROVSKAIA, " Sud'ba amerikanskoi novelly, " *Literaturnaia ucheba*, No. 5, pp. 99-104 (May, 1935).
3. Ia. FRID, " Raskazy Khemingueia, " *Literaturnoe obozrenie*, No. 18, pp. 48-53 (1939).
4. A MINGULINA, " Ernest Kheminguei, "*Kniga i proletarskaia revolutsia*, No. 8, pp. 122-125 (Aug., 1937).
5. Ernest HEMINGWAY, *To Have and Have Not* (New York, 1937), p. 225.
6. The play was produced for the first time in the Soviet Union on July 9, 1962, and received a very favorable review in *Literaturnaia gazeta* (O. PRUDKOV, " K tem, kto boretsia, " July 10, 1962).

7. For a fuller, more comprehensive review of Soviet criticism of Hemingway in the thirties, I refer the reader to Deming BROWN, "Hemingway in Russia," *American Quarterly*, V, 143-156 (July, 1953); reprinted in the same author's *Soviet Attitudes toward American Writing* (Princeton, N. J., 1962).

8. Viktor GOROKHOV, " Kheminguei i ego novaia kniga," *Novoe vremia*, No. 37, p. 27 (Sept. 8, 1955).

9. Ernest HEMINGWAY, *The Old Man and the Sea* (New York, 1952), p. 114.

10. Sergei LVOV, " Mesto cheloveka v zhizni," *Literaturnaia gazeta*, Oct. 27, 1955, p. 2.

11. Vladislav DROBISHEVSKII, " Nepobedimy," *Zvezda*, No. 5, p. 166 (May, 1956).

12. Sergei LVOV, " Replika kritiku Vladislavu Drobishevshomu," *Zvezda*, No. 8, pp. 188-189 (Aug., 1956).

13. V. AGRIKOLIANSKII. A. KRASNOVSKII, and D. RACHKOV, "Pis'mo studentov E. Khemingeiiu," *Inostrannaia literatura*, No. 1, p. 233 (Jan., 1956).

14. E. LITOSHKO, " Sud'ba polkovnika Kantuella," *Moskva*, No. 7, pp. 98-100 (July, 1960).

15. Ernest HEMINGWAY, *Across the River and Into the Trees* (New York, 1950), p. 70.

16. It is interesting to note the table of contents in this collection : Complete translations of the novels, *The Sun Also Rises, To Have and Have Not*, and *The Old Man and the Sea;* all the short stories ; a twenty-four page excerpt from *Death in the Afternoon* (random selections ou bullfighting, a number of exchanges between The Old Lady and The Author on writing and bullfighting, and short selections of Hemingway's comments on a writer's art), and a nineteen-page excerpt from *Green Hills of Africa* (the exchange between Hemingway and Kandisky on American literature, all sections referring to Tolstoy and Turgenev, and the section describing the manner in which America was being destroyed); the play, *The Fifth Column;* the scenario from the film, *The Spanish Earth;* and, what would not usually be included in an equivalent literary collection in the West, a selection of Hemingway's journalistic articles, including " Who Killed the War Veterans in Florida ? " " The Americans Fallen in Spain, " " The American Fighter, " and " The Writer and War. " Absent were *Torrents of Spring, For Whom the Bell Tolls*, and *Across the River and Into the Trees*. The omission of these novels and the limited selections from *Death in the Afternoon* and *Green Hills of Africa* correspond closely to the almost complete lack of comment made on these books by Soviets critics. On the other hand, the complete reproduction of all writing done by Hemingway during the period of the Spanish Civil War (with the exception of *For Whom the Bell Tolls*) is closely correlated with the interest shown by the critics in this period of Hemingway's literary output.

17. Ivan KASHKIN, " Dve novelly Khemingueiia," *Internatsionalnaia literatura*, No. 1, pp. 92-93 (Jan. 1934) ; " Ernest Hemingway : Tragedy of Craftsmanship," in *Ernest Hemingway : The Man and His Work*, ed. John K. M. MCCAFFERY (New York, 1950), pp. 63-93, trans. form *International Literature*, No. 5 (May, 1934) ; " Smert' posle poludnia," *Literaturnyi kritik*,

No. 9, pp. 121-148 (Sept., 1934); " Pereklichka cherez okean, " *Krasnaia nov'*, No. 7, pp. 196-201 (July, 1939); "Slovo o neizvestnom kritike, " *Literaturnaia gazeta*, Feb. 26, 1939; " Ernest Kheminguei, " *Literaturnaia gazeta*, May 1, 1939; " Ernest Kheminguei, " *Internatsionalnaia literatura*, Nos. 7-8, pp. 319-333 (1939); " Pomni o..., " *Literaturnaia gazeta*, Oct. 18, 1954; " Perechitivaia Khemingueiia, " *Inostrannaia literatura*, No. 4, pp. 194-206 (April 1956); " Alive in the Midst of Death, " in *Hemingway and His Critics*, ed. Carlos BAKER (New York, 1961), pp. 162-180, from *Soviet Literature*, No. 7 (July, 1956); " Kheminguei na puti k masterstvu, " *Voprosy literatury*, No. 6, pp. 184-204 (June, 1957); " O samom glavnom, " *Oktiabr'*, No. 3, pp. 215-223 (March, 1960); " Starik i more, " *Sovestkaia kul'tura*, March 16, 1961.

18. Melville J. RUGGLES, " American Books in Soviet Publishing, " *Slavic Review*, XX, 424 (Sept. 1961).

19. Maurice HINDUS, *House Without a Roof* (New York, 1961), p. 94.

20. From publication figures given on the last page of this Soviet edition.

21. Ilya EHRENBURG, " The World Weighs a Writer's Influence, " *Saturday Review*, July 29, 1961, p. 20.

22. Alexei EISNER, " On byl s nami v Ispanii, " *Novyi mir*, No. 8, pp. 169-172 (Aug., 1961).

23. George PLIMPTON, *Inostrannaia literatura*, No. 1, pp. 212-218 (Jan., 1962).

24. Genrikh BOROVIK, " U Ernesta Khemingueiia, " *Ogonëk*, No. 14, p. 29 (April, 1960).

25. Evgenii EVTUSHENKO, " Vstrecha, " *Iunost'*, No. 4, p. 7 (April, 1961). Translated from the Russian by this writer. Conventional capitalization of the first word of each line seemed more adaptable in English than Evtushenko's capitalization of the first word of each sentence.

26. Alexander KORNEICHUK, " Homage to Hemingway, " *Saturday Review*, July 29, 1961, p. 31.

27. EHRENBURG, " The World Weighs..., " p. 20. In the same article, Ehrenburg stated that Hemingway had been his favorite writer for the past thirty years. In a recent excerpt from his memoirs, Ehrenburg made the following remark : " And I, looking back on my life, see that two writers of the number of those I was lucky enough to meet, helped me not only to free myself from sentimentalism, lengthy dissertations, and scanty perspective, but simply to breathe to work, to set out—Babel and Hemingway. " " Lyudi, gody, zhizn' " *Novyi mir*, No. 5, p. 131 (May, 1962).

28. Personal letter from Kornei Chukovskii, Dec., 1961.

NOT SPAIN BUT HEMINGWAY

by Arturo Barea

ERNEST HEMINGWAY'S new novel, *For Whom the Bell Tolls*, was cast for the success it is now reaping along the whole front line from left-wing reviewers to Hollywood producers.

It is a tale of violence, war, and love, blood and thunder on the Spanish soil; it combines the romanticism and glamour of bullfighting with the ugly realism of a civil war; it is heroic, sensational, sensual, lyrical, and honestly antifascist without going in for politics; it contains one set of characters—Castilian peasants—which deserve the cliché praise "*sober in outline like an old woodcut,*" and another set of intellectually intriguing and exotic characters—Russian journalists and generals. It shows the inner problems of the author through his hero, the American scholar and Communist who is serving behind the Fascist lines, a true man of action, yet wrestling with his very un-Communistic, honest-to-God humanist soul. It describes the violence and horror of the Spanish War so that the reader who had been in love with a strange Spain of his own nostalgia sees all his vague imaginings assuming shape and life, and feels himself to be penetrating into the innermost recesses of the Spanish soul. It is written with an excellent technique of realism, and yet spares delicate feelings by putting the foulest oaths and obscenities in Spanish and italics (English readers may or may not look up the words in a dictionary; in any case they would not find half of them), thus noticeably reducing the amount of muckings, sons-of-bitches, and hells.

I myself was fascinated by the book and felt it to be honest in so far as it renders Hemingway's real vision. And yet I find myself awkwardly alone in the conviction that, as a novel about Spaniards and their war, it is unreal and, in the last analysis, deeply untruthful, though practically all the critics claim the contrary, whatever their objections to other aspects of the book :

> You come to understand much of Spain which is not always, or even often, to be found in the histories.
> Hemingway knows his Spain profoundly.... In miniature, Hemingway has written the war the Spanish were fighting.
>
> ... here, in his astonishingly real Spanish conversation, he has surpassed anything I have ever seen.... Mr. Hemingway understands the hierarchy of Spanish blasphemy, the proper place of each rococo phrase.... Horrifying and sickening, the story has nevertheless that theatrical variety of incidents, that primitive realism and capacity to catch every emotion that was felt by the people as a whole....
>
> The Spanish peasants who help him in his dangerous errand are superbly described.... All are alive and astonishingly themselves ; Mr. Hemingway has never done anything better.

As a Spaniard, and one who has lived through the period of our war which provides Hemingway with his stage setting, I came point by point to the following somewhat different conclusions :

Reading *For Whom the Bell Tolls*, you will indeed come to understand some aspects of Spanish character and life, but you will misunderstand more, and more important ones at that.

Ernest Hemingway does know " *his Spain.* " But it is precisely his intimate knowledge of this narrow section of Spain which has blinded him to a wider and deeper understanding, and made it difficult for him to " *write the war we have been fighting.* "

Some of his Spanish conversations are perfect, but others, often of great significance for the structure of the book, are totally un-Spanish. He has not mastered the intricate " *hierarchy of Spanish blasphemy* " (anyhow the most difficult thing for a foreigner in any language, since it is based on ancient taboos and half-conscious superstitions). He commits a series of grave linguistic-psychological mistakes in this book—such, indeed, as I have heard him commit when he joked with the orderlies in my Madrid office. Then, we grinned at his solecisms because we liked him.

Hemingway has understood the emotions which our "*people as a whole*" felt in the bull ring, but not those which it felt in the collective action of war and revolution.

Some of the Castilian peasants Hemingway has created are real and alive, but others are artificial or out of place. Although all are magnificently described, in none of them has he touched the roots.

Ernest Hemingway himself and his book are of such importance that I think it necessary to specify, and if I can, to prove and explain my objections. After all, they cover not only the literary picture of Spaniards and their war, but also the quality of Hemingway's creative work in this instance, and the problem of his realism as a whole. The strength of his artistry makes fiction sound like distilled reality. The reader may well follow the lead of the critics; he may accept the book because it is a powerful work of art, and implicitly believe in the inner truthfulness of Hemingway's Spain. For purely Spanish reasons I want to fight against this danger of a spurious understanding of my people.

The book relates an episode in the Republican guerrilla warfare of May, 1937. It takes place in the Sierra of the province of Segovia, and the *guerrilleros* concerned come from a small town, or rather village, in the province of Ávila. (It is more appropriate to call these *pueblos* "*villages*" than "*towns*," as Hemingway does.) Both the provinces are a part of Old Castile.

The men from those Castilian mountain villages are dour and hard, poor and distrustful. They have grown up on a soil which the snow covers half of the year and the sun scorches the other half. They are walled up in their own narrow lives, each working hard on his meager bit of land and hunting the wild animals in the mountains. Their fierce self-defense against the hardships of their existence and of the very climate makes them shut the doors of their community against any stranger, beyond a momentary and generous hospitality. They do not allow the gypsies to stay overnight in their villages, but often chase them away with stones. They have come to hate their *señores*—all those who exploit them through money, position or power—and when they feel deceived by the highest power, their God, they turn against Him with the same ferocious resentment. They do not talk much, nor do they talk easily; their turns of speech are heavy, simple and direct, with the dignity of simplicity and of pride in their manly strength.

I think Hemingway has seen all this and striven to express it. Some of his *guerrilleros*, above all Old Anselmo and El Sordo, belong to that soil. Yet he does not know the foundations of their lives and minds. Indeed, how could he? This is a Spain he has seen but never lived. And thus he commits the fatal error of putting the men of a Sierra village under the leadership of two people from the Spain he knows thoroughly, from the world of the *toreros* and their hangers-on : Pilar, the old gypsy tart, and Pablo, the horse dealer of the bull ring.

Such a situation is utterly impossible. The men from a township in the Sierra of Avila—from a place as primitive as Hemingway himself paints it—could never have admitted and accepted a Pilar and a Pablo as their leaders. The gypsy and the gypsified horse dealer might have lived, and even become local leaders, in one of those villages in the Sierra of Guadarrama, which Hemingway knows and which live on tourists and weekenders from Madrid; but then again, these villages could never have produced Hemingway's peasant *guerrilleros*. That is to say, the old gypsy whore from Andalusia with her lover, the horse dealer, grouped together with peasants from Old Castile constitute a glaring incongruity.

This lack of realism is, however, necessary for the pattern of Hemingway's book. It permits him to introduce, through Pilar, admirable descriptions of the people of the bull ring a quarter of a century ago. It also permits him to construct scenes of savage brutality built around Pablo, whose whole mind is drenched with the smell of the *plaza de toros* and who is capable of studied, deliberate cruelty. The scenes of the book which seem to have impressed themselves deeply on the minds of every non-Spanish reader as being barbarously realistic and true are thus the result of a purely artificial choice of dramatis personae.

When Hemingway decided not to describe a group of purely Castilian guerrilla fighters led by the most brutal and brave male among them, but to introduce the colorful gypsy woman and the bull-ring assassin, he blocked his own way to the reality of the Spanish War and Spanish violence.

Pilar relates in a painfully vivid narration what happened in the small Sierra township after the outbreak of the Rebellion. First she describes the assault on the barracks of the Guardia Civil, and this part of the tale is perfect in its realism. Just so it happened in many places throughout Spain. Then she tells how Pablo (who, as I must again emphasize, could never have become a leader in such a village in real life) organizes a monstrous and elaborate lynching of the local "*fascists,*" with the underlying intention of involving the whole population in the same blood guilt. He organizes this lynching like one of the old village bull-baitings or *capeas*. The men are in the square, most of them in their festive clothes, all with their wineskins, and armed with flails, sticks, and knives. The doors of the Town Hall open to let out the prisoners one by one; they have to pass through the narrow space between a double line of men until they reach the edge of a cliff. The men in the lines, drunk with wine and cruelty, beat and knife their enemies to death, jeering at them the while. The bodies are thrown over the precipice. The women look on from the balconies, and in the end are shamefully drunk with blood and bestiality, just like the men.

Now, it happened in countless small towns and villages that underfed peasants and laborers killed the local *señores* who had starved them for years and sneered at them : " *Let the Republic feed you!*" At first, there was almost everywhere some man or other, more savage than the rest, who wanted to lynch the "*fascists*" and shouted: "*Let's tear their guts out!*"—guts being a euphemism in place of which Hemingway uses the crude Spanish word in italics. Then two or three of the most hated men would be killed in the streets, brutally, in an outbreak of blind fury; but there was no deliberate torture. The others were shot at night on the threshing floors in the open fields where the women could not see it, nor even hear the shots. They were killed, and then they were buried. Often those who had killed in revenge were naïve enough to give their victims a burial in the cemetery so that they should rest "*in hallowed ground.*"

Hemingway must have sensed this. He had to invent his Pablo, the crafty, potential murderer, accustomed to seeing horses slit open in the bull ring, in order to stage-manage this collective blood orgy. Yet even if a Pablo could possibly have organized such a lynching, it is unthinkable that the community of a Castilian village would have followed him to the end of the revolting butchery, and not sooner have lynched Pablo himself. It is even more unthinkable that the butcher could have remained the leader of honest men who became guerrilla fighters because of their own convictions.

The brutal violence of Spaniards, which exists together with a dark acceptance of life and death, is always individual. It draws strength and pride from a very simple awareness of their own masculinity. In the explosion of that stored-up violence people would agree to kill their enemies, to kill them quickly with a straight bullet or a straight knife, without investigation or trial. Nobody—except of course the few with diseased brains who must have existed—thought, or could have thought, of organizing slaughter like a *fiesta* and of putting on festive clothes to get drunk on blood. In those village bullfights which Hemingway describes through the daydreaming of his young *guerrillero* Andrés, the people would finish up intoxicated with mass cruelty; yet there is still a profound difference. Even if those *capeas* were nothing other than collective killings, the killing was not that of a tame cow but of a wild bull. Brutal, yes; but demanding personal bravery and the risk to life and limb from every individual. Thousands of young men have died in *capeas*. But if instead of the " *bull of death* " a milch cow had been put in the middle of the village square, nobody would have touched her, because a thing like that *no tiene gracia*, it would have held no attraction. The *gracia* does not consist in killing the bull, but in knowing that he can kill you. Everything else would destroy your claim to manliness.

Hemingway has forgotten this when he describes the collective killing of defenseless enemies in a bull-ring atmosphere. And yet, this is the kind of violence the common reader would be apt to expect from Spaniards; the supreme skill of the narration makes it seem stark reality. To me, this is the worst aspect of Hemingway's fundamental mistake : he falsifies most plausibly the causes and the actual form of the tragic violence of my people—not knowing that he falsifies it, because much of what he describes does exist in the Spain of the bull ring, the Spain he understands and seeks to find in every Spaniard.

The chain of errors prolongs itself, always springing from the same main source. Hemingway balances this story of a Republican atrocity with equally realistic-sounding and equally false stories of Fascist atrocities. Again, the most important incident is one of collective violence. The heroine, Maria, has been violated by a group of Fascists, and she tells her lover about it.

At the beginning of the Civil War, Franco's Moorish soldiers committed rape. I myself knew of concrete cases. Afterwards the Spanish Fascist officers did their best to put an end to these outrages, although they themselves went on committing other forms of brutality inherent in civil war and fascist mentality. I have never heard of a collective violation by Falangists, and I do not believe it ever happened. Such a thing is contrary to Spanish psychology.[1] I want to make it quite clear that I do not deny the potential and actual bestiality of Spaniards, but

I do deny the psychological possibility of a collective sexual act. The consciousness of his own virility would make it impossible for a Spaniard to want the union of his body with that of a woman still warm and moist from another male. He would loathe it physically. Again, Hemingway describes most vividly what is intrinsically wrong; again, he is wrong because he fails to understand the individual quality of Spanish violence. Since these are the crucial parts of his psychological pattern, his whole picture of the Spaniards at war is distorted and unreal.

There is, however, another group scene which is magnificent in psychology and detail. The *guerrilleros* feel that Pablo is about to turn traitor, and try to provoke him to a step which would justify killing him. Although they believe his death to be necessary for their common good, they do not attack him together and finish him off, which would be easy; they stage a discussion that proceeds from insult to insult, true to life in its ceremonial violence, and try to incite Pablo to challenge one of them. That one would then be ready to kill him face to face. He would be ready to stab the bull—if the bull accepts the fight.

There are other Spanish scenes and characters which are excellently observed. The old man Anselmo, with his grave problems of life and death, is completely genuine. The Fascist officers are real, although their actions are artificially constructed. Everything connected with the world of the bullfight is vivid and essentially truthful. El Sordo, the peasant leader of another guerrilla band operating near Pablo's, is as much in the right place as Pablo is in the wrong. As far as he is described in his brief appearances, he is typical of his kind : primitive, harsh, straight, and ingenuous, continuing to live and fight though he knows that the future holds no hope. In the end he dies with a simple, brutal, and unsentimental dignity : he dies killing.

But even the genuine characters are curiously detached from their background. One never quite knows why they fight for the Republic; one only feels their stoic loyalty. There is no growth and no future in them. And yet it had been precisely their hope and belief in a constructive future which had set the Spanish laborers and peasants in motion.

Less relevant for Hemingway's treatment of the Spanish War, but interesting in view of his conception of the Spanish character, is the fact that the love story between the young American, Robert Jordan, and Maria is pure romancing, at least in so far as the Spanish girl is concerned. I cannot judge—for I cannot feel and associate in English—whether the love scenes are convincing. They may be good writing, though they do not seem so to me. They are certainly unrealistic in their psychology of the female partner.

A Spanish girl of the rural middle class is steeped in a tradition in which influences from the Moorish harem and the Catholic convent mix. She could not ask a stranger, a foreigner, to let her come into his bed the very first night after they had met. This, however, is what Maria does. She could not do it *and* keep the respectful adoration of the members of her guerrilla group who know the history of her violation. They would call her a bitch in heat, not because she sleeps with a foreigner, but because she offers herself to him at once without even having been asked by him. Maria's ignorance of kissing and love is another impossible fiction. Such mental innocence may be found in other layers of Spanish society, among girls who had no other contact with life but their father confessor and the Holy Sisters of their convent school. In this, the most unreal character of the book, there is also a particularly marked discrepancy between social background and excessively lyrical language. This belongs, however, to the general question of the language used by the Spaniards throughout the book.

It is here that the artificiality of Hemingway's Spain and the gaps in his actual knowledge of the Spanish mind show themselves most clearly. The Castilian peasants speak forcefully and simply. Their language can be austere, it can express a somber kind of hilarity. They often cover their resistance to expressing their own more complicated emotions by fierce blasphemy. All this has been said often, and Hemingway knows it. But when it comes to rendering the dignity and sobriety of their speech, he invents an artificial and pompous English which contains many un-English words and constructions most of which cannot even be admitted as literal translations of the original Spanish. To prove this would require much space and would sound merely pedantic, but I want to give an example :

Agustín says : "*Also I have a boredom in these mountains.*" (Hemingway-Jordan had commented on the fact that Spanish peasants use the abstract word *aburrimiento*, boredom ; in reality, they hardly ever use it.) In such a case, the Castilian peasant would quite simply say : "*Además me aburro en estas montañas,*" or "*Estas montañas me aburren,*" of which the English equivalents are : "*Also, I'm bored in these mountains,*" or "*These mountains bore me.*"

The curious translation, which is no real translation, wants to impress on the reader the abstract quality of the peasant's speech. Yet it is precisely characteristic of the Castilian of the people that it shuns abstract nouns and rather expresses the abstract idea as personified concrete action, such as "*the mountains bore me.*" Hemingway continually sins against this spirit of the language in both the choice of words and the structure of the phrases in his dialogues between Spaniards. It seems to me that poise and simplicity of language should be rendered by equally poised, simple, and natural language. The quality of dignity must flow out of directness, not out of hollow and artificial solemnity. I resent Spaniards in a serious book speaking like Don Adriano de Armado, the "*fantastical Spaniard*" of *Love's Labour's Lost*. As a writer, I would be unhappy if Spanish dialogue I had written were to be translated into something as affected and artificial as : "*I encounter it to be perfectly normal,*" when all I had said in Spanish was : *Lo encuentro perfectamente normal*—"*I find it perfectly normal*" ; or into : "*You have terminated already?*" when I have said : *¿Habéis terminado ya?*—"*Have you finished already?*"

Now, this matter of the treatment of idiomatic speech in a translation is most difficult, in any language. Yet Hemingway's solution, which sounds like utter realism, is in point of fact the very contrary. It makes the understanding of shades almost impossible to any reader who does not know Spanish, and it removes the Castilian figures to a plane of unreality where strange phrases and strange psychology run riot. The fact that genuine Spanish swearwords and idioms are copiously scattered all over the pages only adds to this unreality.

The erroneous use of blasphemy and obscene language reveals very neatly how Hemingway has failed to grasp certain subtleties of Spanish language and psychology. Instead of a long list I will give two instances, among the most striking in the book:

Robert Jordan constantly addresses Maria as "*rabbit,*" in both English and Spanish, in intimacy and in public. Now, the Spanish word happens to be one of the more frequent and vulgar euphemisms for the female sexual organ. Jordan is described as knowing all the intricacies of Spanish double meanings. Had he really addressed his girl like this in public, it would have provoked a truly Rabelaisian outburst.

The other instance derives from a deeper misunderstanding. One of the *guerrilleros* asks Robert about Maria: "*How is she in bed?*" Another, who himself loves Maria and explains to Robert that she is no whore just because she slept with him, says: "*And thy care is to* joder *with her all night?*"
It is strictly impossible for a Spaniard to ask another man how his wife or lover is "*in bed.*" It would break a taboo which is only lifted in the case of prostitutes. No Spaniard would use the word *joder*: the ugliest verb for the sexual act, and one which expresses not the joy but the nausea of sexual union, about a woman he respects and whom the other man loves. It would inevitably provoke a fight. But Hemingway-Jordan discusses the matter serenely, Jordan unaware that he has lost face by accepting an insult, Hemingway unaware that the use of the word by Agustín and its acceptance by Jordan gives away the

fact that his own real knowledge of Spaniards is still confined to the world of *Death in the Afternoon.*

When Hemingway came to Madrid in early spring 1937, he came with the apprehensions of a man who had been hurt and twisted by the Great War, and who was now voluntarily exposing himself to bombs and shells, afraid of being afraid once more and eager to share the experience of a people's struggle. He came with the apprehensions of a man who, many years before, had found an escape from his inner helplessness in the animal brutality of the world of the Spanish bull ring, after having been scarred by the disciplined and dull violence of modern warfare, and who was afraid of having lost the Spain he knew and loved.

I remember him vividly now, as I knew him in those months: big and lumbering, with the look of a worried boy on his round face, diffident and yet consciously using his diffidence as an attraction, a good fellow to drink with, fond of dirty jokes "*pour épater l'Espagnol,*" questioning, skeptical and intelligent in his curiosity, skillfully stressing his political ignorance, easy and friendly, yet remote and somewhat sad.

I think he had once taken Spain, the Spain of *toreros*, wealthy young *señoritos*, gypsies, tarts, tipsters, and so on, rather as one takes drugs. That colorful and purposeless game with life and death which followed rigid and ancient rules must have responded to some inner need of his. He wrote what to my knowledge is the best book on the bull ring, *Death in the Afternoon.* When he came back to Spain into our war, tired of describing and observing the flabby violence of American gangsterdom, he found few traces of the world he knew. The great *toreros* with whom he had been friends were on the side of the Fascists. The gypsies had lost their market and had disappeared, many of them to the trenches.

Hemingway mixed with the soldiers in the bars more than with the pretentious left-wing intellectuals. He made many friends, as one makes friends drinking and joking together. Yet he lived the somewhat unreal life of a war correspondent in the shell-pitted Hotel Florida, among foreign journalists, officers of the International Brigades on leave, and a motley crowd of tourists and tarts. He could speak well with Spaniards, but he never shared their lives, neither in Madrid, nor in the trenches. The commander of the International Brigades, a man who appeared to us Spaniards the epitome of ugly Prussianism, explained to him the strategic and tactical details of the battle of Madrid and the battle of Guadalajara. Kolzov, the correspondent of *Pravda*, gave him his cynical but shrewd explanations of life behind the scenes. Hemingway had access to the strictly guarded world of the Hotel Gaylord and he came to know its inmates, the Russians and the International Communist functionaries. And he admired them, secretly skeptical, and yet with a naïve longing to share their facility of decision. He must have had a bad conscience because he could become part neither of the Spanish fight, nor of that other political fight which seemed so clear-cut to those Russians and Communists.

In *For Whom the Bell Tolls*, there is the sublimation of all those experiences. The world of the Hotel Gaylord is evoked with an astonishing accuracy of detail; the non-Spanish figures of the book are all lifelike portraits, some under their real names, such as the disastrous André Marty; others, like Kolzov, slightly idealized and thinly disguised. What Hemingway did not do but would have liked to be capable of doing, and what he actually felt, is mirrored in his hero, Robert Jordan, who is left dying at the end of the book, not so much because the inner necessity of the tale demands it, as because Ernest Hemingway could not really believe in his future.

And then there is Spain. Hemingway could describe with truthfulness and art what he had seen from without, but he wanted to describe more. He wished for a share in the Spanish struggle. Not sharing the beliefs, the life, and the suffering of the Spaniards, he could only shape them in his imagination after the image of the Spain he knew. His old obsession with violence pushed him into a track which only led him still further away from a share in that new and still chaotic Spanish life.

Thus the inner failure of Hemingway's novel—its failure to render the reality of the Spanish War in imaginative writing—seems to me to stem from the fact that he was always a spectator who wanted to be an actor and who wanted to write as if he were an actor. Yet it is not enough to look on : to write truthfully you must live, and you must feel what you are living.

[Translated from the Spanish by Ilsa Barea]

NOTE

1. While I was translating this passage into English, in 1941, A. B. said to me that the sordid fact of queues in cheap brothels, for instance in the rearguard, did not seem to him a contradiction to his thesis, because there, sexual hunger had become a blinding elemental force. He also mentioned the case of collective rape described by the novelist Pérez de Ayala. A. B. admitted the existence of such explosions by a group of Spaniards whose dammed-up hatred and sexuality found no other outlet, but he considered them psychopathological extremes, while the episode told by Hemingway was meant to be something "normal" in spite of the abnormal circumstances. (ILSA BAREA.)

NOTES ON CONTRIBUTORS

Heinrich STRAUMANN, professor of English literature at the University of Zürich, has published in particular a very popular book on *American Literature in the XXth Century* (1951 ; revised edition, 1962).

Dennis WELLAND, professor of American Literature at the University of Manchester, has published *Wilfred Owen : A Critical Study* and a book on *Arthur Miller* (1961).

Roger ASSELINEAU, professor of American literature at the Sorbonne, has published in particular *L'Évolution de Walt Whitman* (1954 ; American edition in 2 vols., 1960, 1962), *The Literary Reputation of Mark Twain* (1954).

Helmut PAPAJEWSKI was professor or American literature at the University of Cologne when he wrote his contribution to this volume ; he now teaches at the University of Bonn. He has published a book on *Thornton Wilder* (1961).

Mario PRAZ, professor of English language and literature at the University of Rome, is the author of a number of well-known books, including *The Romantic Agony* (1933) and *The Hero in Eclipse in Victorian Fiction* (1956).

Sigmund SKARD, professor of " Literature, especially American " at the University of Oslo in Norway, has published among other books, *American Studies in Europe*, 2 vols. (1958), *The American Myth and the European Mind* (1961).

Lars ÅHNEBRINK, professor of American literature at the University of Uppsala in Sweden is well-known for his study on *The Beginnings of Naturalism in American Fiction* (1950 ; American edition, 1961).

Stephen Jan PARKER is a graduate student in Russian literature at Cornell University.

Arturo BAREA (1897-1958) wrote after the Spanish Civil War, while in exile first in France and later in England, a trilogy which made him famous, *The Forge of a Rebel*.